THE WIZARD OF FESTIVAL LIGHTING

THE WIZARD OF FESTIVAL LIGHTING

The Incredible Story of Sridhar Das

Samragngi Roy

SPEAKING TIGER

SPEAKING TIGER BOOKS LLP
125A, Ground Floor, Shahpur Jat, near Asiad Village,
New Delhi 110049

First published in paperback by Speaking Tiger Books in 2023

ISBN: 978-93-5447-553-5
eISBN: 978-93-5447-560-3

10 9 8 7 6 5 4 3 2 1

Typeset in Minion Pro by SÜRYA, New Delhi
Printed at Chaman Enterprises, New Delhi

Dedicated to the wizard,
the magician, the pioneer himself.

If it doesn't burn a little then what's the point of playing with fire?

—Bridgett Devoue

Author's Note

Writing this book has been a difficult exercise for me. I had to immerse myself in an era about which I knew very little, and plunge neck-deep into a history that almost every single individual around me was a part of, but none were aware of the holistic picture I was trying to paint. I unearthed certain facts and incidents which had been unknown to me, and I have struggled to come to terms with them. These involved people I loved and grew up with, people I thought I knew very closely. However, going back in time, I started viewing these familiar people in very unfamiliar ways. But I can confidently say that this is a story without filters. I have tried my best to present the truth exactly the way it was conveyed to me. There are certain incidents, characters, turns of events, stray bits of information which might seem problematic, but that is because that's exactly how they were remembered. I have not attempted to be perfect as a narrator myself nor have I endeavoured to draw picture portraits of infallible people. What I have attempted to do is to present human beings with all their human follies, biases, imperfections and hypocrisies intact.

And being so close to the narrative myself, and especially fond of the person I have written about, I'm certain that my flaws and biases too have unconsciously shown up at various points in the story.

Another reason why this story was difficult for me to write is because all I had to rely on were memories—mostly of my grandfather's, my family members, relatives, acquaintances, public memory gleaned from newspapers, write-ups, online posts, documentaries and interviews. This makes me an unreliable narrator by default because I started writing this book at a time when my grandfather's memories had rapidly started to fade. Memory, as we all know, is a very slippery thing and I don't want to claim complete accuracy for the stories I have strung together. I know one must not mistake memories for factual truths. However, I have tried my best to crosscheck every bit of information with my grandmother who has been a major part of my grandfather's life and struggle since 1971. Nevertheless, the events from the years prior to that are a mystery to her as well. As there was no documentation available, I had no way to check the accuracy of these events. This doesn't mean that the incidents mentioned never took place. They did happen because they form some of my grandfather's earliest core memories, and he has talked about these at length on various forums too. But at the same time, I had to exercise my creative liberty as an author to fill in some of the gaps, flesh out some of the episodes like one rounds off certain mathematical solutions when they continue indefinitely beyond the decimal point.

While writing the book, I did have the opportunity to

talk to a lot of people in my town, many of whom were old-timers who had witnessed every stage of the evolution of festival lighting in Chandannagar in its full glory. This is where I came across certain controversies when the subject of the rollers was broached. From what I had heard since my childhood, and the reason my grandfather has always been referred to as the pioneer of automatic lighting is because he is famously credited with the invention of the rollers which brought life to the panels through the animation of the miniatures. My grandfather still seems to have clear memories of how he came up with the idea of these rollers, and this story was corroborated by other family members, his helpers and apprentices, and some of his old friends who knew him back in the late 1960s. However, there are some people in Chandannagar who believe that these rollers were already in use before my grandfather had used them in his artistic projects. I was unable to verify this bit of information as the two mechanical artists who were mentioned in this connection are no longer living. From what my grandfather has told me, there were rollers that were used to animate simple mechanical figures without lights and they formed a major source of his artistic inspiration. However, these rollers couldn't be put to use when it came to miniature lamps. The kind of rollers he used at the start to animate his miniature lamps had to be created using an entirely different mechanism and initially they worked only for lamps on panels, not three-dimensional figures. Later on, with the evolution of illuminated three-dimensional mechanical figures, a combination of all these different types of rollers had to be used. What I concluded from the discussion was that there was never a one-size-fits-all mechanism. Artists had to change and adapt these rollers to suit their specific needs.

I have deliberately changed the names of certain individuals or kept them anonymous in order to protect their privacy and avoid any kind of misrepresentation. I'm a firm believer of the fact that truth can never be absolute. Different people have different ways of remembering, understanding and articulating the same truth. Therefore, I have tried to include other perspectives in this story wherever possible. There are chapters narrated by my grandmother and mother each in their own voices because they reveal the dark and oft-neglected side of fame. There are other characters who feature prominently in the interludes and add more dimension to the existing information and my conversations with them mostly follow an informal interview pattern. I wanted to include so many other voices, so many other perspectives, so many other incidents but then this book would never have been finished. I have tried to the best of my ability to stay true to the information I had access to, to understand and explain the technical details of each invention even when my Humanities brain put up strong walls of resistance to grasping the logic behind certain complex mechanisms, and I apologize in advance for any errors that may still remain. Suffice it to say that I tried my best.

Prologue

'As a kid, I just liked playing with torches. That's how it began. And you know the rest of the story.'

The PowerPoint presentation ended with my grandfather's simple words and was greeted by a deafening round of applause from the audience. The stage lights flickered back to life and a saree-clad lady daintily walked up to the podium on the stage and cleared her throat before switching on the wireless microphone. My grandfather has never been an eloquent man. All one could ever expect from him were cold, hard facts. He never made an effort to embellish his story or be philosophical. He has always been a man of few words, who found it difficult to articulate what was going on in his mind. Whenever he was invited to speak somewhere, he never spent a single sleepless night wondering what he would say. He knew that the audience expected something stirring and motivational, something that would inspire them to discover their purpose in life or jar them out of their reverie, but he never tried to live up to their expectations. I think perhaps he enjoyed thwarting these expectations, for he would always grin about it later. It was no different this time. He hadn't prepared a speech. It was a grand event and I was a little apprehensive. But this time, something quite unexpected happened.

My grandfather was nervous. His eyes sparkled, the lines on his forehead deepened, his hands trembled as he gave me a toothless smile. This wasn't familiar to me at all.

'My heart is racing,' he whispered.

'Don't worry,' I took his hand, surprised. 'You've done this a million times already.'

'I don't know what to say,' he confessed. 'I should have prepared for this.'

'You just be yourself, okay?' I told him. 'Be confident. You're a star. Just go up there, shine a little and we will all be dazzled.'

He looked at me fondly and said, 'What would I do without you?'

Try as he might, he could never be impervious to my blandishments. Despite the endless adulation he received from his admirers, what he looked forward to most were my words of praise. From a very tender age, I was overtly conscious of this power that I wielded over him and took immense pride in the knowledge that no one else held the key to his heart. I revelled in making him feel like a celebrity and I wouldn't stop until I could see my own tiny self reflected back at me in his brilliant, happy eyes.

'I hope I don't fall down on the stage,' he expressed his concern. 'It looks so slippery! The steps are so narrow.'

'I won't let that happen. That's why I'm here.' I reassured

him. 'Now calm down and listen to all the wonderful things she has to say about you.'

The spotlight zeroed in on the lady and her silver neckpiece glittered. The murmurs and claps died down and everyone was all eyes and ears.

She began, 'Chandannagar, the beautiful town on the banks of river Hooghly, has always been famous as a former French colony. This little town has attracted tourists from all across the globe like magnets, owing to her picturesque beauty and unique blend of culture and heritage. The Jagadhatri Puja, as we all know, is a major socio-cultural event of this town. But there is something else too that has etched the name of Chandannagar on the pages of history…'

The walls of Swabhumi hall reverberated with the word 'LIGHTS!' and my grandfather and I exchanged glances that were both jubilant and nervous.

'It all started with a little boy who was fascinated by a small electric torch,' the lady continued. 'Curious as he was, he was not content with simply the light of the torch; he wanted to see what was inside it, that is, the mechanical aspects that went into the making of that electric torch. In 1955, when he was just a student of Class VII, he volunteered to do the lights for the grand Saraswati Puja celebrations at his school. He claimed that he could make the lights run. While his friends made fun of his pipe dream, and spent their evening touring the town, this resolute youngster stayed behind the idol's back in his schoolroom with three small bulbs fixed inside three empty cans of barley. The teachers, who had previously doubted his abilities and regarded the boy who paid little attention to studies with contempt, now brimmed with astonishment and pride. And that was the beginning of this young boy's illustrious career and the beginning of "automatic lighting" in Chandannagar.'

My heart swelled with pride and thrilled with anticipation, and I could almost hear the fluttering of my grandfather's delicate heart as he grabbed hold of his walking stick in preparation of what was about to follow.

'Yes, ladies and gentlemen,' beamed the lady. 'He's none other than Shri Sridhar Das, the pioneer of decorative street lighting in Chandannagar! From the august Thames Festival in London to the opulent Festival of India celebrated in Russia, Das' illuminations have immortalized not only his own name but also that of his beloved town, Chandannagar. The Queen's University in Ireland displayed his illumination for over two weeks, a reputed Malaysian company offered him permanent employment with a sky-high salary but Das did not yield to temptation because of his love for his motherland. He has received so many awards and recognitions from India and abroad that the ex-mayor of Chandannagar Municipal Corporation, Mr Amiya Das, considered the possibility of building a tourist gallery solely for the purpose of preserving and exhibiting them.'

She stopped to take a breath and sneaked a peek at the paper she was reading from. I was so overwhelmed that I could barely focus on what she said.

'Today street lighting has developed into a full-fledged industry in this erstwhile French colony, providing livelihood to thousands of people,' the lady continued. 'The lights of this small town have travelled beyond the national borders to illuminate the entire globe! Around ten thousand people in Chandannagar alone and fifty thousand people in the district of Hooghly and its neighbouring provinces are engaged directly or indirectly in this industry. And it all started with an eleven-year-old boy, living in poverty, who dared to be ambitious and worked hard to make his dreams come true!'

She lowered her pitch and said, more serious now, 'At the age of seventy-five, with a walking stick aiding his steps, he still stands tall and strong. So, put your hands together as I call up on stage the legend himself, Shri Sridhar Das!'

My grandfather was close to tears as he feebly stood up from his seat. He leaned on his walking stick, limping a little, looking back at me to make sure I was right behind him. Three of the organizers made their way to his chair, and after touching his feet respectfully, they led him to a gently sloping ramp specially constructed for him so that he'd experience no difficulty in getting up on stage.

Ever since I learnt to walk, I had accompanied my grandfather to every award function he was invited to. I went up on the stage with him to help him carry his awards even when he didn't need any help. During his interviews, I interrupted the journalists, suggesting better questions that they could ask, demanding to be interviewed alongside him so that he didn't miss out on the important stuff, chiming in with funny anecdotes that I had gathered from my grandmother's inexhaustible reservoir of memories. I also boasted about my 'contribution' to his fascinating career back when I didn't even know what the word 'contribution' meant. 'My grandfather invented lights!' I would say to everyone until I was in the fourth standard, which is when I learnt that it was actually Thomas Alva Edison who invented the light bulb, and he looked nothing like my grandfather. But back then my grandfather would enthusiastically indulge all this fuss and introduce me to all his high profile visitors. He always made it a point to call me down to his office whenever a journalist knocked at the door and I was the first one who he showed all his invites to. He even built a separate showcase in his gallery to display my tiny achievements next to his own.

I wasn't little anymore. I grew up, my grandfather grew older, but our relationship only deepened with time. When I was a toddler, I didn't get to spend a lot of time with him. He was at the peak of his career and a workaholic. We were all afraid of him and his unpredictable moods. I would hide behind my grandmother whenever he came back home from his factory and he would be very disappointed with me if I ever bunked school without any valid reason. But in the course of time and especially after he retired from work, he evolved into this inordinately affectionate person. He always loved me immensely but he used to express his love for me solely through his actions. And as a kid, my love language comprised words of praise, physical touch, and quality time, which my grandfather never had the leisure to shower on me. My grandmother used to be my world back then. But over time, he started being increasingly expressive of his love for me. He changed remarkably once he consciously started cutting down his workload owing to health complications in his sixties. But this excitement and apprehension before being called on stage to receive an award, no matter how big or small, was something that had remained constant. I had dressed up brightly for the occasion just like I used to when I was a kid. It was almost as if I was the one receiving an award! But this time, something held me back.

'Won't you accompany me?' my grandfather asked when he noticed that I wasn't following him.

'No,' I smiled. 'I don't want to steal the show, old man. This is your moment!'

'But why?'

'I've been training you all these years,' I replied. 'Now you've got to do it on your own.'

'But what if I fall?' he looked anxious again.

'Well… you've always stood up again, haven't you?'

My grandfather nodded nervously, 'I think so…'

'You'll be just fine!' I encouraged him. 'Go get your award now!'

It was probably the hundredth time I was seeing him on stage receiving an award, but the sight never failed to touch me. There was a lump in my throat and my eyes struggled to fight back sudden tears. I didn't know whether I was right to abandon him like that at the very last moment. But for once I wanted to be in the audience. This was a lifetime achievement award, after all. And there he was on stage, smiling his familiar smile. His eyes searched for me in the audience. He looked like a little child as he raised the spectacular memento proudly over his head to show it to me.

When asked to address the audience, he was too moved to speak at first but when he finally spoke, his voice trembling and thick with emotion, a hushed silence prevailed in the auditorium. My grandfather thanked all his friends and acquaintances who had played a significant role in his life and career. Many of them, whom he held close to his heart, had passed away in recent years and it always made him very emotional to talk about them. The foggy memories of their long time together were powerful enough to move him to tears. He mentioned my grandmother, her tireless effort and sacrifices as she stood by him through thick and thin, my mother who never complained even though she didn't have the best time growing up, and lastly me. He called me his 'guiding light' and pointed at me in the audience, making me feel extremely awkward because a thousand heads suddenly turned towards me and two thousand hands were clapping energetically. He graciously thanked the kind organizers for having him that evening and for bestowing on him so much honour. I gazed at him, astounded at how well he spoke that evening. This was his best speech so far. The audience responded to his humble words with a standing ovation, followed by a rich harvest of press photographs.

One Year Later...

It was around mid-August 2018, when I had the most distressing nightmare. It was about my grandfather and I had had a gut-wrenching glimpse into the worst thing that could ever happen to him.

I woke up panting and reached out for the jug of water on my bed table, spilling it as I poured a glass. My hands were shaking. Every part of my body trembled as I tried to take a sip. My throat was parched, my T-shirt drenched. I couldn't breathe. I had had dreams before which somehow eerily came true. Ominous dreams about the death of family members, miscarriages, unforeseen health issues and even simpler dreams like meeting someone after a long time, or doing badly in a test which I was well prepared for, had come true from time to time. I knew they were all coincidences but a part of me was badly shaken whenever something like this happened. Whenever I had a nightmare involving a loved one, I would plunge into panic and it would torment me for several days. This time it was a little too personal.

'It will be okay,' I kept repeating to myself. 'Calm down. It was just a dream. It's not going to come true.'

I tried to lie back on my bed and practise some of the breathing exercises that my psychiatrist had taught me. Breathe in deeply for six seconds, hold it in for as long as you can and try releasing it slowly in ten seconds. But I ended up staring at the ceiling as the images from my nightmare played on a loop in my head. My grandmother slept soundly by my side. I desperately needed some fresh air. So, I reached for the door on wobbly legs and pulled it open.

A blast of thick air, heavy with the smell of smoke.

And on the garage roof, against the pale blue starlit sky, silhouetted in black, stood my grandfather. Holding a lit cigarette in his hand. I could finally release the breath

I had unconsciously been holding for so long. I wanted to cry in relief at the sight of him.

'Why are you awake?' I called out instead, drowning my sorrow in feigned anger.

He turned around, squinted at me and then said, 'You're awake too?'

'I can't sleep,' I told him. What I couldn't tell him was how relieved I was to see him there, living and breathing.

'I was just thinking about you,' he said. 'You don't write anymore, do you?'

I shook my head. 'But why are you thinking about that now? It's almost four a.m. You should be in your room, asleep. And definitely not smoking.'

He put out the cigarette immediately and tossed it away. I went up to him, gave him my hand, and slowly led him back to his room. He followed me without a word.

'How long have you been awake?' I asked.

'About an hour, I think,' he said.

'And so you came up here to smoke?'

He looked apologetic.

'How many did you smoke?'

'Umm… one.'

But my eyes had already caught sight of two more discarded cigarette butts by the flower pot.

'You shouldn't be smoking. You know it's bad for your health. You have a pacemaker. You have COPD. You know how dangerous it is! I thought you'd quit. So, this is what you've been doing, huh? Smoking at night when everyone's asleep.'

He didn't speak a word. He just went quietly to bed.

I don't know why he was awake, why he was smoking despite having breathing problems or why he had asked me that question. I went back to my room, but I couldn't stop thinking about what he had asked me. Why did I stop writing? Maybe because I had lost faith in my ability. Perhaps because I had run out of imagination. The scathing criticisms of the book which I wrote and published as a teenager, the countless rejection mails from various publishers, the heaps of half-finished manuscripts that stared blankly back at me whenever I switched on my laptop, the lines I had written, rewritten, deleted, the voices in my mind that kept repeating, 'You're not good enough. You'll never be good enough.'

A few months ago, I had been diagnosed with clinical depression. Having bought the antidepressants, I tucked them away and never spoke a word about it to anyone. I felt that no one would understand. No one in my family had a history of depression. Each one of them was self-made. Both my grandfather and my father were complete strangers to privilege and both had gone through enormous hardships in life. Just like my grandfather, my father too had started working at a very young age to provide for his family. My mother, in spite of being my grandfather's daughter, grew up all alone, deprived and neglected because my grandfather was still a striving light artist in her growing years and could barely pay her school fees in time. And my grandmother, who was going through several personal tragedies of her own alongside doing all the household chores and taking care of her young siblings, could barely give her own daughter the time and attention she needed. My mother was a victim of tremendous abuse in various spheres and at various stages of her life. She was the strongest and the most hardworking woman I knew despite all of that. How could I have expected any of them to empathize with me? More than that, I didn't want to appear weak in their eyes. 'Depression' was a word which was quite foreign to their ears.

I had witnessed my parents' struggle for the majority of my childhood and I barely got to spend time with them until I was eight, when my brother was born. But I never blamed them because I knew they were working extremely hard. My grandmother brought me up and we led a minimalist life, buying only what we really needed, eating in moderation, spending a lot of time reading books and never indulging in any kind of luxury. My grandfather might have been famous but he was not a spendthrift. He has always been extra careful with his money and looked down on any kind of unnecessary extravagance. As a kid I had very few demands and many young uncles and aunts. They were all cool and fun and I always looked forward to their visits because they brought me toffees and other titbits. But I missed my parents very much. I was constantly anxious for them and perpetually lonely.

My life changed significantly during my teenage years. My parents finally had stable jobs and could now afford the luxuries that we were once strangers to. Our standards of living naturally went up and I was happy that they were doing so well, but happier because now I could spend more time with them. We could finally go on trips and celebrate festivals together. Our house was renovated. It was bigger now and felt so much livelier with my baby brother around. I tried my best to make friends because I really wanted to feel accepted in school. But my schoolmates looked at me with a cold, distant look in their eyes. There was a major part of my story that none of them knew.

Very early in my childhood I went through a series of terrible experiences which left me with major trauma and trust issues. I suffered from tremendous OCD, so much that it was difficult for me to function normally and perform my daily activities. I was physically weak but academically very strong. In fact, I was addicted to the kick I got out of it. It almost made me feel invincible. I kept to myself most of the time and wrote extensively about my day-to-day experiences in my diary because I experienced significant difficulty in communicating with others. My diaries were my only friends.

I had attachment issues and social anxiety, too. I must have seemed distant and unapproachable, but all I ever tried to do was keep my guard up to protect my sanity. I never felt like I truly belonged anywhere. While I was in school, I never thought much about these problems. I didn't mind being lonely. It helped me focus on my studies and get good grades. It gave me a lot of free time to write. But once I was out of school, something snapped inside me. I became even more detached and distant.

A year before I was diagnosed, my grandfather, who was seventy-six years old, had been diagnosed with cerebral atrophy which, unlike my depression, couldn't be kept under wraps. He often lapsed into fits of dementia, developed speech problems and was unable to comprehend simple things or register a lot of information at once. His steps were unsteady, his actions bungled and to top it all, he soon complained that he couldn't see or hear clearly.

All in the course of just a year.

From a towering stature, over six feet tall, with piercing eyes and a striking personality, my grandfather had been reduced to a shaky and unconfident old man. Since 2005 he had relied on a pacemaker to keep his heart going but it never felt like he was not in good health or that a vital part of him depended on a machine. He used to be so steady, so active. Now his hands trembled like jelly, he could barely keep his balance when he walked and the very sight of him sitting alone in his room all day, not being able to remember things, not being able to speak without stuttering or hear without being shouted at, was excruciating for me.

'Make him remember things from his childhood,' the family physician suggested. 'Ask him to narrate in detail incidents that happened long ago. Make him read a few paragraphs from the newspaper and ask him questions about it. Tell him a story twice in the morning and ask him to repeat it in the evening. Sadly, cerebral atrophy is not something medicine can cure. The next stage of it is Alzheimer's. You cannot avoid it but you can delay it with the help of these brain exercises.'

When I was a child, the very thought of my grandfather getting old and disappearing from my life one day would terrify me and keep me up at night. Now it only made me feel helpless. In difficult times, it was he who I always looked up to for inspiration and strength. I had taken for granted that he would stay the same forever, that nothing would happen to him. Finally faced with the harsh reality, I couldn't think of a life without my grandfather. The house that I had lived and breathed in for the past twenty years, the house that he had erected himself thirty-seven years ago, had become a symbol of him. The walls bore his touch. He laid the bricks with his own hands back in the 1980s when he couldn't afford to pay for construction. He had painted these walls that guarded so many of my secrets. I couldn't think of the house without thinking of my grandfather.

These anxieties soon transcended the realm of the conscious and infiltrated into darker, murkier territories. Outside the window, the sky was slowly awakening to the first rays of the morning sun, red and gold amidst waves of brilliant blue. The birds had started to twitter and I found this comforting. It was probably half past four when I fell asleep.

'You know what?' I told my grandfather the next morning while we were having tea, 'I think I'm going to start writing again.'

His eyes sparkled with happiness.

'I'm going to write a book,' I added. 'And I'm going to finish it this time.'

'You should,' he responded, taking a sip from his cup.

'And… I'm going to write about you.'

He looked at me in surprise now.

'Why?' he asked, the cup of tea quivering in his hand. 'Why would anyone want to read about me?'

'For the same reason that they read about other people,' I shrugged.

'But t-they can easily know about me… from… from the magazines and newspapers or watch the d-documentaries,' replied my grandfather, frowning.

'Yes, but then they will only know about your achievements,' I put my cup of tea down. 'They'll never know your story.'

'But there are l-lots of other famous people,' stammered my grandfather, 'who are more popular. I'm just a... a... small town artist. Why would anyone want to read about me?'

'Because you are self-made! You never had any formal education, nor did anyone give you the technical knowledge or expertise you've gathered in the field where you excelled. You did it all through trial and error. And today our town is internationally famous for its lights. And thousands of people are earning their livelihood from the industry you once started. Can't you see how fascinating that is?' I let it all out in one breath.

He didn't seem to. The smile I was looking for wasn't forthcoming.

'Why don't you write about something else?'

'Please, Dadu! Please let me do it!' I begged, not knowing how else to change his mind.

'But what about your studies and… and exams?' he asked, worried.

'I'm not going to compromise on them,' I turned to him and took his trembling hands. 'I promise you. I won't let it affect my studies. I've wasted enough time already. I spend hours doing nothing. I must do something productive.'

He didn't look like he thought it was a good idea.

'Please don't say "no". It's something I've been planning for quite some time now. I need to do it. Not just for you, but for myself too.'

'I… I don't think I understand. For yourself?'

And then I gave up and told him the truth. 'I haven't been feeling well lately.'

I saw my grandfather looking at me with renewed interest now.

'Are you sick? What happened? What's wrong?'

Now I had made him anxious.

'No, no. Not physically sick. I just don't feel right.'

'I noticed that you haven't b-been yourself lately,' his eyes were full of concern. 'You have been unusually quiet. But I thought perhaps you were busy with c-college and exams. So, I didn't bother you. Whenever I see you, you're… you're either sitting alone in your room or typing on your phone.'

I gave a hesitant nod.

'What's the matter with you?'

'I don't know,' I said, unable to meet his eyes. 'I can't explain. It's been this way for over a year now.'

'For over a year?' his eyes widened.

'Yes,' I replied. 'This constant feeling of being worthless and incapable.'

I looked at the floor, toying with the old red thread tied around my wrist.

'I feel like I can't even think straight now,' I struggled to explain. 'I can't take anything lightly. I don't know how to talk to people. I don't know what to say most of the time. And when I do, I don't think they get what I am saying. I have to think a lot before I speak so that I'm not misunderstood.'

He patiently waited for me to continue.

'I look around and feel like everything's wrong with the world, like everything is meaningless! I look at my face in the mirror and feel nothing but disappointment. I never feel good about myself. There are these... these voices inside my head, saying I will never be good enough. I have tried writing. I didn't want to give up. That's the only thing I wanted to do.'

'Then why did you give up?'

'Because I am never satisfied with what I write. I have tried sending out my short stories and poems to different magazines. Rejected. Every time. I think I've either lost the ability to write or I never possessed it in the first place.'

'You know that's not true at all. You are not even twenty years old yet. You have your whole life to work on your writing.'

'All my dreams look impossible,' I told him. 'And I no longer have interest in the things I've always loved doing, like painting, listening to music or reading books outside the course syllabus, above all writing. It's so frustrating!'

He looked at me, a little confused, as though it was all too much for him to understand. And then he asked, 'What do you think will make you... happy... right now?'

'To be able to write,' I replied after what seemed an eternity. 'To write about you. I want to forget about everything else and write again. And I'm really not bothered about whether or not it affects my academic performance. My third semester has been a disaster, even though I worked the hardest for it. I just want to breathe a little now. I'm not even sure if I made the right choice in taking up English Literature.'

'What are you saying?' he looked really worried. 'You've always been a good student!'

'I don't know what you mean by a good student,' I said. 'Scores are just numbers on a piece of paper. The whole education system is screwed! All it's ever taught us is to compete with each other. What an unhealthy way of thinking it has instilled in us! We can no longer be happy for others.'

'I agree,' he replied. 'But… you've wanted to s-study literature ever since you were a child. Just because one semester t-turned out bad, it… it doesn't mean you should give up.'

I didn't know what to say.

'I want to be like you someday, Dadu,' I told him. 'I mean, I know I can never boast about being self-made. You couldn't study beyond Class VIII. But you followed your calling, you did what you were good at, and you succeeded. Since my childhood, the only thing I was somewhat good at was writing. I'm not great at it, there's room for loads of improvement, but this is the one thing I've always wanted to do.'

'I know that.'

'But I haven't been able to work on the only thing I love doing because I've always felt obliged to work on my studies, just to go on being a "bright student". Right now, I feel like I'm stuck in a creative limbo. I don't have a story to tell. It's like all my creative juices have dried up. I can't think of anything.'

He nodded gravely.

'But I think I've found one now. Why should I look for a plot elsewhere when I've got a brilliant one right here?'

He looked at me and smiled. Finally, he was beginning to understand.

'And you know what,' I continued. 'If I'm actually able to write about you, I think I might be able to get over all this negativity. I'll be engaged in something, at least. I really want to get well, Dadu. And there's only one person who can help me and that's you.'

'You really think so?'

'I do,' I replied. 'But the one thing that I'm really worried about is whether I can do justice to your story. I know there are writers out there who are infinitely better than me. I'm just an amateur.'

'Oh! But there's one big difference between them and you, my dear,' he grinned, his bleary eyes sparkling. 'You know me in a way they never will. They know me as an artist. They can write only about my achievements. But you know me as a *person*. It doesn't matter if you're an amateur. None of us is perfect. We all make mistakes. God, I've made hundreds and thousands of them in my life! You can never achieve anything if you let mistakes and criticisms deter you. Take them in your stride.'

'Okay, then!' I smiled for the first time that morning.

I hadn't expected him to be able to say so much without stammering. More importantly, I hadn't expected that talking to him about my state of mind would be so easy. He understood me. I felt more confident in my hunch that this would be good for both of us. I decided to push him a little further.

'But I'm not the only one who's going to make an effort,' I told him. 'You need to help me out by doing some thinking and remembering of your own. Why should I read magazines and newspaper articles, when I can have it all straight from your mouth?'

After being lost in thought for the entire day, my grandfather went to bed that night at the usual hour but it took a very long time for him to fall asleep. I had given him some memory homework before I said goodnight and that was to think of a day in his life before he had discovered his calling. He was to think back to the time when he was just a little boy, like any other ordinary little boy, living in Chandannagar in the mid-twentieth century, except for the fact that this little boy, a stranger to luxury and privilege, had his eyes fixed on the stars. With my mind brimming with new ideas for my narrative, I gulped down my sleeping pill and slumbered peacefully that night for the first time in months, while he lay awake in bed, lost in thought till the small hours of the morning. The next day, after our chores were done and we had some time in the morning, I settled down with my notebook, switched on the recorder in my phone and he began to tell me of a day he remembered from a vanished time when he was just eleven years old. The summer of 1955. This is his story.

1

Summer of 1955

'Eggs for lunch! One for each!' I sang on my way to school that day. 'One for each! *One for each!*'

When I was a child, I never had to feign illness to avoid school. While the other boys my age faced serious trouble if they were ever found bunking classes, I never had to think about it twice. It's not because I was too fond of going to school. For the record, I wasn't. But my father was too busy with his job at the mill and my mother too engrossed in cooking, cleaning, feeding and looking after the new-born to enquire about my whereabouts, and I usually took full advantage of the situation.

My father, Prafulla Chandra Das, worked as a labourer in the Alexander Jute Mill and my mother, Saraswati Das, was a homemaker who struggled to prepare decent meals to feed a family of thirteen, suckling my youngest, eleven-month-old brother, even as her belly was slightly swollen with yet another unborn sibling on the way. They were both very hardworking. My father displayed his expertise in the public sphere, my mother in the private. The home was her only world. Just one small hut tucked away in the suburb of an underdeveloped country which had acquired independence from British rule just eight years ago.

But what was special about our town was that it had been under French rule, unlike the rest of the country. So, in a way it was like one small world of its own. It never belonged elsewhere. It had a distinct culture of its own, a different flavour altogether. Many of the people we knew could speak in broken French. Fewer people could speak English. I could speak neither. And that never irked me, though I could say it irked some of my friends. They considered it a major drawback. I never understood why. I was content knowing my own language which was Bangla. Why would I learn someone else's? Did they ever try to master my language? Hardly. But they always expected us to master theirs as though we weren't up to the mark unless we could speak their tongue.

Oh, how glad I was when we attained freedom! We would finally be free from such expectations, I thought. I could speak my own language proudly and be content with the colour of my skin. The constant presence of the French around us, and even a mere glimpse of their white faces from across the street was powerful enough to induce strong feelings of inferiority in oneself. We were many, they were few, yet we stood out like contrasts next to them in the land which was supposed to be our own before they brought in their ships for trade. However, it didn't take me long to figure out that I was mistaken. Even though the pale faces were gone, we were far from free. Speaking English and French were still considered to be the hallmarks of literacy. Anyone who didn't conform to these standards was deemed illiterate. The colour of my skin still stood out like a sore thumb and even my mother mocked me at times for being the darkest member of the family. She said I was never going to get married or be able to do anything significant in life since I was both poor and dark, unlike my other siblings who were just poor.

To my mother, the four moss-laden walls of our house were limits she never had the will to explore beyond. She was content living within those walls and felt blessed that she had a roof over her head. She had no complaints, no demands. And if any of us ever complained about our sorry state, the cane would do the talking. In those days, boys of my age would be beaten black and blue by their parents for the slightest misdemeanour. I was no exception. However, I was never punished by my mother for bunking school. If my mother ever saw me at home during school hours, she would either ask me to help her clean or hold my baby brother, Ganesh. And my father, who was the only one in the family concerned about my education, would be out all day working in the mill, so he wasn't much of a threat either. Had he been home, I would never have had the liberty to remain absent from school. A year ago, I remember having been beaten up by him severely for the very same reason. But the mill demanded more of his time now, his pay was increased by two rupees by way of justification, and he was barely around. And when he came back, there were so many of us that he often kept losing track and sometimes called my brother Kartik, 'Balaram' and Balaram, 'Krishna'. We weren't even sure when we were born or how old we actually were because nobody had the leisure to remember such details.

All my brothers were named after characters from Hindu mythology but none of them looked like the characters they were named after. Not even close. Except for Ganesh. No, no! He didn't have the head of an elephant. But his features were blunt, his eyes brown and large, his limbs plump and short and his belly, round and flabby. In other words, he was the healthiest kid in our family with an insatiable appetite. All he lacked was a trunk. What an unfortunate oversight!

I had a few sisters who had greater responsibilities. Of course, they didn't go to school. That was pretty much out of the question for girls back in those days. They helped my mother cook, wash the potatoes, chop the vegetables, boil the rice and lentils, mop the floor with rags which had long outlived their utility. And in their leisure time, they either sat at the door of the kitchen separating mussels from their shells or sucked on the sour slices of mango pickle stored in the old glass jars, clicking their tongues and occasionally licking their brown, chapped lips. Baba hardly ever bought fish or meat for our family, for the little pond situated right behind our house was full of small fish and freshwater mussels. While my elder brothers spent hours on the steps of the ghat with a ball of dough, two small fishing rods and a very old rusty iron bucket, fishing all weekend, my sisters would float large coconut leaves near the banks to collect clusters of mussels that drifted on the water. And our mother would cook small portions of them over the week.

Krishna and I often stole mangoes from either the biscuit factory orchards near our house or the numerous tall trees standing proudly amidst the green thicket lining the dirt road on our way to school. Even though I loved mangoes more than any other fruit, I found the date palm trees particularly interesting. With earthen pots tied to their trunks to collect sweet palm juice, they reminded me of the fat, black leeches that refused to let go of my legs that one time we went to play hide and seek in the dark and gloomy bamboo forests of Kalupukur, in our neighbouring locality. It was the kind of place that sent shivers down one's spine after nightfall, a den of ravenous jackals, boggarts and ghosts from the cemetery, enchanting shapeshifters, raucous crickets, fiery glow worms, sometimes dacoits. Acres and acres of tall bamboo, so green and wet during the day and so cold and dark during the night that one could get frightened of the sound of one's own footsteps and shiver all the way back home, repeating Lord Rama's name one hundred and eight times.

Our little cottage made of mud and straw in Bidyalanka, at the heart of Chandannagar, wasn't big enough to house all thirteen of us when I think of it now, almost sixty-four years later, but it was home to us back then and most of us could never have dreamt of anything bigger or better.

'Don't be late today,' my mother called out from the kitchen one morning. 'I'm making boiled eggs for lunch, one for each.'

I almost thought I was dreaming because, one, my mother was hardly sweet to me. She barely even cared whether I came back home from school or was knocked out on the way, but today she was actually asking me to come back home early for lunch. Number two, she was making boiled eggs for us. Most importantly, one for each! Oh, it was nothing less than a dream come true to me! I had never had a whole egg in my entire life.

'Eggs for lunch! One for each!' I sang on my way to school that day. 'One for each! One for *each*!'

It was drizzling and the narrow, unmetalled dirt road was full of potholes and muddy puddles but I didn't care, whereas, on any other day, I would have jumped in those puddles and drenched myself at the tube-well. It was a common and quite popular strategy back in those days. My friends and I would deliberately forget to carry our umbrellas and often drenched ourselves at the tube-wells or any random pipe oozing out water on rainy days so that our teacher sent us back home the moment we stepped inside the classroom with our pants dripping. I remember Bhola smelling like a sewage one rainy day and I instantly knew that he had stood under the wrong pipe.

'You look very happy today!' Bhola slapped my back. 'What's up?'

'Maa is making boiled eggs for lunch!' I replied gleefully. 'One for each!'

'You are such a lucky boy!' he said, enviously. 'My mother seldom lets me have a full egg! She cuts each egg into three pieces for the nine of us to share. And dada always gets the biggest piece.'

'I know, it is very unfair,' I replied. 'I never had a full egg in my life! I once had half an egg, stole dada's piece when he wasn't looking and blamed it on Kartik who is my mother's favourite and hence never gets scolded. This will be the first time I get to eat a whole egg! I have to get back home early today because I don't want to miss it.'

'So, you won't play with us today?' my best friend Vikash asked me, disappointed.

'Sorry, no.'

'But the team needs you, Sridhar! We have to defeat the bullies from Lal Dighi.'

'I promise I'll stay back tomorrow. Today is a very special day!' I rubbed my hands excitedly, imagining the taste of the hard-boiled yolk melting slowly in my mouth and my uneven front teeth biting into the white, solid albumin. My mother was probably cooking those gigantic pearls right now! Visualizing it all in slow motion, I relished it in my imagination bit by bit. I wasn't sure how long I was going to sit there on the cold earthen floor sucking on that one egg in the afternoon. However, I was determined to make the most of the opportunity and savour every molecule of that blessed egg till my mother slapped me out of my reverie and told me to go wash my hands or fetch some firewood for the hearth or fuel for the hurricane lamp before darkness engulfed our little cottage.

The hours in school seemed extremely tedious and tiresome that morning. The sharp bristles of the coarse sacks we sat on poked through the cheap fabric of our pants and scratched the skin of our thighs till they were sore. The ceiling was made of cheap asbestos, making the heat all the more unbearable and we were sweating like horses and smelling like dogs. While we kept repeating the same stanza of Tagore's poem, 'Taal Gaach', over and over again in chorus and in a distinct nasal tone for special effects, till we got sick of the sound of our own voices, our teacher, Babulal Pramanik, dozed on his wooden chair, cane in hand, the vigilant mole below his right eye looking stern and taut as though it wouldn't permit even the slightest nuisance. And then there was this wretched fly, that had developed an unnatural fixation with Babulal Sir's precious mole and continuously tried to settle on it. His vain attempts to make a pass at the comely mole often interrupted Babulal Sir's slumber and he woke up with a start but then dozed off again in a few seconds, lulled by our monotonous incantation of Tagore's energetic verse. I regretted coming to school that day. Oh, how I wished I had stayed back home!

'It's intolerable!' Bhola whispered to me from behind. 'Do something, Sridhar!'

'Like what?' I whispered back.

'Something! Anything! This is torture! We will be half asleep by the time we reach the field and the Lal Dighi dogs will cheerfully kick our butts instead! Let's run away. I don't think he's going to wake up any time soon.'

'And get whipped by my father if he comes to know?' I exclaimed. 'I cannot do anything risky today!'

'Boiled eggs! One for each! One for each!' a voice in my head reminded me, and I was cautious.

Needless to say, there was surprise and envy on the faces of my friends when I told them after class that I was going to have a whole duck's egg in the afternoon. That was precisely the reason why I had gone to school that morning, to break this fabulous news to them. I remembered Chandu calling me 'the poor worker's son' one day and I wanted to make it known to him that my father had become rich enough to afford eggs for all of us.

'Who is the poor worker's son now, huh, Chandu?' My best friend Vikash had taken my side.

'Who cares about stupid eggs?' scoffed Chandu. 'I have them every day. And he's still a poor worker's son anyway! Look at the torn straps of his sandals held together by pins, the unwashed shirt he's worn for four days in a row. My father earns twenty-five rupees every week. That's one hundred rupees per month! How much does his father earn? Ten? Twelve? Probably less than that.'

'He's just jealous, you know,' Vikash whispered in my ears. 'Don't bother. He's telling lies simply to torment you.'

'I know,' I whispered back, even though I knew Chandu had absolutely no reason to be jealous of me. He was better than me in every way. He was a Brahmin, upper caste, fair and healthy looking. I was a Vaishya, dark and thin. His father was a manager, he earned a hundred rupees a month, my father was merely a labourer. He was not too bad at studies either and was Babulal Sir's favourite student. I was the one who bunked classes and was always the victim of his wrath. I had no idea why Chandu was so bitter towards me. He had everything. I had little. It was not like I could ever be his rival. He was way beyond my league. Perhaps his bitterness was habitual. Vikash too was fair. He was the most handsome boy in our class! He too came from a rich family, but he was never bitter towards anyone. He wouldn't hurt a fly!

'Hey, why do you think Chandu hates me so much?' I

remember asking Vikash later that afternoon while we were perched on the parapet, eating his tiffin.

He thought hard about my question for about two seconds and then answered, 'Because he's afraid you're better than him.'

'What?' I laughed, relishing the *dum-aloo* that his mother had prepared so lovingly. I never carried any tiffin to school. But Vikash always brought some extra so that I didn't go hungry.

'Yes,' he replied. 'What he sees in you is… what do they call it? Potential! He sees potential in you. You can solve any sum. Even the ones that Babulal Sir cannot solve, let alone Chandu or any of us.'

'Is that why he hates me?' I asked. 'Because I am good at solving sums?'

'Of course,' said Vikash. 'He's afraid that your *potential* might take you places someday, maybe you'll become a mathematician like Ramanujan, or… or a scientist like Einstein! He definitely cannot stand "the poor worker's son" being better off than him one day.'

'But I don't want to be a mathematician or a scientist,' I told him.

'Then what do you want to be?'

'I don't know. I have not given it much thought yet. I want to do something different. Something no one's ever thought about.'

'You'll definitely do something great, my friend!' Vikash encouraged me. 'You have it in you. I can see it.'

'Have you seen the lights at the bazaar, Vikash? The long ones?'

'The light tubes at Sudha Kaka's shop, you mean? Yes, I have seen them. Why?'

'Aren't they fascinating?'

'They seem pretty ordinary to me,' he scratched his head. 'They are just lights in long tubes.'

'I want to create something beautiful,' I told him. 'Something so beautiful that people will stop and stare...'

And no sooner had I uttered those words than I felt a violent blow on my back and fell flat on my face on the ground along with the little tiffin box. A group of boys stood by and laughed, some peered over the rails curiously to look at me.

'You see?' a familiar voice cackled. 'You don't always have to create something beautiful to make people stop and stare.'

'What the hell, Chandu!' Vikash cried out. 'This is not funny!'

Chandu and his sidekicks stood there mocking me, roaring with laughter, calling me all sorts of names. Vikash, being the peace-loving person he was, didn't attack them physically but he lashed out at them verbally, promising to take the matter to Head Sir's office. I stood up, brushed the dirt off my uniform, and picked up the pieces of *dum-aloo* that had fallen to the ground. My forehead hurt, my eyes stung and one of my knees was badly skinned. I felt a lump in my throat, but I swallowed it. I didn't want to shed a single teardrop that day. With the sound of Head Sir's scooter arriving at the gate, Chandu and his lackeys fled from the scene, while Vikash escorted me to the tap and helped me wash away the dirt from my bleeding knee lest it get infected.

'I hate those people!' Vikash fumed through gritted teeth as he wildly splashed water on my knee, almost drenching my pants. 'I have never, in my entire life, hated anyone as much as I hate them! Let's go straight to Head Sir's office. Right now!'

'Let it go,' I said instead. 'I don't want to create unnecessary trouble.'

'Unnecessary? If you let it go now, they'll keep doing this to you,' he cried. 'This is what they do. These bullies, they prey on innocent people! This needs to stop!'

'We'll go some other day, Vikash,' I told him. 'I have to return home early this afternoon. I cannot be late today. Let's take this matter up some other day.'

'Some other day might be too late!'

'I don't want to get involved in any scene today,' I told him. 'My mother's making eggs for lunch. I cannot afford to ruin the mood.'

And indeed, nothing could ruin my joyous mood that day. And I wasn't the least bit disappointed when I got back home, for all my dreams came true that afternoon!

To start, we had crispy bitter gourd, cut into thin round slices. This was followed by mashed potatoes seasoned with finely chopped onions, chillies and a few drops of mustard oil. For the main course we had white rice with watery *arhar* daal. And then came what we had all been waiting for, the precious, mouth-watering, hard boiled duck's eggs still warm in their shells! Oh, what a luxury!

For the first time in my life I was this happy at lunch! My mother's eyes sparkled with contentment as she served the eggs. I couldn't believe that I had one whole duck's egg sitting on my plate, right before my eyes, waiting to be relished. Knocking it softly against my plate with trembling hands, I broke the shell and took great pleasure in peeling it off from the shiny surface of the solidified albumin. And there she was! The beauty! Exactly like I had imagined! What happiness! What inexplicable fulfilment!

However, it didn't quite go as I had imagined. I had planned in my fantasy to sit with that egg for an hour, relishing it bit by bit, sprinkling salt in layers on the orange yolk. But when faced with the temptation in real life, it took only a few minutes for the succulent egg to completely disappear from my plate and right into my stomach. So, instead, I burped all afternoon and relished every single one of them.

We didn't have a camera back then to capture that moment of joy, so I etched it indelibly in my memory and today, almost sixty-five years later, even though I have forgotten most of the events of my life, this memory remains crystal clear, the memory of the day I was allowed to eat one whole egg for the very first time. And such was the taste that it kindled a blazing fire in a poor boy's heart, a desire to be well off, so that he could have another egg, and two more if that's what he wanted, without having to beg, borrow or steal. I wanted to show Chandu and all his rotten sidekicks what I was capable of.

The fire burned that afternoon and gathered momentum by dusk when my mother asked me to pay attention to my studies instead of playing with the torch and wasting the battery as well as my time.

'Why do you always keep messing with that instrument,

boy?' she cried as she patted Ganesh's back over and over again to put him to sleep.

'I like how it glows on its own. Just like a firefly. Isn't it, Maa?'

'Why don't you devote the same energy to your studies for a change?' she scowled.

The golden flames of desire blazing within me manifested in my complaint about the weak light of the hurricane lamp which was too dim for me to read even a line.

'I can't read in this darkness. My head aches.'

'It doesn't ache when you play with that stupid light, does it? Only when it's time to study, your head aches.'

'Why don't we have brighter lights, Maa?' I asked.

'Because we are poor,' my mother replied imperiously, pouring water into a bowl of flour while Ganesh sucked his thumb on her lap.

'I can't read in this light,' I complained again, switching the torch on and off.

'What's wrong with you?' she snapped. 'You never complained about the light before.'

'I have seen better lights, Maa. Brighter ones!'

She pretended she hadn't heard me.

'I saw Sudha Kaka at the Laxmiganj Bazaar repairing them in his shop. They are real lights, in long tubes. Nothing at all like the hurricane lamps! And they are so bright that everything seems blurry after you've looked at them for a while.'

'So, that's what happened, huh?' my mother hissed now, kneading the dough with violent intensity. 'Those lights seem to have blinded you and now you can't see anything else. If I ever find you looking at those lights again, *khoka*, I'm going to make you starve for a week!'

The forbidden fruit is always sweet. So, I went to look at those lights again the very next day. And the day after. And the day after. Even though I knew I would be skinned alive if Baba ever caught me there. There was something pleasantly uncanny about the lights. They were so strange and beautiful! I had never seen anything like them before. The longer I looked at them the more restless they made me. It was an unsettling feeling, yet I longed to be closer to them. I wanted to touch them, feel them with my hands, and fall asleep next to them. They had triggered something in me, some emotion that I had never experienced before, a sense of urgency. I could see the world in those tantalizing lights, a world calling out to me. I often dreamt of them, and in those dreams, I could see myself being anything I wanted to be. Soon enough, these lights were all that dominated my waking hours and they were all I went to bed thinking about.

'Mother was right, Vikash. The lights have blinded me. I can't see anything else anymore.'

'Boy, oh boy!' he grinned from ear to ear. 'You're in trouble now, aren't you?'

2

Autumn of 1955

'Why are you standing outside, child?' asked Sudha Kaka, a small earthen cup of lemon tea in one hand and a rusty aluminium kettle in the other. 'Come on in.'

I had been standing outside his shop, Sadhu Electric, for months looking at all the electrical appliances that his men repaired. The walls were stained and greasy, of a yellow ochre colour, there were several hinges all around and containers with different kinds of oil, bits and pieces of cloth, all old and torn and stained. There were a number of big and small instruments strewn across the old, cracked mosaic floor. They fascinated me to no end. Switchboards, screwdrivers, nuts and bolts, cables, bulbs and tube lights, stand fans, ceiling fans, tins of heavenly smelling kerosene oil and a machine that emitted a shower of sparks and had to be wielded with extra care. I wanted to touch them, but I didn't dare.

'I'd like to see how you work with all these,' I told him. 'Can you teach me, Kaka? I will work for you.'

'But you are too young for this kind of work,' said Kaka, his kind eyes wide with astonishment. 'It's risky job, kid. Like playing with fire. People get injured doing this kind of work.'

'The thing that passes through those wires is *current*, right?'

'Yes. It is called electricity.'

'What exactly is electricity?' I asked him out of curiosity. It was all very alien to me. 'What does this electricity or current do that makes all those bulbs glow and the fans spin?

'Well child, there are two types of current,' replied Sudha Kaka. 'AC and DC. In Chandannagar we only have AC. Whereas in Kolkata and other big cities you will find DC...'

'What's the difference between AC and DC?' I cut him off in excitement.

'AC is alternating current which changes its direction at regular intervals,' Kaka informed me. 'Whereas DC is direct current which flows in one particular direction.'

I couldn't really comprehend what he had said. All I gathered was that there was something called current, also known as electricity. It flowed through wires. And it also made lights glow and fans spin. At times it changed directions. At times it didn't. I could still not understand how it made those lights glow and curiosity was killing me. The more time I spent standing there watching Kaka's men pinching snuff and smoking *bidis*, pausing to take sips from their cups of lemon tea but all the time working on those lights and fans like experts, the more my curiosity grew. It seemed like they knew everything about electricity! How did they? And why did I not know anything about it? Was it something they had learnt at school? I couldn't remember being taught anything like that. All they made us do was sit with books and recite the same inane poems over and over again or do sums that even a donkey could solve. Was I not paying attention when all that was taught? Had I bunked school on that day?

'Where did you learn about this from?' I asked them one day. 'School?'

They looked at me for a moment, in absolute silence, and then burst out in booming laughter, all five of them together, as though I had said the funniest thing ever. There were people around in all the other stores and even the ones standing across the street buying cream and butter from the dairy looked in our direction. All this time a cow stood by me busy chewing cud, looking blankly at a pariah dog playing with her pups, but now she paused her cud chewing and turned around to look at me. I could say with certainty that she too was amused.

I squirmed with embarrassment.

'Well, which school do you go to, lad?' one of them asked me, wiping a tear from his eye.

'Narua Shikshayatan' I scratched my head. 'You?'

'We don't even know what a school looks like from the inside,' he replied.

'All we know is that they don't do you any good,' added another, putting on his helmet.

'They only turn you into big, fat idiots with lots of money and no zest for life!' their group leader chimed in. 'They tell you when to sit, when to stand. They beat you when you don't obey. You can't even pee without permission! Think of that! I went to school for a few days, they didn't let me pee when I asked to go. So, I peed all over the place and never went back. They tell you to shut up when you ask questions they can't answer. And then when you score poorly, you're whipped at home as well. There are no schools. Only prisons.'

I looked at him with swelling admiration.

'At times, I feel the same.'

'Yes?' he looked happy. 'You feel that too, boy?'

'Yes,' I replied. 'I don't like school. The bullies are never punished.'

'You're a good lad! Come, you are one of us!' the group leader patted my back.

You are one of us, that phrase stuck with me for an entire day and I felt an inexplicable sense of pride and belonging every time I thought about it. If I could just work at Kaka's shop for a few days, I would learn everything there was to learn about electricity. And my house would never be dark again after nightfall.

'I want to know how the electricity passes through those wires,' I told Kaka. 'Where does it come from? Who makes it? What exactly happens in those glass bulbs when they come in contact with electricity? Why do they glow? What about the fans?'

'You are too young for it,' Kaka repeated. 'I will teach you all about electricity once you turn fourteen.'

I was disappointed. I wanted to learn about it right then, at that very moment. But Kaka was busy and so were his men and I knew it was not a good time to pester them. At least he allowed me to watch his men while they worked. I was afraid I would be barred from doing even that if I interfered too much or seemed too excited. I considered going back home and opening up my torch. I was certain that it had something to do with electricity. How would it glow otherwise?

But the moment I was about to rush in through the gates of my humble abode, I was rudely grabbed by my collar. I choked and coughed a little, and was about to react violently because I thought it was one of my brothers but then I turned around to discover that it was none other than my father. He had come back home from the mill early that afternoon and wanted me to lend him a hand in carrying bricks from our house to the front yard of a rich man who had recently moved into our locality. No sooner had he issued his orders than a trolley piled with bricks arrived at our gate. Our wealthy neighbour had apparently got them really cheap and hence bought the entire load of bricks and a few sacks of cement for the purpose of building a boundary wall along the length of his garden.

'I got you a present today,' Father said, trying to tempt me. 'Do your work sincerely and you will get it.'

At the end of the day, after I was done shifting the mountain of bricks and my hands and legs were sore, my neck and shoulders stiff, my backbone almost numb, I discovered that the 'present' that my father had been brandishing as his bait all day was nothing but a bunch of dull, yellowish papers that he had brought back from the mill. He now wanted me to help him stitch them into notebooks and use them for my classes. I think the disappointment showed up a little too clearly on my face because my sore back got spanked hard three times soon after.

'This boy has no interest in studies!' he brought his fist down on the table with a loud bang while I stood there rubbing my aching back. 'All he's good at is bunking school and loitering about in Laxmiganj Bazaar! He's USELESS!'

'You went to the bazaar again?' my mother glared at me.

'Yeah t-to bring some firewood…' I stammered. 'For the hearth.'

'Well, where is the firewood then?'

'I… I didn't find any. There was n-none of it in the market t-today.'

'But Hari from the fish market told me you were there in Sudha Sadhu's electric shop all day,' my father looked enraged. 'Was he lying to me?'

'I… I wasn't there today, Baba,' I lied instinctively. 'I… I went there… y-yesterday.'

'Let me refresh your memory then, YOU RASCAL!' my father roared. 'The truth is, you go there EVERY DAY!'

'Every day?' my mother cried. 'Did I not tell you never to go there again?'

'EVERY DAMN DAY!' my father hollered. 'In fact, Sudha told me himself! Why would he lie to me? He bunks school, he lies to you at home to go and sit there with Sudha Sadhu and his lads, smoking *bidis*!'

'Is that true, *khoka*?' mother enquired.

'I don't smoke *bidis*,' I protested. 'I never smoked *bidis*.'

'I didn't say that, YOU JACKASS!' shouted father. 'Don't feign innocence! I know you're not innocent. You have disobeyed me! You've disobeyed your mother! How dare you live under my roof and disobey me?'

I didn't speak. I didn't know what to say.

I was beaten black and blue and made to starve that night.

The following afternoon, when my mother was busy in the kitchen and my sisters were busy arguing with each other about what they would name our new sibling once it was born, I succeeded in opening the torch. I expected to find the universe encapsulated within it, like Yashoda Maa found in Lord Krishna's mouth, but all I found was a paltry spring, a trifling battery with its butt attached to the spring and its head touching the lamp, and a thin bronze plate, about the size of a lottery ticket folded five times, which was connected to the switch. Was that all I was going to find? I was a little disappointed. But the moment I pressed the switch, the bronze plate touched the lamp and it glowed. The moment I released the switch, the bronze plate drew back and the lamp ceased to glow. Interesting!

'The battery and the bronze plate definitely have something to do with electricity!' I told myself.

I wasn't wrong.

Winter of 1956

I was quite proud about the new developments that had taken place in the course of the last four months or so.

Number one, my father had introduced electricity in

our house. We now had a switch board with many funny switches on it. A network of wires ran through the walls of our house. There was just one fan and two lights of the cheapest quality, but it brought me unlimited joy and satisfaction. Sudha Kaka's men had done the wiring in our house, and I had observed the process keenly, taking in as many details as I could with the intention of conducting a similar experiment soon.

Number two, I chanced upon an old homeopathy medicine box under the bed and collected in it the most interesting objects I could find. For example, a pair of pliers, a screwdriver, some iron nails, a bunch of wires, some holders and bulbs, a string of lamps, a few sheets of cellophane paper and the like. And I hadn't begged or borrowed or stolen any of it. I bought them. Each and every one of them. I saved the little handouts my father often bestowed on me on the rare occasions when he suddenly wanted his generosity to be acknowledged. I also helped Sudha Kaka with little odd jobs like bringing tea, getting his *bidis*, making a few small deliveries and he let me keep the change. I judiciously invested all my savings bit by bit to procure the paraphernalia of electrical spare parts and other necessary appliances that would aid me in my experiments.

School got over earlier than usual one day, and I came back home to find my mother suckling my new-born brother and my five sisters busy in the kitchen. My father was at the mill, my four elder brothers had all gone out to work. Kartik and Ganesh were with our mother, playing with each other and entertaining the new baby with their antics. Krishna was out there somewhere, fishing perhaps or playing with the neighbours' ferret-faced son who never missed an opportunity to remind me how ugly and awkward I was. Talk about the pot calling the kettle black! It had just been a week since my mother had delivered my new-born sibling so she wasn't quite active. My coast was clear.

I opened my precious box and picked up a bulb, a holder and a bunch of wires. Fixing the bulb in the holder, I attached the wires to it the way I had seen Sudha Kaka's men do, and the other end of the wires I inserted into the plug point on our switchboard. And then I stood still, my heart palpitating.

Should I press the switch? What if it didn't work? All my hopes and dreams would crumble to dust on the ground. All these months that I had bunked school and stood outside Sudha Kaka's repair store watching the men work, observing all their activities minutely, getting whipped and beaten by my father every time the teacher complained about my poor attendance and lack of attention in class, all of that would go to waste if the bulb didn't glow.

The bulb attached to the holder and the wires lay there on the ground mocking me, as if asking, 'What now? What do you want to do?' I could hear the cuckoo cooing outside in the balmy afternoon sun, I could hear the lapping of the water from the pond nearby. Mani Kakima was probably washing clothes, I could hear them being beaten against the hard steps of the ghat. A few boys were out there bathing, splashing water at each other, laughing like maniacs and swearing away to glory, words that I couldn't utter without immediately running the risk of being buried alive by my father. A delectable smell of fresh pickle made from the jujube fruit and home-made spices wafted through the air and hit my nose. I knew what my sisters were up to as soon as I heard the familiar clicking of their tongues against the roofs of their mouths, but I felt so detached from all of them. As though I had never been a part of their lives. As though I was never meant to be.

I was no longer even interested in going out and playing *gulli-danda* with my friends. They often dropped by to catch up on my affairs, asking if I wanted to go play but I turned them down every day, feigning illness, errands or something or the other. Electricity had devoured me. Nothing else mattered as much. All my sense of belonging lay there in that homeopathy box. This side of my personality was new to me and strange though it might sound, I was proud of every bit of it.

My hands trembling, I finally pressed the switch and then, for a while, I looked at everything but the bulb that lay on the ground. Never did my heart beat so fast and so loud while I tried hard not to concentrate on something. Not even when my mother screamed that she was dying in the throes of labour. I whistled some stray, unfamiliar tune that I had cooked up at that moment, I looked out of the window to see the tops of the tall coconut trees swaying, I dug my nose with a look of deep contemplation, I looked up at the ceiling to notice the cobwebs that had accumulated there, I looked around everywhere but I didn't look down for fear that my hopes would be shattered. I touched this and that aimlessly, straightened some of the objects on the table, wiped the dust off the rails with my sweaty fingers, and noticed the dirt that had accumulated beneath my fingernails.

And then my eyes caught a faint flicker. And finally, looking down, out of the corner of my eyes, I saw the bulb glowing gently on the ground with faint, weak and unsteady light. A loud, triumphant cry of delight rent the air!

My first experiment was a success.

Saraswati Puja 1956

'As you all know, each year it is the students of class seven and eight who organize the puja in school,' said Babulal Sir. 'So, I would like you all to sit in groups, divide the responsibilities and come up with ideas. The puja is next week on Thursday, so I need a plan by the end of the day.'

Vikash, Bhola and Chandu readily volunteered to be a part of the donation camp or *chanda* party which required the members of the party to go around and knock on every door, or stop every passer-by on the streets and shamelessly demand *chanda* or donation for the puja. Not everyone was willing to pay all the time, and they often had to be really persuasive and demanding. As a consequence, they often got insulted, slapped, shoved across the street and rudely rejected with a swear word or two but our parents had definitely prepared us for life, and we had all developed a thick skin. Hence, we were immune to every possible kind of public humiliation by now. It was all in a day's work for us.

A few brave ones volunteered to be a part of the skit

that Babulal Sir presented each year. On such occasions, Sir's cane was his constant companion and he often liked to acquaint the backs of the actors with his beloved cane in case they missed a line or delivered it late and when their facial expressions didn't fall in line with their dramatic dialogues. He made them keep chillies in the corner of their mouths and bite on them when the scene required them to cry.

'It makes the tears look natural,' he would proudly proclaim.

He even made some of them dress up as girls and speak in a high-pitched voice and taught them how to walk with short steps and sway their hips with each step. His live demonstrations were fascinating to watch. Oh, how his hips swayed! I tried many a time to copy them when I was alone. I never succeeded, and instead I ended up looking clumsy and laughable. It was so difficult. I could never understand why the boys made fun of him and called him all sorts of names. They were all ignorant juveniles who probably had no eye for art.

The next week, just three days before the puja, as the various groups sat there in the school compound discussing their share of last-minute responsibilities, I had the courage to stand up and say, 'I'll do the lights, sir!'

'What?' he looked at me from over the rims of his spectacles, his eyes bulging out. 'What did you just say?'

'I said I'll do the lights, sir.'

'But we have lights already.'

'Yes, but they are fixed,' I explained. 'I can make the lights run. We never had running lights before in any of our pujas. I'll do it this time. It will be something new.'

'And how exactly do you plan to make the lights run?'

'I don't know how to explain, sir,' I said. 'But I can show you how to do it. The lights will glow and fade, glow and fade, and change colours, one after another. I... I can make them do that.'

'So, all you want to do for the puja is stand by the stupid switchboard and press the darn switches on and off and make the lights glow and fade, glow and fade, till you get an electric shock, the lights stop working altogether and the puja is ruined?' Sir asked sarcastically, mocking me.

The class of twenty-five rolled on the floor with laughter. Except Vikash.

'No sir, I didn't say that...'

'Look Sridhar, if you don't want to volunteer or help, that's fine,' he growled. 'You are not indispensable. But you think you're an upstart, huh? That's where you are mistaken. That attitude should change. You think you can stay at home every day and pass your exams. You think you can teach me how to do maths. And now you think you can do the lights too! What did you have for breakfast today, kid, that has made you this delusional? Which world are you living in?'

'Sir, will you please give me an opportunity?' I requested. 'I won't touch your lights, I'll bring mine. I'll cause no harm to any of your switches, and the puja will not be ruined, I promise.'

It was at that moment that our Head Sir, Lalit Mohan Chatterjee, stepped in to know what was going on and why Babulal Sir sounded so furious. After being acquainted with the matter, Head Sir called me into his room and asked, 'How do you know so much about lights, child?'

'I have learnt about them from Sudha Kaka's men,' I told him, scratching my head. 'I... I work for them.'

That wasn't completely true but at that moment I didn't have a better explanation.

'You really think you can do what you're saying?' he asked, his tone kind and understanding.

'Yes, sir, I have done this before. Many times.'

'You've made lights run?'

'Yes, sir. I have.'

I had never done anything like that. But I knew I could, if only I was given a chance.

'Okay, then you do it.'

'Really, sir?'

'Yes, if you think you can, you do it.'

'But Babulal Sir won't give me permission.'

'Okay, I'm giving you permission,' he told me, smiling. 'I'm your Head Sir, aren't I?'

'Yes, sir,' I replied shyly.

'So, bring your lights tomorrow and show me what you're planning to do,' he said. 'If I like what I see, I'll let you do what you want to do.'

It was one of the happiest days of my life! But there was one tiny glitch.

'That won't be possible, sir,' I told him, sadly. 'I have to get fresh lights for the event. I'll require a few other things too. And I need some time to gather all of that.'

'But the puja is in three days, son.'

'I can guarantee you that it will all be ready by the puja,' I assured him. 'Please give me a chance, sir. I promise I won't disappoint you or cause any damage to school property.'

So, it was decided then. I was going to do the lights. Head Sir gave me three rupees to buy the fresh supplies and I was overwhelmed not only with gratitude but also with a sense of responsibility. I couldn't afford to disappoint one who had so much faith in my abilities. Now I wouldn't rest until my work was done.

Finally, the day of the Saraswati Puja arrived. I remember that year it fell on the 16th of February and was celebrated with much pomp and grandeur throughout the town. People woke up early in the morning, washed, got dressed in new colourful clothes, mostly bright yellow, to go to the various puja mandaps and offer *pushpanjali* in an attempt to impress the Goddess of learning and pass in all their exams. It was a day when no one was allowed to even touch books since they had to be consecrated at the Goddess's feet for twenty-four hours. Hence, we looked forward to it every year.

Girls dressed in bright yellow or orange sarees and boys dressed in colourful dhotis and kurtas. We hardly got to wear new clothes on Saraswati Puja. Father couldn't afford new clothes for so many of us. Every year perhaps three or four of us received new clothes by turns and we wore the same for the next three years. The older boys exchanged their kurtas with each other even though the clothes didn't fit us perfectly and the girls exchanged their sarees, so that they got to wear something different each year.

This year too I was wearing one of my elder brother's hand-me-downs. It was ill-fitting since I was the tallest and the thinnest boy in the family and he was quite plump and of a shorter stature. Krishna said I looked like a scarecrow and then teamed up with the neighbour's ferret-faced son to make fun of my appearance. However, I was least bothered since I had bigger fish to fry that day, and trying to look good wasn't one of them. And I had already made peace with the fact that with a face like mine I had a zero in ten probability of looking good no matter how expensive or well-tailored my kurta was.

I walked to school with three empty cans of baby food, three holders, three bulbs, three iron nails, a dozen wires, a wooden board, and some cellophane paper in different colours. Reaching the school gates, I headed straight to the room where the idol was to be worshipped. My friends were already there fulfilling the duties allotted to them, some drawing the *alpana*, some decorating the idol with marigold garlands and *chaand-malas*. A few of them sat in one corner chopping fruits for the *prasad* and a few others decorated the gates and pillars with the cheaper sort of garlands, hand-written banners and posters with drawings by the junior students of our school. Vikash waved at me as I arrived. He looked cheerful and handsome in his bright orange kurta and crisp white dhoti. He was not only the best-looking boy in our class but also the best mannered.

I sat behind the idol, and took out all the equipment one by one with the utmost care. I had a spare bulb and a few holders in case one of them failed me. Vikash sat beside me, looking at my precious collection with curious eyes.

'You know I'm your best friend, right?' he asked me out of the blue.

'Yes, why?' I questioned, confused.

'If you need any help you can tell me,' he put his arm

around my shoulder. 'I know you can do this, Sridhar. You've always been a genius!'

Vikash's words functioned like a catalyst for me and filled me with a sense of motivation to nail my objective and prove Babulal Sir wrong.

I set about working, first cutting open the closed ends of the cans and inserting the bulbs through them. Next, I covered the cans containing the bulbs with the coloured cellophane papers—one red, one blue and one yellow—and tied the ends of the paper with fine cotton thread. Vikash stared at it all, his eyes full of awe and wonder.

'What are these colourful papers for?' he asked.

'The bulbs are going to glow through these papers in three different colours,' I told him.

His eyes widened with excitement.

Following that, I went about preparing the board that was to be connected to the plug point. Hands shaking, I twisted the wires, attached the nails to the board and did everything that I had learnt from my own experiments. It was a long process and a complicated one, but over the last few nights I had replayed all the steps over and over in my head so that nothing could go wrong that day.

When both the board and the three tins of light were ready, I connected the two wires to the plug point. My heart beating loud and fast, I said a quick prayer and pressed the switch.

Nothing glowed. Not a single bulb.

'What's wrong, Sridhar?' asked Vikash, anxiously. 'Why aren't they glowing?'

'The light show is over, boys!' ridiculed Babulal Sir

with a guttural laugh that made my blood boil. 'You can go home now! Well done, Sridhar! I haven't seen anything like this in my entire life!'

This was followed by peals of laughter from Chandu and some other boys of my class who delighted in making fun of others. And then I grabbed hold of the free wire and pressed it gently against a nail on the board. And just like I had planned, the game changed.

'It's glowing! It's glowing!' cried Vikash in amazement and joy. 'The red lamp is glowing!'

I touched the wire to the nail connected to the blue lamp next and there was a gasp of surprise from the boys and then I touched the nail connected to the yellow lamp's wire. Another gasp. Next, I placed the three tins right next to each other horizontally, their fronts facing the idol, and repeated the act with the wire, making it touch one nail at a time. And soon the light ran from one can to another, changing the colour of the idol in quick succession and all I could hear next were claps and expressions of surprise from not only my batchmates but also our Head Sir who had dropped in without my noticing.

'What have you done, Sridhar?' he exclaimed in astonishment as the idol glowed red and blue and then yellow. 'This is excellent! How did you even come up with this idea?'

I only smiled, nervous and shy. My light show was the talk of the town that evening and people thronged to our school to have a glimpse of it. They arrived in multitudes. Never before had anyone done something like this in any of the puja mandaps in town! And never before had our school been visited by so many people on Saraswati Puja as in 1956. I had not only made the lights run but also made the beautiful idol glow in a different colour every three seconds. The soft lights filtering through the cellophane layers augmented the idol's beauty, making the sequins on her saree sparkle. The tiny stones studded on her crown glittered and the colourful *chaand-malas* appeared bigger and brighter.

One look at the Goddess' eyes and a shiver ran down my spine. They seemed to look right into mine, trying to tell me something, trying to convey some secret message. I knew I could get lost in those eyes if I looked at them for too long, so I focussed on my work instead. And the pride in our Head Sir's voice, as he introduced me to all the visitors, was something I knew I would never forget in my life!

While all my other friends had filtered out slowly one by one to visit the other pandals, Vikash, like a true friend, stayed back for a very long time, offering me tea and biscuits every now and then to keep me going. I couldn't leave my lights alone for even a minute because people kept coming and going and I had to keep working the wire through all the three nails so that the lights ran in sequence, jumping from one can to another. It was a lot of manual work and I hardly got a break that evening. I didn't visit any other pandal apart from the one in my locality. It was exhausting yet exhilarating and I enjoyed every bit of it, especially the part where the visitors asked me my name, where I lived, which class I studied in and other associated questions. I had never felt more important or proud! Even Babulal Sir came to me later that evening and offered me his apologies.

'It's okay, Sir,' I replied. 'I didn't mind.'

'You know I was kidding, right?'

'Yes, Sir, absolutely,' I nodded, smiling. 'You don't have to worry about it at all.'

'It wasn't my intention to hurt you.'

'I wasn't hurt at all, Sir. You told me at the very beginning that you haven't seen anything like this in your entire life.'

'I haven't,' he said guiltily.

'So, of course you wouldn't know what to expect, Sir,' I replied. 'It wasn't your fault.'

Interlude

'That was a really cool reply!' I remarked. 'Did you get into trouble for saying that?'

'No, I didn't,' replied Grandpa. 'In fact, Babulal Sir was never rude to me after that day. Nor was Chandu.'

'Good for you,' I laughed.

'Indeed.'

'So, you left school in the year 1957, after finishing class eight, am I right?' I scribbled in my notebook.

'Yes.'

'What did you do next?'

'I worked in the jute mill for a few months and then I was turned out of my house,' he chortled.

'You were turned out of your house?' my little brother, Bonny, who was sitting right next to our grandfather fiddling with one of his TV remotes, now took an active interest in our conversation.

'Yes,' agreed Grandpa, looking at him. 'I had just sat down to eat one night when my father appeared out of nowhere, kicked my plate of rice, splashed a glass of water over my head and turned me out of the house.'

'But why?' my brother asked, choking with laughter.

'I had refused to work in the stupid mill, that's why.'

My eleven-year-old brother guffawed like a maniac which amused my grandfather a lot and thus he explained it all over again, and my brother's hilarious reaction to the tale had me in stitches. It had been quite a while since I had seen Grandpa indulge in light-hearted amusement and it warmed my heart.

'Where did you stay after that?' I asked him.

'I lived with my friend Vikash in a nearby locality called Palpara,' he said, fondly remembering the old days. 'He gave me shelter in his house. His mother treated me like her own son. She's one of the kindest women I have ever known. Not only his mother, his father, grandfather, sisters were all very generous and caring... Vikash and I... we... we were almost like siblings'.

'I know,' I replied, remembering him.

I used to call him 'Kaka' just like my mother did. Even though he was my grandfather's age he looked extraordinarily youthful and handsome, almost like a 1970s movie star. My grandma had once told me that he had often performed in theatres and when he was in his late twenties and thirties everyone said that he looked like Rajesh Khanna, the superstar of Indian cinema. His eyes were of the kind that warm one's heart, brown, sparkling and good humoured. Like yellow carnations and a pocketful of sunshine, he radiated positive energy and spread happiness wherever he went. I can still recall how I used to perch on his lap, with my two ponytails, a colouring book in one hand and a box of wax crayons in the other, while he tirelessly narrated to me funny little anecdotes from his past and the age-old stories of Gopal Bhar, Akbar and Birbal, Vikram and Betal, yarns from Thakumar Jhuli, *and small episodes from the two great Indian epics, the Ramayana and the Mahabharata.*

'He was a very rare human being,' my grandfather broke into my thoughts. 'You won't find another person like him.'

I knew he was right. My mother often said that Kaka was the one who had brought her up since my grandfather used to stay busy most of the time. He was like a father to her. He helped my grandmother cook, sometimes brought her groceries from the market, helped my mother with her lessons, gave her all the love and attention that my grandparents couldn't. Our dogs always swarmed around him since he brought them little treats every day. In other words, he was everyone's favourite. A brother from another mother, he was perhaps the greatest well-wisher my grandfather ever had. From giving shelter to him when he was homeless, he saw my grandfather through both his highs and lows and stood by him like a rock in times of adversity.

He passed away almost six years ago, and I have still not been able to accept the fact that he is no more. Especially because of the unnatural way in which he died. Whenever I think of that kind face, those benevolent eyes, I feel a painful lump in my throat. The sound of his gentle voice, the way he threw his head back and laughed heartily and the way his eyes lit up at my every little achievement, be it a ten on ten in my class assignments or an A+ in my drawing exam, shall never fade from my memory. He was dear to us all, perfectly healthy and hearty, and we lost him even before we knew it. And what's even more tragic is the fact that he was on his way to our house when he met with the terrible accident that took his life.

'Don't worry about me,' he had held my grandfather's hand and uttered painstakingly before his broken body was wheeled into the ambulance. 'I'll be fit as a fiddle in a couple of days.'

And he never came back.

'It's sad that we don't have such friendships anymore,' I said. 'Friends who are like family, who love you and care for you without any ulterior motives, who are always ready to stand by you, come what may.'

'The times have changed,' replied my grandfather. 'Children nowadays, where do they have the time to actually bond with other people? Look at your brother. He's never had a friend come over to our house.'

'I don't have close friends,' he said. 'There's one boy, roll number thirty-five, he's good to me. I like him.'

'What's his name?' I asked my brother. This was the very first time he had mentioned a friend.

'I don't remember his name. But I don't like roll number twenty-two. He eats all my tiffin and copies all my homework.'

'What is this weird roll number thing? You guys don't call each other by your names or what?'

My brother shrugged in reply and got busy with the TV remote again.

'See,' said grandfather. 'Most of the time they are glued to these devices, doing what... I don't really understand. Things don't work that way. You weren't like this when you were a kid. You would read and sing and write, help

your grandmother with her chores, play with the dogs. It was all very different back in our day. We were more interested in going out to play with our friends. People across different paras *played together. We used to have* gulli danda *matches every week. We had only one world where real bonds were made and cherished. Also, there was little access to information. Hence there was the urge for experimentation, the chance to make mistakes and actually learn from them.'*

'And now we mostly choose to walk the beaten track. It seems like there's nothing new to discover. Everything's already been said and done,' I said.

'There's always something new to discover,' he told me. 'You only have to be willing to sacrifice.'

'Sacrifice what?'

'Whatever pulls you away from the road to discovery,' he said. 'In other words, distractions. Whenever you are on the path to a new discovery, the world will try to distract you in various ways. If you think of the world as a person, it's a person who is very secretive. There is so much more to it than what it shows you. It often lies to you and misleads you in order to protect its secrets. Most of us remain satisfied with the world just as we see it. But there are some who are never satisfied, who can see right through the disguise. They start exploring, to unveil the world's secrets. And the moment the world gets a whiff of that, like any human being, it gets defensive and sends forth various obstacles to block their path. It acts out of self-preservation. These obstacles take the form of... of people and circumstances in your life, all of which try to lead you astray from the path to discovery.'

I nodded, amazed at how well he was articulating his thoughts.

'And you must realize that it's got nothing to do with either the people or the circumstances,' he continued. 'They are not the ones at fault. It's not like they are bad people. It's just that their priorities are very different from yours. So, they are not the ones you should be fighting. It's all between you and the world. And here's where you are faced with a choice, to give up or to keep going. If you choose the latter, you must give up on the people who try to lead you... lead you astray. You must distance yourself from them, seek isolation if that becomes necessary. Once again, I am not saying they are bad people, but they might never understand where you're coming from... because... because...'

'Because they are not me,' I finished.

'Yes,' his eyes lit up. 'And you also need to stand strong in the face of any misfortune that might come your way, no matter how physically or emotionally taxing it might be. Life goes on. You need to go on, too. You cannot remain stuck where you are. We don't have all that time. Do whatever you can to pull yourself out of the problem and stand up on your own two feet again. We cannot control what happens to us... but... but to some extent we can control how we respond to it. Never give up on life no matter how hard it gets. Survival is the greatest challenge. Everything comes after that.'

I nodded again.

'Things will never happen the way you want them to. But if you want to be successful, you have to get used to the chaos. You have to sacrifice the comforts. You cannot expect to have a very comfortable life, taking your meals at the right

time, sleeping for ten hours, spending time with family and friends, practising your hobbies and so on, if you are really after something. We... we don't have all that time, dear. A good life is something that is exclusively available to the privileged, the ones who don't have to worry about what they are going to eat at night or where they are going to sleep or what they want to do with their lives.'

'That's so true. You're absolutely right, Dadu.'

'But then again, you should also know your limits. We all have our limits. Not everyone is built for everything. We are not all created in the same way.'

'How do I recognize the people who might try to lead me astray?' I asked.

'Your gut will tell you that,' he replied. 'The gut never lies. They might come in the form of friends, relatives, loved ones, strangers or even parents.'

'Like your parents.'

'Yes. They never supported me. So, I... I had to distance myself from them, even if I didn't want to. If I had taken their advice and kept working in the mill, I would never have been able to chase my dreams. I'd never be the person I am today.'

'What if I'm not strong enough to give up on those people? What if they are too close to me?'

'Don't worry about that,' he replied with a smile. 'The right ones will always stick around. Like your grandmother. She never gave up on me no matter how difficult things got for her. She made countless sacrifices so that I could work on my goals. I feel really guilty whenever I think about how she had to waste her own potential so that I could achieve

my goals. Back when I was young, I was too hot-headed and proud to acknowledge all of this. Now I feel very guilty. The fact that your grandmother couldn't fulfil her own dreams in order to look after the family is one of my biggest regrets in life. But she never complained, and she always stuck around.'

'What if they don't stick around?'

'Well then, you need to let go of them,' he answered. 'If you've really set your heart on something, there's always a price you need to pay. Be around people who will help you grow, not the ones who'll try to stunt you.'

'Do you believe in luck or destiny?'

'I would like to believe that we make our own destiny,' he said. 'And luck is but a lump of clay in our hands. It takes whatever shape we are able to give it. But sadly that's not true. I have never believed in astrology or horoscopes but I know that privilege definitely gives you a head-start. You're already ahead in life if you have a strong support system, if you are able to feed yourself thrice a day. Not many people are lucky enough to have all that. You can't change where you're born. But to a certain extent, you can change what happens after that. But once again, this doesn't apply to everyone. Whether you're able to change your circumstances in life or not depends on a variety of external factors which might not be in your control. So, umm... I have no answer to that question.'

'I'm very lucky that way. I have the required head-start.'

'True,' he nodded. 'But what makes me really happy is the fact that you never take that for granted. You're a strong kid. You have gone through a lot very early on in life but... but you never allowed yourself to be treated like a victim. I am extremely proud of you.'

I felt a simmering ache in my heart which threatened to drown me but I tried my best to not show it.

'It has been possible for me because I have always had a strong support system,' I told him. 'Something you never had growing up.'

'Your mother didn't, either,' he looked down. 'Even though she was my child. I could barely take care of her. That is another major regret I have. She deserved so much more.'

'I went through a lot, I agree, but I have always been taken care of,' I told him. 'At times I wonder if that's a bad thing.'

'Why does it seem like a bad thing?' He looked at me quizzically.

'I constantly feel like I owe a huge debt to the Universe for being born here in this family. And whenever I feel dissatisfied about something, whenever I feel like I have been wronged in some way, I wonder if I should even allow myself to feel disappointed. Do I even deserve to complain?'

'It's good that you're aware of how privilege works and you're not afraid to admit it,' he said. 'But that doesn't necessarily mean that your experiences are not valid. It's true that I did not have certain privileges which you have had growing up, like a supportive family who has helped you grow, a good place to stay, and all other necessities of life, but you didn't have the easiest time growing up either. There's absolutely nothing that you ought to be ashamed of.'

The lump in my throat was back again.

'You are a good person,' he continued. 'A little lonely. Always minding your own business. Doing your own thing. But you've always gone out of your way to help others in need. And... and you have never abused your privilege.'

'That's a lot of praise. You're embarrassing me now.'

I scratched my temple. I wanted to change the topic because I had started feeling self-conscious. 'Can you tell me a bit about your parents? Why did they not support you?'

'My mother was always allergic to all the things we couldn't afford,' he told me. 'I couldn't understand why. To her, anything better than what we had was unnecessary, and expressing a desire for them was sinful. We had to be strictly satisfied with our lot and never open our mouths to complain. Even as a child, I found something inherently problematic about her way of thinking. Unless we had dreams and aspirations, how would we ever change our situation? How or why is it wrong to dream? But according to my mother, we did not have the right to dream of a better life because we were poor. We weren't allowed to indulge in dreaming because she thought it was a luxury. My father's attitude was also similar. He liked playing safe, doing the same thing over and over again. That was perhaps because he had so many mouths to feed. He couldn't afford to be adventurous. Later in life, I could understand why he was the way he was. I'm not saying they were wrong and I was right, but I knew I was very different from them.'

'I see.'

'I could never imagine being perfectly content with my lot,' he added. 'Settling down seemed like accepting defeat. I can't say if I was right or wrong but I wasn't happy with the way things were. I wanted to be able to hold my head high with pride. I wanted to create a better life for myself. I never blamed anyone for my situation, least of all my father. But the thought of spending the rest of my life like my father,

cooped up in a small town, working away all my hours in a factory or a jute mill, completely oblivious to the rest of the world, apathetic towards a better life, unnerved me. There was a whole world out there waiting to be explored. So many places to see... so many lands to visit... so many different things to do and just one life to accomplish all of one's heart's desires.'

I nodded, smiling.

'It is frightening how little time we all have!' he continued. 'I couldn't afford to spend my entire life in anonymity and then die someday without having left a mark. It didn't seem to me like a life worth living. I had dreams. Being perfectly content with my lot and never daring to take risks didn't seem like a good way to live.'

'What exactly transpired between you and your parents when you refused to work in the mill?'

'I had refused to work in the mill which would have guaranteed me a stable income every two weeks. That was a huge risk considering my family's financial condition at that point of time. Naturally I was called "selfish", "the black sheep of the family" and so many other names by my own parents and siblings. But I see it all as a part of my struggle. In fact, I look back now and see it as a blessing. If I had my way with them easily, if I had all the comforts and privileges, the sense of security and stability, I would soon become complacent. It is my struggle that taught me to value every little thing I achieved later on. It also granted me a sense of fulfilment because I know how hard I worked for every bit I earned. Nothing was ever given to me on a platter.'

'Tell me more about it, please.'

3

Summer of 1957

'Your mother told me that you haven't been going to school lately,' my father broached the subject one morning while he rubbed a piece of alum in circular motions over his freshly shaven cheeks.

'Yes,' I replied, fearless. 'I don't see the point in going to school anymore. None of my brothers studied beyond class eight. I have been working like them, earning money.'

'You mean, fixing a few lamps and fans here and there and bringing in hardly five rupees a week, eh?' said my father with some mockery in his voice.

'I've just begun, Baba,' I explained. 'Give me some time. And I have been doing good work. You can ask anyone in the neighbourhood, they will tell you. Slowly I'll expand this, take up more and more repairs and when I have enough savings, I can open a shop of my own like Sudha Kaka.'

'We don't have the luxury to wait, *khoka*,' Father replied. 'We don't have the luxury to dream big either.

And you want to open a shop? Do business? How old are you? You're barely fourteen! What will happen when your business suffers loss? Who will pay your workers? And how long exactly do we have to wait before you set up your own shop and start making profit?'

'A few years.'

'How many do you mean by "few"?' he asked sternly.

'I can't be sure.'

'That's the problem with business,' said my father. 'One can never be sure of anything. Laxmi has come of age. We have started looking for a suitable match. And you know what those words mean?'

'Which?' I asked, confused. 'Suitable match?'

'Yes,' he nodded. 'It means more dowry. You have five sisters. Do you think your two elder brothers and I can finance all their marriages alone? Kartik is still too young to drop out of school and find work. Krishna has to study another year.'

'What can I do to help, Baba?'

'Leave all this electricity madness and join the mill,' replied my father. 'I have been working there for over twenty years now, I can easily get you a spot. You have to go to work every day but you will get good money. Almost double of what you are earning now.'

'But, Baba, this is what I have always wanted to do. I don't want to work in the mill.'

My father, who was knotting the thread of his pajamas, turned around to look me in the eyes. He didn't say a word. Only his eyes spoke. And this time they were glaring at me. He tossed his piece of alum out of the window, put his glass of water down on the table with a sharp bang and shouted for my mother.

'SARASWATI!'

She hustled out of the kitchen instantly with unkempt hair, the loose end of her torn and discoloured saree tucked at her waist, holding an oily spatula in one hand and the rolling pin in the other.

'What happened?' she asked, flustered.

'Is my tiffin ready?' he asked with authority.

'Yes, it is.'

'Then what are you waiting for?' he hollered. 'Give it to me!'

Mother hustled back into the kitchen, dropping her spatula in haste and then panicking because she couldn't find the box. Father didn't want to wait. He wanted my mother to feel guilty and responsible for the whole event and this was his way of doing it. The anger he originally felt for me, he wanted to take it out on my mother because she was an easy target for him. She never talked back, she never questioned him, she took it all in and suffered silently. So, he left without the tiffin that she had so painstakingly prepared for him. He knew she was sick, but he still chose to be merciless. He slammed the door on his way out, muttering under his breath that he couldn't stand the sight of us any longer. When my mother came out of the kitchen with his tiffin he was already gone. She slumped on the floor with a heavy sigh, her hands all sticky and white, her forehead streaked with perspiration.

'That man can't wait for a minute,' she muttered breathlessly while I offered her a glass of water and rubbed the sweat off her forehead and neck with a ragged towel.

She shoved me away with utter distaste, 'Get away from me! My hips are tearing!'

My father didn't return home that night. He sent the news through Vishnu Kaka, his friend and co-worker, that he would be working overtime for a few weeks to earn extra money for Laxmi's wedding. So, he might not be able to return home every day. Two days passed without much ceremony. On the third night, he returned home, several hours after Rampeyari, the lamplighter, had climbed up and down his old ladder multiple times, trimmed the wicks of the street lamps, wiped the oil stains and meticulously poured oil in each of the lanterns lining the road outside our house.

Father didn't speak to anyone. He barely even looked at me. He ate his dinner silently, went to bed early and then groaned all night, keeping each one of us awake. He had a body ache, apparently. Mother stayed up all night massaging his hands and legs even though she had barely eaten anything herself over the last two days. I couldn't say whether my father was really sick or he was just putting up an act to make me feel guilty. But as soon as the cock crowed next morning and the flames in the lanterns died down one after the other, he sat upright on his bed, took a hurried bath, chewed some stale chapati, downed it with water, and left for the mill. He didn't return home for another four nights. My mother's constant apprehension about my father's health made me feel miserable. She implored me to join the mill and help him out, so that he didn't have to work overtime at the cost of his health.

One day I overheard her saying to Laxmi, 'Your poor father is working so hard day and night to give you a good wedding but look at your brother, sitting on his arse all day! I cannot imagine how a child can be so immune to his father's misery.'

I couldn't imagine how a mother could be so oblivious to her child's struggle! I wasn't sitting on my arse all day. I was hardly at home. In fact, I had taken up more repair work, increased my rates and had earned a lump sum amount of ten rupees just the previous week. That was exactly how much I would be earning at the mill. I didn't take any breaks. On some days I even skipped lunch. Mother knew about that. I made it clear to her that father didn't have to work overtime, that it wasn't really necessary. I had also been apprenticing under a carpenter in Bagbazar who taught me some woodwork. There too I earned a small stipend. It seemed that unless I joined the mill, nothing I did would ever be acknowledged. And then Bishnu Kaka dropped in that evening to inform us that my father had fallen seriously ill and had to be rushed to the hospital that afternoon. My mother burst into tears, now openly accusing me of being the reason behind all of it. I was at my wits' end.

The next morning, I rose early to bid my dreams adieu. I wore a clean old shirt, a pair of half pants and my customary chappals and set off for the mill with an empty stomach, a broken heart and tears in my eyes. A twenty-minute boat ride across the river Hooghly and I was there. But what took me by complete surprise was the fact that my father too was there at the mill and he didn't look sick at all. I was greatly relieved but also taken aback. He didn't seem happy to see me at the mill and at that point I didn't even care. My stomach growled every now and then and I yearned for some of the tea that the workers around me enjoyed. As I was being enrolled, my father kept up a facade which seemed to tell me that it didn't really matter to him whether I joined the mill or not because he was quite capable of doing the needful on his own. He didn't look unwell, just sleep deprived. He walked around quite effortlessly, speaking to the other workers, examining the machinery, looking out for necessary repairs. He wanted to let me know that he didn't need me to be there for him. But I knew I had to be there, even though I didn't want to be, that this was all a ploy to get me enrolled as soon as possible. I was sick of the accusations and mockery, sick of hearing time and again that I was born to devour my family and that I had absolutely no concern about anyone apart from my own self. Now that I was there in the mill, doing exactly what he wanted me to, he still wouldn't acknowledge me. That was fine. I would at least have some peace. I'd rather he didn't speak to me than always ridicule me whenever I tried to initiate speech. For I knew if I stayed back home and continued my repair work, all my meals would stick in my throat, my bed would feel like a rock and I would be reminded day in and day out that I ought to be ashamed of myself for living under his roof and not paying enough rent.

'You will not regret this decision.' Those were the only words he spoke to me while we were on our way back home that evening. 'Beggars can't be choosers, son.'

'Hmm,' I replied, stifling a yawn. I could tell him that it wasn't really my decision, that he was the one who had manipulated me into all of this, that I would have earned more from my repairs and carpentry work. But it was not as though he wasn't aware of any of this. When it came to Baba, reason didn't apply, obedience was all that was valid. Unwavering, unquestioning obedience. Whether what he proposed was logical or not, we had to obey him. However, I refrained from opening my mouth because I didn't want to stir up any more trouble. Besides, the rocking motion of the boat coupled with the gradual darkening of the evening sky was making me feel drowsy.

Over the next couple of days, I learnt in detail about how raw jute was turned into cloth. It was an elaborate process and for the first few days I enjoyed it. Enormous barges loaded with bales of jute arrived by the river each morning. The bales were then unloaded and kept in the godown where they were eventually classified on the basis of their quality. There was soft jute and hard jute, each used for making different items. The bales were then loosened and treated with the jute batching oil, or JBO, a chemical that disentangled the fibres and gave the brown strands of jute a hair-like appearance. The untangled mass of jute was then passed through the spreader machine which had a bunch of comb-like structures which straightened out the jute fibres. It reminded me of how my sisters took care of their lush, black, tangled hair, first releasing it from the tight hold of their buns, then oiling it meticulously from the roots to the ends and then slowly smoothening it out with combs.

I loved seeing how jute cloth was made. I was learning something new, and this was definitely very different from whatever I already knew. There were so many machines that I never knew existed, the carding machine, the drawing machine, spreaders and spinners. But one month in, the repetition of the entire process seemed to suck the lifeblood out of me. There was no room for innovation, no place for the imagination. Repetition! Repetition! I was living my life by the clock and doing the same unthinking thing every day like a machine. I didn't feel like a human being. I felt like a number, a pair of hands attached to some nondescript structure which wasn't allowed to have any desires or volitions of its own. I wondered how my father had managed to work here for over two decades. I looked at my fellow workers and wondered how they found contentment in the work they repeated every single day for years. We were all stuck in some sort of a paralysis, our existence reduced to nothing but mere hands. How could they not see it? The *maalik* didn't even care whether we lived or died.

Besides, there was a lot of disunity among the workers. They often got into brawls, arguments, and misunderstandings and it seemed like there was always some sort of unspoken war going on between the Hindu workers and the Muslim workers. With every passing day, my motivation waned. The only part of the day I looked forward to was the journey back home, the boat rides across the river, the evening trance stirred up by the singing of the boatman, the setting sun streaking the sky with hues of tangerine, vermillion and aubergine, the soft sounds of the river water rippling past the oars, awakened on the banks by a small cup of lemon tea, and then walking back all the way home with heavy steps and a head full of dreams.

And then one day, one of us demanded more wages.

'But you have just joined!' replied the manager.

'Why should the others get more wages for doing the same work that I do?' Rahim bhai asked.

'For the simple reason that they've been working here for years. They have more experience. You're still learning. Once you've learnt the whole process and have worked here for a while you will be paid just like them.'

'But I already know the whole process! I have been working here for over three months! I'm contributing to the production as much as they are.'

'Listen, man, rules are rules. They must be followed. I am a manager, I don't pay the workers. I myself am a paid employee just like you are. If you want more wages, I'm afraid you must talk to the *maalik*.'

I saw Rahim bhai leaving the manager's cubicle with a distressed look on his face and later that afternoon, when he sat all alone in a corner drinking his tea and eating a few pieces of bread, I went up to him and asked, 'What's the matter, Rahim bhai?'

'The manager won't increase my wages,' he replied, without looking up. 'He says it all depends on the *maalik*. Amma is very sick. My four sisters are all unmarried. I am the only earning member in my family. I don't know how long I have to work here to earn as much as the others. How much do they pay you?'

'Ten rupees,' I replied.

'And you've been working here for…?'

'A month.'

'Only a month…' he laughed. 'I've been working here for over three months. And they pay me only seven rupees.'

'This is so wrong! I didn't know about that, Rahim bhai,' I told him. 'Let me go talk to the manager.'

'What for?' he looked at me in disbelief. 'You know it won't end well for either of us.'

'Why not?' I replied. 'This isn't right. They should pay you ten rupees too. You've been here longer than I have. We must speak out against this. I'm sure the others will stand with us too. Will you come with me?'

When we went back to the manager's cubicle, he was leaning back in his chair, twirling his moustache and smoking a *bidi*. We stood outside his open door, hesitating. And then I finally cleared my throat and said a loud and unmistakable, 'Sir'.

He looked up at me, his spectacles hanging at the tip of his nose.

'What is the *jhamela* now?' he asked in his throaty voice.

'Sir, I think there has been some mistake.'

'What kind of a mistake?' he inquired coldly, releasing a thick stream of smoke through his nostrils.

'Sir, I've been working here for only a month yet I get paid more than…'

'Look, boy,' he raised a hand stiffly, cutting me off. 'You've come here to advocate on behalf of that Mussulman chap, haven't you?'

'His name is Rahim, sir.'

'I don't care what his name is,' he waved his hand dismissively. 'I know what you're here for and before you speak on his behalf, let me inform you that it is really not my responsibility. If you want, you can talk to the *maalik* about this. I'm merely following his orders. It is he who decides who is to be paid how much.'

'But this is not right!' cried Rahim bhai, frustrated. 'Whenever I come to talk to you, you say the same thing! I have never seen the *maalik*. Not once in three months! Where am I supposed to find him? Aren't you the one who is supposed to communicate our grievances to him? Isn't that your job?'

Five seconds of absolute silence followed.

'How dare you stand in my room and talk to me in that tone?' the manager left his moustache alone, sat up now and readjusted his spectacles fiercely. 'You're not paid to remind me what my job is.'

'Sir, please don't get offended,' I tried to placate him. 'Rahim bhai's mother is extremely sick. It's been very difficult for him to manage a family of six...'

'I am not talking to you!' he rudely cut me off again.

Rahim bhai stood next to me, his eyes fixed on the ground. And at that very instant I knew there was nothing we could do.

And then it all began, that afternoon, after lunch. A brawl broke out between Rahim bhai and some of the other workers. I didn't know what it was about but from what I gathered, Rahim bhai had probably dropped a can of batching oil by mistake. It spilled all over the place. Someone slipped and fell flat on their butt. That created a ruckus. The manager came over and accused him of having dropped it intentionally because his wages were not being increased. In his anger, Rahim bhai shoved the manager away from him and a few of the other workers ganged up to attack him immediately. That was the first time I saw Rahim bhai cry. When the others accused him of having lost his temper because he was a 'beef-eating Mussulman,' the other Muslim workers were naturally upset and that's how the brawl broke out. I received a few blows myself when I tried to intervene on behalf of Rahim bhai and was later slapped across my face by the manager in front of everyone for having done so.

'I've been paying you ten rupees just because your father came to me begging!' he shouted at me as I stood before him in his cubicle. 'His wages would have been increased a month ago if it hadn't been for your father's pleas. And this is how you show your gratitude! By siding with the enemy! You're FIRED!'

That's when I realized that I needed none of it anymore. I didn't need the mill job. I didn't need any wages. I didn't need my father to go begging for me. I couldn't afford to waste another day in the mill. I didn't care whether I was fired or not. I was not one of them. I never could be. What hurt me most was when the manager revealed that Rahim bhai's wages would have been increased if I hadn't joined the mill. But just because the manager was close to my father, he acted on my father's request and decided to give me the wages that actually belonged to Rahim bhai. So, all the trouble that Rahim bhai had to go through, was actually because of me. And I wasn't even aware of my involvement in this whole mess!

'I'm never coming back here,' cried Rahim bhai, as he left the mill that evening, crying.

'Me neither,' I told myself. I would go back home and talk to my father.

For the first time in thirty days, the boat ride back home was not enjoyable. The sky was a reddish orange that evening, slowly turning purple. The birds were stitching up the sky as the last of the daylight started to fade. Soon it would all be dark. The river water softly lapped all around me. Somewhere far away in the horizon, I saw a group of people, clad in mourning white as they carried out rituals at the river. The corpse lay on the steps of the ghat. The smoke from the incense twirled up over their heads and spiralled into nothing. It chilled me to the bone, even though I didn't know the deceased person. One day my lifeless body would be lying on those steps. Would anyone cry for me? Would anyone know whose corpse it was? Would my absence be felt? Would my presence make any difference?

The sad cries of the boatman as he sang about his long-lost brother cut through me deeply and jaggedly. As he sang '*Praan kande, kande, praan kande re, bhaai er dekha pailam na, pailam na...*' (My soul cries, my soul cries out in pain,

for I could never see my brother again) I was close to tears myself. I had never lost a brother I loved, or a friend. I couldn't relate to the song on any personal level. Nevertheless, I felt strangely touched by it. There was something about the atmosphere that evening and the melody of the song which made my heart ache tremendously. I too would be burned on a pyre someday, turned to ash. And then from ash to dust, I will be nothing. Just a name on the lips of a few successors if I was lucky. How many of my ancestors did I remember? I barely knew my great grandfather. No one ever talked about him. No one ever asked what kind of a person he was. The ripples of the water made me feel like I was running out of time. All I had was this life. I had to make the most of what I had. I couldn't allow myself to fade away like these ripples and drain into the ocean of oblivion someday. I felt that extreme sense of urgency once again, the way I used to feel when I gazed at the mesmerizing lights in Sudha Kaka's store.

It had started to rain when we reached the bank. Hence, no lemon tea. The road was gloomy, drenched and deserted. Soon it was raining cats and dogs. I didn't carry an umbrella so there was nothing much I could do. I walked all the way back home in the rain, every inch of my body wet and cold, my pajamas sticking uncomfortably to my legs. The water dripped from my hair into my eyes, interfering with my vision. I didn't know what to expect when I got back home. The closer I inched to home the more distant I felt. My footsteps on the asphalt sounded alien to my own ears. I had often heard people say that home is where the heart is. I envied them. How lucky they were to be able to relate to such sayings! To have a home to go back to at the end of a maddening day, people to cherish and be cherished by, someone to snuggle close to for comfort, somewhere to belong. Where could I go to find solace? I was homeless, even though I had a home. Never had I felt so lost before.

Father was examining a chink on the roof when I reached home. There was rainwater collecting in a tiny tin bucket placed on the ground below it. Mother was sitting in a corner, rubbing Kartik's head dry with a towel lovingly with a little smile of contentment on her face.

'You will be the death of me someday,' she fondly scolded him. 'Never thought what would happen to your poor mother if you caught pneumonia, did you?'

It felt like someone was whetting knives against my heart.

'Mother, I am home,' I called out, standing at the doorway drenched from head to toe.

She looked up at me, the smile on her face instantly fading. My heart ached to hear a kind word from her but my head cautioned me against the inevitable heartbreak.

'Go and take a bath,' she replied without any emotion and then went back to rubbing Kartik's head.

I quietly took a towel, a bucket and a mug and made my way to the nearest roadside tap. It was still raining heavily and with the rain beating hard against my back, I filled up the tin bucket and poured the ice-cold tap water over my head a few times, my only source of warmth being the tears that ran in streaks down my cheeks as I walked back to the inhospitable hollow that I called home.

And then it happened at dinner. We were all sitting down together to eat our meal on the floor in a circle. Mother had prepared rice, daal and something with potatoes. Father looked like he was in a very bad mood. He snapped at one of my elder brothers without any reason. I poured some daal over my rice and tried to swallow a mouthful but it didn't feel right. Unless I had bared my heart to him, I knew nothing would feel right. I was aware of the grave consequences that might follow as a result of my confession but I was determined to stand my ground and make him understand.

'I've been fired,' I finally declared.

No one paid any attention to me. Father continued to eat, mother urged Krishna to take some more rice. It was like they hadn't heard me at all.

'Father,' I called him now to draw his attention.

'Ahh! Let him at least have his food in peace,' Mother intervened. 'This is not the time to...'

Father raised his hand, Mother stopped speaking.

'What do you have to say?' his inflamed eyes bore deep into mine.

'I... I've been fired from the mill,' I confessed.

'Fired? How on earth did you get yourself fired?'

'Did you... umm... ask the manager to pay me more than the other new labourers?' I asked him.

'I might have. How's that your business?'

'I didn't know about that,' I told him. My hands had started to tremble.

'GET TO THE POINT!' he glared. 'How did you get fired?'

'Today Rahim bhai asked me how much I was being paid and... I... I told him,' I explained. 'We both realized that there must have been some mistake, so I went to the manager's office to talk to him about it. The manager said that he had nothing to do with it, he was just carrying out the *maalik's* orders. Later on, in the afternoon, Rahim bhai spilled a can of JBO by mistake and the manager accused him of having done it on purpose. The other workers said some really bad things and that's how the fight began. I tried to defend Rahim bhai and… and… that is why the manager fired me. Then he told me all about what you had requested him to do.'

'I'll go and talk to the manager tomorrow,' declared my father. 'Be prepared with a proper apology.'

'I don't want to apologize, Baba,' I told him. 'I don't want to go back.'

'What did you just say?'

'I said… I don't want to go back.'

'And why is that?' he inquired. 'You were doing good work at the mill.'

'What was happening there wasn't right,' I somehow found the courage to say. 'I can't earn the share of wages that someone else deserved. And the atmosphere is very unhealthy there. There's so much prejudice, so much hostility! I was not at all happy working there. Besides, the work was so tedious.'

'You don't work for happiness, son. You work for wages. You work to eat.'

'But I was earning so much more from my repairs and carpentry work,' I argued. 'And it would only have increased with time.'

'Your repair work was not a stable source of income. Today you have repairs, tomorrow you might not. Some other person might open a repair shop next to yours and your earning will go down instantly. The mill gives you a fixed amount of wages every week. You don't have to leave things to chance.'

'Sorry,' I told him. I don't know where I got the strength from. 'But I can't do what you're saying.'

I shall never forget the look on his face when I said that. But I kept looking right back at him, right into his eyes as I continued, 'I want to live my life my own way. I know for sure I will earn more from my repair work with time. And who am I doing all this for? For our family. Whatever I have earned till today, I have given it all to my mother. And I am ready to work as hard as I can to help you finance Laxmi's wedding, but not this way. I want to have something of my own, Baba. Something I can be proud of. I don't want to work in the mill. I feel like a machine there, not a human. Please understand, Baba. Please have faith in me. I shall not let you down.'

I couldn't read the expression on his face when I was done speaking. For a moment I thought he had understood what I was trying to say. For a moment I thought he was willing to cooperate, for he was silent. But the very next moment, my white shirt was smeared with yellow daal and my rice lay scattered all over the floor. A glass of water came flying towards me, the water splashing all over my neck and chest. I dodged just in time so the glass hit the wall right behind me and fell to the ground noisily. My father pulled me up by my shirt collar and jostled me out of the room.

'I would rather die than call you my son!' I heard him say. 'You deserve to live on the streets. GET OUT OF MY HOUSE!'

I looked at my mother helplessly. She stood by the door, silent and submissive.

'GET OUT!' yelled my father. 'And never come back here again!'

With tears streaming down my face, I looked at my house for one last time and walked out. I didn't know where to go, I didn't know what to do. I was hungry, heartbroken and penniless. And it was still raining.

Around eleven thirty that night, I found myself knocking on a familiar door in Palpara. I felt extremely embarrassed but at that point, I couldn't think of any alternative. He was a sight for sore eyes as he opened the door but his face fell at the sight of me.

'Sridhar!' he exclaimed. 'What happened? What are you doing here in the middle of the night? Is everyone alright at home? You look devastated!'

'Can I please stay here for a few nights?' was all I could say.

'Of course you can!' he replied. 'That goes without saying. You are my best friend!'

'Thank you, Vikash. Thanks a lot.'

'What are you thanking me for, silly? Come on in. You're freezing!'

And that's how I found my home.

Interlude

'What happened?' my grandfather jarred me out of my reverie. 'What are you thinking?'

I replied, 'I'm just a little jealous of you right now.'

'Why so?' he asked, amused.

'You had one thing that I always wanted,' I told him. 'A best friend.'

He smiled with a faraway look in his eyes.

'Anyway, what was the environment like in Palpara?' I got back to questioning him.

'Refreshingly different from that of Bidyalanka,' replied Grandpa. 'Or perhaps I simply felt like that because I... I was away from my house. Any place away from my house was like a respite to me. I had many friends in Palpara, they all helped me in different ways. I started my business with two hundred rupees offered to me by a man named...' he paused to recall. 'Su-Subhash, I think his name was.'

'It's okay, Grandpa, you can take your time and remember. There's no hurry.'

'His name was Subhash Ray, I think,' Grandfather recalled after some thinking.

'Who was he?' I asked him. 'A relative?'

'No, he lived near Vikash's house,' he replied. 'That neighbourhood was almost like an extended family. Everyone was extremely friendly to one another. And since he was especially close to Vikash's family, he often came to visit. That's how I got to know him. He was a rich man. He had inherited a lot of wealth from his forefathers. He was much older than me but had great affection for me and believed in my capabilities. He often stood by and watched while I experimented with my lights. He was a really kind and magnanimous person! He did for me what my family never bothered to do. It's because of him that I could give wings to my dream. Two hundred rupees was an enormous sum back in those days. People who earned a hundred rupees per month were considered extremely rich.'

'And how much did your father earn?'

'My father earned fifteen rupees every week from the mill. And he had to feed fourteen people in the family.'

'Why did people have so many kids when they knew their incomes wouldn't support them?' I wondered.

'There was no family planning in those days,' replied my grandfather.

'And I suppose the idea was to have as many male children as one possibly could.'

'Yes,' replied my grandfather 'For the dowry they would bring. Also... the boys could start earning from a very young age, which would mean more income for the family. Till I was fourteen I had siblings almost every year. A few of them died soon after birth. My last sibling... umm... the one who was born after Ganesh, died when she was two or three months old.'

'It must have been really painful.'

'Only temporarily,' he replied grimly. 'We had gone through it many times. It was nothing new... Besides, it was a girl. An extra mouth to feed. Had it been a boy, my parents would have been upset for a very long time. The death of a baby girl would mean less expense for the family. You wouldn't have to bear the burden of getting her married. But a son could work and earn extra for the family, bring a wife and so on.'

'Wasn't it hard for your mother?'

'The death of the baby girl?' he asked. 'No, it wasn't as hard as being pregnant all year long, cooking, cleaning, looking after all of us, and on top of that, going through the painful process of labour m-multiple times and then enduring my father's mood swings.'

My heart couldn't help but reach out to the women who were expected to function like vending machines every year, disgorging one baby after another, at times in twos and threes, and then being treated like they didn't matter at all. As though the excruciating pain, the incessant bleeding and unfathomable physical discomfort meant nothing. As though they were somehow obliged to go through all of that and keep performing strenuous duties while neglecting their own wellbeing in order to take care of the family just because they were women. Yet it was always the men whose mood swings and anger issues would be given a free reign as if they had somehow earned the right to be terrible human beings.

'In my later years, when I was comparatively well established,' my grandfather broke into my thoughts, 'I had two other benefactors. One of them was a very kind man

called Sudhir Bose, who gave me a substantial amount of money to buy my first batch of 6.2 miniature lamps. And the other man was... I think his name was Sailendranath Ghosh. People fondly called him Madan Da.'

'I think I've heard that name before.'

'You've met him, too,' replied my grandfather. 'He used to visit us often when you were little.'

'How did he help you?'

'I often ran out of spare cash in my early years, since I used to juggle several projects simultaneously. Madan Da was the owner of a shop selling electrical goods at Laxmiganj Bazaar. I used to purchase loads of goods from his store on credit, goods worth thousands of rupees... and pay him back as and when I earned money, be it six months or a year later. He also took great care of me. He was always concerned about my health and wellbeing. And he trusted me so much that he never pushed me for the money, nor did he take any interest. He knew I would pay him back the moment I received my payments.'

'That was so kind of him.'

'It certainly was,' he reflected. 'When I think of it now, I can't help but realize that even though I was kicked out of my house, I never really lacked a family.'

'That's exactly what I was thinking!' I told him. 'The Universe always put kind people on your path who helped you advance towards your goal. I guess that's how the Universe works for the ones who are really determined.'

'I don't know if it was God or the Universe,' he said. 'But without these people I would have been nothing today. Perhaps this is how luck works for some. Little acts of kindness can transform someone's life.'

'That's how I have always felt too,' I told him. 'But sometimes kind intentions get interpreted in very negative ways. Even if you genuinely try to help, people often say that you're doing it for attention or to feel good about yourself.'

'Why do I feel like this is personal?' My grandfather was quick to detect something underlying my words. 'Have you experienced something like this?'

I nodded. 'Last year a few like-minded people and I started a small group to help really underprivileged people with food and other basic necessities. We had to largely depend on fundraising which was possible only through social media since our own circles were limited and being students, we had no income of our own. But some people thought we were trying to help ourselves.'

He shook his head sadly. 'That's sad. But I can tell you one thing, when my family abandoned me and I had nowhere to go, when I had no funds to start my own business... at every step of my journey whenever I was faced with difficulties, it was kind people who helped me sail through. Whether they were doing it for attention or just to feel good about themselves, I can't really tell, but I benefitted immensely from their help. And in a country like ours where the concerned authorities don't take the necessary steps to minimize poverty and inequality, willing people like you help a lot. So, never let useless comments discourage you from doing the right thing. Instead, try harder to use the donations you receive in the most efficient way and do let me know if you need any help. I want to be a part of your group too.'

I felt a strange sense of relief. His words felt like a breeze blowing through my hair and left me feeling warm and complete.

'You're in, Sir!' I said happily. 'Now, let's talk about what happened after you left home.'

'Nothing significant for a few years,' he replied. 'I worked in a carpenter's shop and was known as "that Bidyalanka chap who can solve any electrical problem". So, whenever people in the neighbourhood or in the near vicinity faced any troubles... be it a tube light or a bulb that had gone out of order or a fan that had stopped spinning, they always summoned me. And I went to help them readily and earned some money.'

'How much?' I asked him curiously.

'Maybe two or three rupees. A five-rupee coin was a luxury back then.'

I scribbled down every word that dropped from his mouth in spite of having the recorder on my phone switched on.

'It was sometime in the early 1960s perhaps, when I was paid fourteen rupees for decorating a cycle shed in Ashok Palli for the Durga Puja,' said my grandfather.

'Fourteen rupees!' I exclaimed. 'You must have been over the moon!'

'Oh, I was! I remember suddenly feeling extremely rich!'

'Where is this place Ashok Palli exactly?' I tried to test his memory.

'It's not a part of Chandannagar. It's a part of a neighbouring town, right across the moat that surrounds our town.'

'Yes, the French had constructed that moat all around Chandannagar to fortify our town against intruders,' my brother, who had been silently listening to our conversation all this time, added proudly and received a pat on his head from our grandfather.

'So, how did that Ashok Palli work go?' I jumped to the next question.

'The puja was to take place inside a cycle shed. But the problem was that there was no electricity in that particular area since it was pretty remote,' said my grandfather.

'Then how did you decorate the shed without power?' I wanted to know. 'Did you use portable batteries?'

'No,' he replied. 'There was power available all over Chandannagar which was about half a kilometre away from Ashok Palli. I took permission from the Electric Supply, and attached long cables from one of the light posts in Chandannagar to the cycle shed in Ashok Palli.'

'How's that even possible? You said it was half a kilometre away and there was a moat in between and so many houses!'

'Yes, I had to carry the cables over the roofs of the houses and across the moat. There was even a women's college on my route. They probably thought I was some lunatic because I noticed a couple of them sprinting away in the other direction the moment they noticed me.'

He stopped there and burst into a fit of laughter in which my brother enthusiastically joined.

'Oh, Dadu!' he said, wiping away tears. 'I can't stop laughing!'

I couldn't help but partake in their gaiety.

'You're really one of a kind, you know,' I told my grandfather. 'And what did you decorate the shed with?'

'Very basic stuff,' he recalled happily. 'Brackets, tube lights... umm... tiny chandeliers and small disco globes. 6.2 miniature lamps weren't yet in fashion.'

I scribbled in my notebook, still chuckling. 'I can't believe you actually carried the cables over people's roofs.'

'Oh, I did!' he replied. 'Even though the struggle was hard, those were the best days of my life.'

That's when my mother peeped in through the gap between the two doors to inform us that Bonny's maths tutor had arrived. My brother, thoroughly disappointed, scowled at her for being the bearer of ill tidings and dragged himself out of the room reluctantly.

'I got a bigger project after that one,' my grandfather recollected a few moments later. 'I think it was the year 1966. It was my first attempt at street lighting for Jagadhatri Puja.'

'How did it go?'

'My lights were rejected.'

'What?' I exclaimed. 'Your lights were rejected?'

'Yes,' he frowned. 'It was a neighbouring locality. I had made a tunnel of lights with... umm... 25-watt bulbs. We used rollers for the first time.'

'Rollers?' I asked him. 'What are they?'

'The lights operated on their own with the help of the rollers,' he replied. 'They didn't require any manual effort on my part. Each arch of the tunnel had its own separate roller. Remember how in the Saraswati Puja in my school I had to sit by the idol all evening pressing the wire to each nail to create the running effect?'

'I remember. You couldn't leave the venue for a single minute.'

'That's precisely what the rollers did now,' he said. 'I wouldn't have to be present all the time. I would just have to connect the rollers to the power source and the lights would run automatically.'

'There were two great artists in my time, Prabhash Kundu

and Jiban Bhar. I was greatly inspired by their mechanical work at the Lalbagan Durga Puja, but what they used were not fit for what I wanted to do with my lights. So, I had to think of something different.'

'So, where did you find these rollers? Were they already available in Chandannagar?'

'No, I made them myself,' replied my grandfather.

'What?' I asked him, amazed 'You made the rollers? How?'

'That's a whole new story!' he smiled.

'A story I would very much like to hear.'

'Okay, then. Let's begin!'

4

Autumn of 1965

'Your ideas are unique!' Vikash told me one day. 'But have you thought about what you'll do when you have to work with more than three lights?'

'I have been thinking about the same thing,' I replied. 'I can manually control four or five lights in a single row, a dozen at most, but not more.'

'And you have to be there with them the whole time,' added Vikash. 'That is very inconvenient. Isn't there any way the lights can run automatically without your involvement? That way you can take up several projects instead of focusing on one at a time.'

'There's definitely a way out,' I mumbled. 'There must be! It's just that I haven't been able to think of one yet.'

'I'm sure you'll figure something out soon,' he encouraged. 'I have faith in you.'

It was seven years since I had been thrown out of my own house for refusing to work in the jute mill, and had sought refuge in my best friend Vikash's place. Since then

I had lived there off and on. It was a very old house but a magnificent one, like those belonging to the zamindars, with an open courtyard in the centre, and big, spacious rooms constructed all around it. There was a separate room for prayers situated in the inner quarters of the house and a *tulsi mandap* stood austere in a corner of the courtyard. We weren't supposed to venture anywhere near it wearing unwashed clothes.

Every evening his mother, who I called Kakima, worshipped the enormous idol of Lord Krishna in the prayer room and then, clad in a white saree with a broad red border and *champa* flowers in her hair, she came downstairs and lit candles and oil lamps at the foot of the *tulsi mandap*, leaving a lingering trail of fragrance behind her. A heavy burst of sandalwood, incense and flowers. There was grace in her gestures, kindness in her eyes and abundance in the palms of her hands. With her hands joined close to her bosom, she knelt before it in prayer and then went from room to room distributing sweets from the prayer room among all of us.

'May you live a very long and prosperous life, my dear,' she would always say as she offered me the *prasad*, smiling brightly. 'You are a very good boy.'

I often wondered if my mother would be a totally different person if she had had the good fortune of marrying into a well-to-do family. She probably would. We would be different too. Circumstances change people. I knew it better than anyone else in my family because over the last few years I had experienced what it felt like to be on the other side. Hearing words of praise and encouragement from elders, having people around who have faith in your abilities, can really make a difference to one's personality. I could breathe in Vikash's house, I felt good about myself; I grew more confident, all because they never made me feel like I was hopeless, they admired my efforts and valued me for my work. They never made me feel inferior or unworthy or selfish. Kakima always had a kind word for me. She often expressed concern about my wellbeing, took care of me whenever I was ill and asked me every day if I had eaten well. But I couldn't understand why my mother found it so difficult to say something along those lines to me. It was not as though she was incapable of it. She was always showering her love and affection on Kartik, even when he sat around doing nothing. She wasn't too bad with my elder brothers either. Why was I always treated like an exception? Like some vermin that she would love to squash under her foot?

Vikash had a huge family and several uncles, aunts and sisters. So, whenever there was a festival, his house buzzed with swarms of people ranging from infants to old grandparents who were all so humble and jovial that I felt perfectly at home. They never made me feel like an outsider. In fact, I was as important a member of the family as Vikash himself and their kindness towards me was unconditional. Hailing from a family like that, I knew kindness was a virtue that my best friend was born with. Or was kindness just a virtue that sprouted alongside privilege? The more privileged one is, the easier it is to be kind. But what I admired most about Vikash was his humility. He could have easily befriended one of the richer boys in school, like Chandu, but he chose me. And he stuck by my side and helped me through thick and thin. He didn't need to. What was there in it for him? Nothing. But he had simply chosen to. He treated me like his own brother.

And then the day arrived. It was Vishwakarma Puja. Several of our school friends had been invited to his house that morning. We were supposed to have a kite fight on his roof at noon. It was an annual tradition and the one whose kite survived for the longest period of time without its string being cut by the sharp *manja* of the other kites, would win the tournament. The special kite string called *manja* was made by us with our own hands. The stronger one's *manja* the higher the chance of winning the competition. So, the making of the *manja* played a very important role in these competitions. For the last seven years, it was either Vikash or I who won the competition and we never cut each other's kites. It was a little tradition of our own that we had never formally agreed on but we both followed. We used twisted polyester thread for our *manja* and coated it with a specially prepared glue and finely powdered glass. It was so sharp that it could slice through one's flesh if not handled carefully. Our victory, we knew, was guaranteed this year too.

The kite fighting tournament would be followed by a sumptuous meal of hot, puffy pooris, *chana masala*, spicy *aloo-dum*, eggplant cut into fat round slices, fried in pure mustard oil and a special fish curry made of fresh *kaatla mach*. Merely thinking of the lunch made my mouth water all morning. Besides, I could smell the different items being prepared in the kitchen, the many spices being ground, the ones stored in the big glass jars finally being put to use, the rich aroma of the pooris being released into the hot, boiling oil, the filets of fish being marinated with salt and turmeric powder, coated with a mixture of onion, garlic and ginger paste, the ingredients of the *aloo-dum* and *chana masala* being poured into the huge pans one by one and the spatula stirring them into thick, delectable pastes. The different aromas wafted through the air playing tricks with my self-control and making me impatient, jumpy and abnormally hungry. So, when Chandu tried to pull my leg for dropping out of school years ago and still not having a stable job, I wasn't intimidated one bit. Instead, my stomach and I growled at him in unison, loudly and menacingly.

'If you don't shut up, I'll electrocute you in your sleep!'

He looked at me as though I was completely out of my mind. But something in my face perhaps indicated that I wasn't kidding, for he could not be seen anywhere near me for the rest of the morning.

It was finally noon and we were all on the roof, nine of us, with brand new kites and spindles. I hadn't bought a kite, nor a spindle. It was not like I couldn't afford them but I simply didn't want to. I invested most of my earnings in buying fresh lights and other equipment for my experiments, and the rest I spent in buying groceries and other necessities for Vikash's family even though they had strictly told me not to. I was an able-bodied twenty-one-year-old man and I liked to pay for my share. I couldn't let them offer me food and shelter indefinitely without making any contribution. It stung my self-esteem. I would have to do the same for my family if I was at home. So, it wasn't anything out of the ordinary. Besides, they had done more than enough for me and I couldn't afford to fritter away my meagre earnings on kites and spindles for a morning's entertainment. Vikash had several old kites and spindles which were as good as new, so I used one of them.

Looking up at the sky, I was tantalized by the hundreds of kites that were already up in the air competing fiercely against one another. That was one of the best things about Vishwakarma Puja. The sky! Hundreds of bright, colourful kites flew freely, floating gaily with the wind, looking like exotic birds of every hue and size. Some flew kites purely for the love of it without intending to cut off other kites or compete against their neighbours. And some, like us, found nothing more invigorating than a tooth and nail kite fight. Winning or losing didn't matter to us. We signed up for the thrill, the fun, the loud cursing and swearing which we were allowed to exercise with full liberty since we had already sailed into adulthood, and the sumptuous feast that followed after a long and gruelling cut-throat competition.

The kite fight began, and in about fifteen minutes, I had successfully defeated two of my friends, as well as an unsuspecting neighbour. 'BHO-KATTA!' my friends screamed each time and came over to pat my back. In the next ten minutes, Vikash had cut off two other kites. Four kites down, only five kites remained. Bhola, Chandu, Parashuram, Vikash and I were engaged in fierce competition. Soon Parashuram cut off Bhola's kite and his kite was in turn cut off by Chandu. Two more kites to go, apart from mine, my best friend's and my arch enemy's. I decided to vanquish the latter and then call it a draw.

But just when I was about to do so, the sight of the spindle rolling effortlessly in my hands gave me a brainwave. I stood there for a moment, transfixed, gazing at my spindle like a lover gazing deeply into the eyes of his beloved.

'What's wrong with you?' Bhola cried out. 'Get his DARN KITE down!'

Instead, I rolled in my *manja* as if in a trance.

'WHAT ON EARTH ARE YOU DOING?' yelled Parashuram.

Deaf to all their exclamations, I slowly brought my kite down and handed it over to Vikash.

'Are you backing out?' he asked me, surprised.

'I just had an idea!' I uttered, dazed. 'Can I borrow this spindle for a while?'

'Of course, you can!' he looked perplexed. 'But why not finish the game first?'

'I... I think I found a solution!' I cried.

Vikash looked at me as though I was speaking in a foreign tongue.

'I have to go right now!' I insisted.

'Okay! Go!' he looked excited and then he stepped close to me and whispered in my ear. 'I'll join you as soon as I've kicked Chandu's ass.'

And then I rushed to my room with the spindle in my hand, laughing.

'He's gone completely mad, hasn't he?' I heard Chandu remark as I clambered down the cold, hard mosaic stairs, but nothing mattered to me then.

I had to attend the call of an invention!

For the next few days, I visited several carpenters across

the town to get a small, cylindrical, spindle-like wooden structure made for me, with a hole drilled through the length of it. I also spent a major portion of my month's savings on the motor of a table fan, the essential part of the whole arrangement. It was this motor that would make my spindle spin once connected to a power source. Once my spindle was ready, I placed it within a wooden framework horizontally and drew five vertical lines with equal spacing between them on its body. Then I planted one copper plate on each line, diagonally one below the other, with no two plates planted right next to each other. And I placed one lone copper strip on one end of the roller that went all the way round like a continuous ring.

'What's that one for?' Vikash asked me one day.

'That will be my conductor of electricity,' I stated proudly.

Next, I connected all the five copper plates to the conductor with tiny copper wires so that once the power reached the conductor, all the tiny plates would be electrically charged. And I fixed a separate and independent wire loosely to my conductor. This would be connected to the plug point and function as the continuous supplier of electricity. I chose five bulbs from my collection. Each of them had two wires. I took one wire from every lamp, and fixed them with duct tape on the framework exactly side by side in such a way that the ends of the wires just touched the five corresponding lines on the roller. The five remaining wires, I joined together to form one common wire that was connected to the plug point. So, there were two power sources, one exclusively for the roller and the other for the table fan motor.

My heart skipped a beat when I switched on both the power sources and the roller slowly started spinning. The wires taped to the framework were fixed but the roller spun. And I was washed over by a feeling of ecstasy when I saw that as my wooden roller spun, the fixed bulb wires touched the electrically charged copper plates one after the other, and the bulbs glowed and faded out in a line one after the other. I leapt in joy and almost brought the ceiling down with my cries of delight!

'Vikash! Vikash! Come and see what I have made!'

I was so overwhelmed that I couldn't keep my tears from flowing!

'You should have been an electrical engineer, you know!' Vikash cried when he saw it. 'You will go far, my friend!'

'It's all because of your help,' I told him. 'I wouldn't have been able to do this if you hadn't been there by my side.'

'I did nothing! It was all your idea, your design.'

'You gave me a place to stay,' my voice was heavy with emotion. 'You lent me your spindle. You've always believed in me. I don't know if I can ever repay you.'

'You don't have to!' he cried. 'Just don't forget me when you become a star.'

And that's when we started laughing through our tears.

The rollers served a dual purpose. First, after connecting my table fan motor to the power source, I just had to stand back and watch my roller do wonders with my lamps. Secondly, the lamps all glowed at different times, depending on the position of the copper plates. Had I planted the plates side by side, they would all glow and fade out together. But since I had planted the plates diagonally, the lamps flickered one after another in a line.

Eventually I developed my rollers, learnt to make newer mechanisms that allowed hundreds of lights on a panel to operate on a single roller, creating light and shadow effects and animation effects all depending on the strategic location of the copper plates on the surface of the roller, catering to the different designs and specific requirements of each panel. It was one of my most significant innovations, the one whose blueprint was revealed to me by a paltry spindle.

I used my rollers for the first time to illuminate the streets of a neighbouring locality for the Jagadhatri Puja. More than the Durga Puja, it was the Jagadhatri Puja that I awaited each year with bated breath. I didn't care much about the message of Durga Puja since I looked a little like the asura myself while the rest of the entourage looked lovely and fair. The people playing asuras in the locally staged skits would either be dark complexioned or covered with dark paint. A few times, I was invited to play that part and my brothers delighted in making fun of me. So, it wasn't something I looked forward to. Jagadhatri Puja was the festival celebrated in our sleepy little town with more pomp and grandeur. New dresses were bought, houses cleaned, old shoes polished, faces beautified and the town dressed like a newly-wed bride as it prepared to welcome guests from far and wide. It was a time of revelry and reunions, of homecoming and social gatherings. People from all over the country came back home to celebrate the five auspicious days of the puja. Previously, in the absence of electricity, they would burst firecrackers and use lit torches around the *mandaps* and during the immersion. As I later learnt, these practices were all started and inspired by the French who would organize huge firecracker shows on the fourteenth of July every year in our town to commemorate the fall of the Bastille and these traditions continued to be upheld even after they were gone.

When I was a kid, I had learnt from my elders that Maa Jagadhatri is an aspect of Maa Durga herself. And while I could never remember the elaborate tales of Maa Durga and Maa Kali and often mixed up one with the other, I always remembered Maa Jagadhatri's story.

'The story goes that after creating Maa Durga, the Gods Indra, Varun and the others started considering themselves omnipotent. They refused to acknowledge Shakti, the primordial cosmic energy that ran the entire Universe. They made the heinous mistake of thinking themselves to be mightier than her.' Dada had said.

'What happened then?' I had asked eagerly.

'That enraged Shakti of course and she decided to take them to task. So, she appeared before them in the disguise of Maya, let a patch of grass grow before them and asked each one of them to try to pluck the grass if they could. They all made fun of Maya for giving them such an easy task but then one by one, each one of them failed the test. That's when Shakti appeared before them as Goddess Jagadhatri sitting on a lion.'

'What about the elephant then? What is its significance?'

'The Gods soon realized their mistake and their pride took the form of an elephant. And that's how we worship

Maa Jagadhatri, a Goddess seated on a lion with an elephant under her.'

Maharaja Krishnachandra Roy of Krishnanagar, West Bengal, as I later learnt, was known to have first started the Jagadhatri Puja. He had been imprisoned by the Nawab of Bengal, Aliwardi Khan, for refusing to give away his kingship to him and was released on the day of Durga Nabami which was the last day of the Durga Puja. The Maharaja was extremely grief-stricken for not being able to enjoy the one festival that he looked forward to every year and his imprisonment ruined the festivities of Durga Puja in his kingdom. Maa Jagadhatri is said to have visited the Maharaja in his dreams asking him to worship her on the next Shukla Nabami. He obeyed the Goddess' instruction to the letter and started the Jagadhatri Puja. The puja eventually spread to other towns and cities, Chandannagar being one of them.

Like last year, this year too, the people at Ashok Palli wanted to hire me for the decoration of their shed, this time for the Jagadhatri Puja. They were willing to raise the amount to eighteen rupees but I wanted to do something different this time, something bigger. I wanted to put my invention to use. While I was still thinking about whether or not I should take up their offer, a few men from a neighbouring locality dropped by at Vikash's place wanting to see me.

'How did you find me?' I enquired, a little confused.

'Subhash Babu gave us your address.'

They wanted me to decorate their street, the one leading up to the pandal, and said that they would let me have my way as long as my work was impressive. Also, they were willing to pay me twenty-five rupees for my work.

I came up with the idea of making a tunnel of lights using arched strips of bamboo with bulbs lined along their lengths. Every arch had a separate roller with diagonally planted copper plates that would make the lamps run from one end to the other end of the bamboo strips. It was a major project since I would now have to decorate an entire street. They would pay me twenty-five rupees which was an amount way beyond my expectations. But considering the idea I wanted to work on, I knew twenty-five rupees would barely cover the costs. Nevertheless, I was ready to do it. Back then, I gravitated towards newer innovations like a moth to the flame and was willing to take the risk to present something new and different this time.

My friend Parashuram and I spent sleepless nights working extremely hard to create around twenty-five rollers. It cost me fifty rupees, which was double the amount I was promised, and I knew I would have to fall back on my savings to finish my work. But I wanted to earn praise, more than money. I wanted people to stop by and appreciate my work. Probably because I was so starved of admiration growing up that I hungered for it throughout my life. Money never mattered to me as much as respect and admiration did. It took us more than a month to create all the rollers but we thoroughly enjoyed the process.

A few days before the puja, we went to inspect the street once again, noting down all the necessary measurements and finalizing our deal with the committee members. Two days later, we were at the site, sticking small equidistant bamboo poles on either side of the street and connecting each pair across the street with thin arched slices of bamboo shaped in huge half circles with the crown extending almost ten feet above the ground. It looked like the entrance to a cave which ultimately led to the main pandal. Then we attached several 25-watt bulbs wrapped in yellow cellophane all along the length of the bamboo strips.

'Why yellow?' Parashuram had questioned me. 'Why not red or blue or green? Why don't we use all the colours?'

'Yellow will be the best,' I explained, visualising the arches glowing at night. 'It's the brightest colour. The bulbs will glow like fireflies in the dark of the night.'

The brilliant picture in my head fuelled me to put my nose to the grindstone and work hard on the arches all day. I wanted to breathe life into my imagination and the very excitement of doing something new had made me immune to the pangs of hunger and thirst. By the evening, we had finished installing the arches along almost half of the street. And just like I had imagined, the arches looked breathtakingly beautiful when we conducted a trial after dusk. It was almost like I was walking through some enchanted tunnel lit by glow-worms and fireflies, and I couldn't help but hum a few lines from one of my favourite songs written by Tagore.

'*O Jonaki, ki shukhe oi daana duti melecho!*' (Oh firefly, how merrily you flutter your wings!)

'You were right,' Parashuram patted my back with sparkling eyes. 'It looks wonderful! I can't imagine what it will look like once we've installed all the arches. Nothing like this has ever been done here before.'

I was so excited that I could hardly sleep that night. I kept humming Tagore's melody over and over again and even thought of suggesting to the committee members the next day that they play that song in the puja pandal. Little did I know that I was in for a nasty shock the next morning, for when we went back to work on the other half of the street the following day, we saw that all our lights along with the bamboo strips had disappeared. Only the bamboo poles and the rollers remained, the rollers on which we had worked so hard all day and all night for over a month.

We rushed to the pandal immediately to talk to the puja committee members, thinking perhaps it was a case of theft or robbery. We definitely weren't prepared for what we were about to hear from them.

'What happened?' Parashuram asked one of them. 'Where are the lights?'

'We've kept them behind the pandal,' he replied, stroking his chin casually, hardly looking at us.

'Why did you remove them?'

'Look chap, let me be honest with you,' he looked a little annoyed at being questioned. 'It is not quite the sort of thing we wanted. We wanted something bigger and brighter. These lights are too dim! The street looks dark and gloomy. It's ruining the essence of the festival. If you can do something with readymade tube lights, that would be great. We will pay you for the tube lights. But don't expect us to pay for the bulbs, because when we approved of your plan, we didn't expect your work to be so clumsy.'

'But we haven't finished our work yet!' I cried, tears stinging my eyes. 'We had installed just ten arches. There are fifteen more. We can install more arches if that's what you want. Why don't you understand? It's incomplete! It will look extremely bright once it's complete!'

'If you can do something with tube lights you are most welcome to do so,' he declared. 'Otherwise you're free to go work elsewhere. Your bulbs are behind the pandal, collect them at your convenience.'

When we ran to the small patch of marshy land behind the pandal to see if our lights were safe, we found all our bamboo strips strewn about carelessly on the ground. For the first time in my life, I trembled from top to bottom like a man standing barefoot on a live wire. I wouldn't mind if they had just rejected my idea, but they had gone one step further and disrespected my art, they had tossed it on the ground like pieces of garbage. I would not let them get away with it so easily.

'Don't lose heart, my friend,' Parashuram tried to console me. 'I'm sure we're going to be accepted somewhere next time.'

'I'll show these men what I can do!' I tried to choke back my tears.

'I am sure you will.'

My anger had died down, my lights lay strewn about, my pocket was empty and my heart broken.

'I will make them pay for what they did,' I sobbed on Parashuram's shoulder.

'It will all be okay,' Parashuram assured. 'Trust me!'

'I will never work for them again!'

'You don't have to.'

And I never did. I never worked for that committee

again in my entire life. No matter how hard they pleaded with me later on, no matter how much money they were willing to offer to me. My art held as important a position in my heart as God. And I owed it not to myself but to my art that they received the retribution they deserved.

Interlude

'So, what did you do then?'

'I went and lit the street up with a bunch of tube lights like they wanted,' my grandfather shrugged. 'I needed money. I had spent every bit of my savings on the tunnel. So, I attached the tube lights to the bamboo poles just like they had asked me to, and took my rollers and arches back home. The street looked awful!'

'That's so disappointing!'

'But I made the same tunnel with bigger bulbs and rollers for Bidyalanka next year and won major appreciation. Bidyalanka attracted the biggest crowd that year,' his eyes glowed.

'So, your efforts didn't completely go down the drain.'

'No, they didn't,' he smiled. 'And then came the transformative panels in... in... 1968, I think. They were rectangular structures designed with thin, flexible strips of bamboo which could be patterned in the shape of flowers, animals or whatever designs you wanted. And along the lines of the patterns you attached the 6.2 miniatures.'

'I don't quite understand,' I said, on purpose. I wanted him to remember.

'Okay, consider a page from a drawing notebook,' my grandfather sat up, his confidence renewed. 'You first draw the four margins, right?'

'Right.'

'Those are the four sides of a panel,' he replied. 'The frame.'

'Uh-huh.'

'Now where do you draw the... the... outlines of a flower or an elephant or whatever it is that you want to draw?'

'Within the margin or frame,' I answered.

'Absolutely,' he nodded. 'You do the same here. Except, you don't use a pencil to draw the outlines. You use thinly sliced strips of flexible bamboo, which can be cut into pieces and bent like clay to form any shape you desire.'

'Okay,' I finally understood. 'There must have been some base on which you attached these patterns, right?'

'Of course, that's common sense! The designs would fall off otherwise!' my grandfather laughed, thinking what an idiot I must be to even ask questions like these. 'The base was made with stronger and thicker strips of bamboo placed both horizontally and vertically to form a grid-like structure that held the designs.'

'And all of this was your idea?' I was spellbound.

'Not really,' replied my grandfather. 'I had seen the men of Sudhir Dhara and Deben Sarkar do something similar for the Bagbazar Puja Committee the previous year. They had used 12-volt lamps found in car headlights, and arranged the lamps to portray a scene of marriage.'

'How was that?' I asked, absolutely thrilled at the number of details he could recollect.

'It was very nice! I was fascinated. That was the impetus which gave rise to newer ideas in my head. But they had used fixed lights. I wanted to do it differently.'

'So, what did you do on your panels?' I pushed him on. 'What kind of designs did you make?'

'Since it was my first time working with panels, I didn't do anything complicated, I kept it simple,' my grandfather explained energetically, sitting up straight, his eyes sparkling. 'There was one panel on which I showed a flying pigeon made of miniature lamps. There were panels with the Bengali alphabet. Panels with flowers and fishes and so on.'

'All of these lights were moving?

'Yes, each one of them,' he replied. 'The bird fluttered its wings, the flowers bloomed, things like that. No one else knew about this technique back then. In the course of time, I taught different people how to make rollers and bring the designs to life and then they taught others, and this is how the art spread through Chandannagar.'

'Wow! And who drew these designs?'

'There was a great artist back in our time. His name was Mahadev Rakshit. He was the one to draw all my designs on paper. Then we made the structures accordingly. After his death, a man named Satinath took over. Both of them were incredibly talented.'

'And were these designs moving or still?' I could almost hear my heart beating in my chest in excitement. I couldn't believe how well he remembered everything! So many details from his past! Every single name! And he hardly stammered while he narrated them.

'The ones on the paper were not moving, of course,'

he replied in a matter-of-fact manner. 'It was just as in animations... you know... figures moving, colours changing and everything. We created those effects with the lights. On paper, we only had the drawings, the measurements and so on. The movements of the lights all depended on the positions of the copper plates on the roller.'

'It must have been extremely difficult to connect the intricate designs of an enormous panel to a single wooden roller.'

'It was,' replied my grandfather. 'One had to have sound technical understanding to be able to properly plant the plates on a roller. Everything depended on the position of the plates.'

'I remember Grandma telling me that she had planted the plates on several rollers herself. Was she really good at it too?'

My grandfather nodded gravely for a while and then to my surprise, he suddenly doubled up with laughter.

'What is it?' I asked him, amused. 'Let me hear the joke too.'

'Don't tell your grandmother I told you this,' he chuckled. 'But none of the rollers that she worked on could ever be put to use!'

'Really?'

'None of them,' he replied. 'She had no clue what she was doing. She planted the plates randomly, wherever she liked. But it made her extremely happy that she was helping me. So, I let her do whatever she wanted to do.'

I laughed. 'She still believes she's a pro at planting plates on rollers! In fact, she told me that with so much confidence,

I believed her too! She said it's like the easiest thing ever and that anyone could do it if they only knew the technique.'

My grandfather laughed even louder at this. So did I. It was indeed a hilarious discovery!

'Having inflicted her expertise on my rollers, when your grandmother went back home to prepare meals, my workers would plant the plates back in their proper positions. And then she'd return again the next day, by the time the rollers were ready, and she'd point at the glowing panels and cry out in delight, "See... see! Those are the ones I made! And you thought only you could do it!" I'd listen to her fondly and let her know that the ones she'd made were the best of all. And the happiness in her eyes would make my day!'

I couldn't help feeling a little overwhelmed at that. I could visualise my grandmother, young, beautiful and a little hare-brained, working hard in the factory amidst all the workers, with her long, dark hair tied in a bun decorated with white jasmine, nailing copper plates on a roller with a hammer. And my grandfather standing right next to her, looking down at the mess she'd been busy making with admiring eyes, secretly grinning to himself, but at the same time letting her believe that she was doing a good job, just to see the delightful smile on her face when the panels glowed.

'The following year I displayed lights underwater,' my grandfather said.

'Yes, I've heard a lot about that. Everyone talks about the underwater lights. It was a turning point in your career, as far as I know.'

'Oh, it definitely was,' he said with a faraway look in his eyes. 'The stakes were pretty high too. I could have lost

my life. In fact, I was almost about to, at one point of time.'

'Grandpa, I want to know all about it, every single detail!' I insisted.

'Well then, come back after lunch,' he told me enthusiastically. 'I... I'll try to recall the details and tell you everything.'

When I went to his room that afternoon with my notebook and phone, I found him sleeping. I gazed at him fondly for a while, the streaks of grey hair on his head peppered with strands of black, the skin on his hands and face which had wrinkled with age. Sleep seemed to lend a strange dignity to his features. You could see the strong personality that once lay underneath the soft, wrinkled exterior. But when he woke up, he was a different man, a man fumbling for his spectacles and hearing aids, shaky and unconfident. He had overcome his speech and memory lapses to a great extent and I felt extremely proud about that. In fact, that was precisely what kept me going. I would have given up ages ago and sunk deeper into the abyss of depression had he shown no signs of improvement.

I nudged him gently to wake him up. He slowly opened his eyes, looked at me and asked me what had happened. But when I reminded him about the story of the underwater lights that he was to narrate to me, he looked at me with blank eyes.

My heart skipped a beat.

'What a-are you t-talking about?' he asked me weakly.

'I'm here for the book, Grandpa,' I told him. 'The book I'm writing about you. You told me to come to you this evening.'

'The book?' he looked perplexed. 'What book?'

'Don't you remember?' Something within me shattered. 'I've been interviewing you all this time. You've been telling me all about your life.'

'What are you s-saying?'

'You really don't remember?' my voice was barely a whisper.

He simply looked at me, speechless, as though I was a complete stranger to him. And for a moment, the world around me came to a standstill.

'I... I don't think I understand.'

'It's okay,' my voice shook. 'It's okay... You sleep now.'

I made my way out of the door, cold, numb, and silent. A stream of tears flowed involuntarily out of my eyes. I hurried to my room and bolted the door to avoid prying eyes and ceaseless enquiries. I didn't like crying in front of others. As a matter of fact, I didn't like crying at all. My tears made me feel extremely self-conscious, almost naked.

'It's all going to be okay,' I told myself as I sat down on my bed in the silence of my room, rubbing the tears from my eyes. 'He'll remember. He'll remember everything.'

I felt like an idiot for crying and tried hard to be optimistic, to convince myself that it was all temporary. But as I sat there alone, in the silence of my room, I couldn't help but picture my grandfather's old and wrinkly face as he sat up energetically and spilled out all the details of his life, his bleary eyes sparkling, his eyebrows almost touching his forehead whenever he recollected something that he thought would interest me, and the funny way he moved his hands back and forth in explanation. He would be alright. He was getting better. He had stammered several times, but it was okay. I could see how hard he was working and his helplessness moved me but when he finally succeeded and spoke long sentences without stuttering or losing the thread of his thoughts, I could see his face light up with hope and joy and that in turn made me feel alive.

Perhaps my grandfather's degeneration was one of the many reasons why I went into depression. Since childhood, he'd been my role model. Before every little exam, I would sneak into his room to seek his blessings. His words always worked like a catalyst for me. His faith in me pushed me to work harder.

One evening, in the middle of my exams, I received a call from one of my uncles who told me that Grandpa had met with an accident while riding his scooter. A few minutes later, he was carried into our house by three burly men. He looked so terrified and infirm clinging on to them for support that I wanted to burst into tears. I tried to make light of the situation by endeavouring to make him laugh instead.

'How did a grown man like you fall off a tiny scooter?' I asked him as I applied ointment to his wounds. 'I didn't expect this from you, Dadu.'

He only flinched in response as his wounds stung.

The X-ray reports later revealed a serious injury to his knee and he was bedridden for almost four months after the accident with his knee in a cast. For most of this period, he either slept or spent hours despairing that he would never get back on his feet again, for he could not even stand the slightest pressure on his knee.

In those four months, he underwent a visible breakdown,

both physically as well as emotionally. He cried too easily, smoked excessively, coughed his lungs out, dropped his cell phone multiple times because his hands just wouldn't stop shaking, and couldn't remember most of the things that happened every day.

One afternoon, he called me to his room and told me the worst thing he could have ever said. The light in his eyes had started to fade. He couldn't even turn on the light in his room because it hurt his eyes and caused headaches. The lights which he had once so passionately loved had now become almost repulsive to him. His watery eyes couldn't endure their brightness anymore.

He held my hand, and with a lot of difficulty, said, 'I can't do little things anymore… I-I forget everything… I can't hear. People get irritated when I speak. They scream at m-me. The lights hurt my eyes. I-I can't even speak without getting stuck. I can barely get up…'

'You'll be okay, Grandpa,' I tried to assure him.

'No, listen to me,' he insisted. 'I… I won't be okay. I can feel it. I'll never be okay.'

His eyes were two hollows of complete darkness. I don't remember having felt so traumatized before. I had cried in my pillow bitterly all afternoon and ended up having a fit of high fever for three days straight.

And that's how I stepped on my downward spiral.

5

Autumn of 1968, 1969

'Don't do this, Sridhar,' Vikash had warned me several times 'It's okay to come up with new ideas but this one is too dangerous!'

'Let me at least try,' I had told him. 'Let me see if it's even possible.'

In 1968, when I was hired by the Bidyalanka Puja Committee for the purpose of providing street lighting, I had volunteered to additionally decorate the banks of our old pond too for three primary reasons. Number one, I had grown up next to it. Number two, it had been the source of some of our most sumptuous meals in childhood. And number three, it had been the setting for several of my childish shenanigans. However, when the lights glowed around the pond after sundown, the space enclosed by the banks of the pond looked extremely empty. But of course, I couldn't have done anything about it because the enclosed space contained nothing but neck-deep water.

That's when I first contemplated the possibility of

making lights glow under water and laughed at myself for being so impractical. But then the idea stuck with me for a while and what had seemed impossible in the evening had started to seem like an idea worth giving a shot by the night. I wasn't even sure if the idea was feasible since it was unprecedented. Besides, making the 25-watt lamps glow under water was itself a very risky business. And if I had to make those lights glow under water, I would obviously have to step inside the water to fix them, test them and do whatever else was needed in that situation, and that would expose me to the perils of a major electric shock in case the fixtures exploded for some reason. However, I was curious, and I always wanted to try something new, to do something unique, even if it was risky. I made up my mind to test my idea regardless of the risks involved.

So, one fine day, my friend Parashuram and I lowered a small panel decorated with 25-watt lamps in the Bidyalanka pond to see if our plan was even feasible and also to get an idea of the probable risks. Standing knee deep in the water, I debated how we could approach the task without hurting ourselves. The lamps glowed bright and colourful. We had absolutely no idea what to expect.

'Are you sure you want to do this?' asked Parashuram with a nervous laugh.

'Hmm,' I nodded gravely without looking at him.

'But… what if we die?'

'You can stand on the bank if you like,' I told him. 'I will test it and let you know. If things go wrong, at least one of us can get help.'

It seemed that was exactly what he wanted to hear from me.

So, Parashuram waddled across the pond, climbed out of it, stood on the steps on the bank and offered me moral support while I bravely stood in the water, holding a stick in my hand. I knew we had no alternative. Every new invention begins with someone who is willing to shoulder the risks. I had to do it sooner or later, and the sooner I was done with it, the better.

'Listen, Parashuram,' I told him. 'If I get a shock, don't rush into the water to get me out. First turn off the lights, unplug the main wire, wait for a few minutes, and only then help me out.'

He nodded.

'Please don't ignore my warning,' I told him again. 'Even if I die here in the water, you have to do what I said. Step by step. Don't rush in impulsively.'

'You won't die, stop saying such things,' he told me, even though it was he who had first broached the possibility of death. 'And yes, I will follow your advice to the word.'

'And if I come out alive,' I smiled. 'We will go to Bimal Mishtanna Bhandar, okay?'

'Yes, sir!' he cried. 'You treat me to samosas and I will treat you to jalebis.'

'And we will smoke afterwards. Deal?'

'Deal!'

There was so much to live for. I was eager to stay alive. And I knew I'd be much happier if our experiment proved successful. The jalebis and samosas would be so much tastier and smoking afterwards wouldn't make me feel guilty. In fact, I would feel like I had earned the right to smoke.

So, I closed my eyes, muttered a quick prayer and used my stick to smash a glowing lamp.

Then I waited for the impact.

There was none that I could feel.

My muscles, which had been tense and stiff all along, slowly relaxed. Parashuram and I looked at each other, and my gentle nod was met with a happy little jig that he performed on the steps of the ghat, bursting with excitement. 'WE DID IT! WE DID IT! YES!'

That afternoon we discovered that the idea of underwater lights was not only feasible but also pretty risk-free because only a tiny patch of water around the broken lamp would be electrified, not the whole pond. Our fears had basically been built on a bedrock of myths! Overjoyed, we filled our stomachs and our hearts that afternoon and then I set about working on my new project. The puja committee members had requested me to arrange the lamps under water in such a way that they formed the letters of the word 'Bidyalanka' written in Bengali. That was fine with me. In fact, that seemed like an easy, hassle-free project. So, I readily agreed to their proposal.

'I will do it,' I told them and watched their faces light up with joy.

For this project, I didn't use the soft slices of flexible bamboo. Instead, I used thick pliable wire to create the letters of the word and then framed the word with thick bamboo strips. After a couple of weeks, the word was made, the letters looked excellent and the lamps glowed bright as ever. But two days before the Jagadhatri Puja, on Chaturthi, when we had just lowered the frame into the pond to test the lights, a group of electrical engineers from the Bhar Company, the only electric supply company in Chandannagar, appeared out of what seemed like thin air and ordered that I should stop the work immediately since it was dangerous and could pose a fatal threat to the visitors.

'But these aren't dangerous,' I insisted. 'I've tested them.'

'You never know what might happen, young man,' cautioned one of the engineers. 'Who will take the responsibility if someone is injured?'

'There will be no injury,' I kept saying. 'Even if a lamp explodes in the water, it's quite safe.'

'No chap, we cannot allow this,' another engineer said, adamant.

'Let me at least show you,' I requested. 'I've worked extremely hard for this. Let me show you what I'm talking about. Then you can decide.'

After a few long minutes of tireless persuasion, they decided they would give me a chance.

I immediately signalled Parashuram to switch on the lights and then took a stick that was lying nearby, went waist-deep into the pond confidently and burst one lamp in front of them. And then I burst another.

'Are you alright?' Parashuram asked.

'Absolutely,' I shrugged.

The engineers looked surprised. I could have burst the lamps of an entire letter and recreated it again if that was what took to convince them that it was safe. Anyway, I was lucky. They were convinced after I had burst three lamps and said that they would let me go ahead with the plan.

The solicitous engineers, however, had a fence constructed around the pond for the safety and security of the visitors which I had no reason to disapprove of.

The underwater lights were a phenomenal success that year and in the following year, the founders of Boroline Company offered me a handsome amount of money to advertise the name of their company with underwater lights in the same way as I had done for Bidyalanka the previous year. And that was the year I could have died because of my overconfidence.

The lights were lowered into the Bidyalanka pond once again in the autumn of 1969, the white and green 25-watt lamps forming the letters of the word 'Boroline'. It was only Panchami but Bidyalanka was congested. People had arrived in multitudes and thronged the banks of the pond while I stood there in the water signalling Parashuram, as the lights glowed at my feet underwater. Fully aware of the hundreds of eyes watching me from behind the fence, I expressed my disapproval at the lights and decided to do something about them just for the heck of it!

'They're too dim,' I yelled at Parashuram even though he was standing almost right next to me and then I shook my head vigorously without any reason.

'What are you saying?' he looked confused. 'They look so much better than last year!'

'Nah,' I replied with my hands on my hips, striking the pose of a know-it-all for my audience to see. 'Something is wrong. The wires need to be tightened.'

There was nothing wrong with the lights. The wires were perfect. But I wanted the people to see me at work in the pond, vulnerable to their imaginary perils while the lights still glowed underwater. To them it was something lethal and dangerous and I wanted to bust their myths. Some of them stood there trembling with anxiety, the palms of their hands pressed against each other, terrified, praying for my safety. I loved the attention. It made me feel like a local celebrity! I loosened a couple of wires on purpose and meddled with them, connecting them, disconnecting them and then connecting them again while the corresponding lights flickered in the water, and the people around me gasped in surprise and fear.

'Look, that's Sridhar Das!' I heard someone say. 'Quite a daredevil, that young lad!'

'Where is he? Where is he?' said some others, probably the ones standing behind, who could not see the pond.

'Oh, there he is! He's so young!' said someone else.

'Nevertheless, so brave!' replied another.

And the lamps weren't the only things which glowed that evening.

Then there came a moment when the crowd on the bank got a little too enthusiastic. Suddenly, there was a loud explosive noise as the fence failed to hold back the riled-up crowd and soon gave way. The mortified screams of the people who stood nearest to the pond caught me off-guard and the loose wire caught my finger, burning my skin. The electricity made my entire hand tingle. When I tried to free it with a jerk, it fell on my back and burnt a patch of skin there too. Next it fell in the water right where I had been standing.

I don't remember what followed because I blacked out instantly. So much for overconfidence!

I was immediately carried out of the pond in an unconscious state. Someone had already called for an ambulance. Most of them thought I wouldn't make it out alive because my pulse couldn't be detected for a while. And the rumour spread throughout the town that I had died with my boots on.

'Death by misadventure,' they called it.

However, it was all a false alarm and they were soon proven wrong when I was resurrected at the local hospital three hours after my misadventure.

Parashuram had fixed the wires I had loosened on purpose right after I was carried out of the water and the pictures of my lights reached the black and white pages of the local newspapers and magazines, including detailed accounts of my death followed by my 'miraculous resurrection'.

I thought that was the end of my promising career but within a week's time I was flooded with newer projects, not only from all across the town but also from Kolkata. Some big shots from Paikpara wanted to book me in advance for the Kali Puja next year. The College Square Puja Committee wanted my underwater lights. I received several calls from neighbouring states, all offering to pay me handsomely and there was no looking back after that.

Interlude

I was in my room and my grandfather was sitting on the edge of the bed with a tender smile on his face. Rubbing the sleep off my eyes, I sat up at once. My favourite song, 'The Winds of Change' by the Scorpions, was playing on my phone. I realized that I had fallen asleep while I'd been listening to it. I turned it off and checked the time. Four thirty, the clock in my phone said.

'I was waiting for you,' he said. 'You said you'd come to take my interview in the afternoon.'

'You remember the interview?' My heart leaped.

'Of course, I do! Why would I forget?'

'I went to you this afternoon,' I told him. 'I woke you up. But you didn't seem to remember anything.'

'That's probably because I was umm... sleeping,' he replied with a laugh. 'It takes me a few minutes to remember things after I wake up.'

I heaved a sigh of relief. I thought he had completely blanked out and was experiencing some kind of memory loss. Now I felt like an idiot for overlooking something so obvious and indulging in a full blown pity party.

Grandpa laughed some more at the confused expression on my face and then asked me to freshen up and have some tea first because he knew I couldn't function well without it. I splashed some water on my face and tried to convince myself that I was feeling better. I knew I had no reason to be upset anymore. Everything was alright. Grandpa was absolutely fine.

I shuffled into my grandfather's room soon after I had drunk my tea. I was surprised to find that this time I didn't have to ask any questions. He was ready with the answers already. He had even written some of the facts down on a small postcard-sized medicine envelope. There was no dearth of those tiny envelopes in his room. Looking at the paper from time to time, he told me at length about the first time he worked with the underwater lights, and the terrible shock that he received the second time.

'It was all because of my overconfidence!' he told me, while I listened to him in wonder.

'Tell me something, Grandpa,' I said, after he had told me all about the underwater lights. 'Before you started working with lights, was there no street illumination or puja procession during Jagadhatri Puja in Chandannagar?'

'Yes, there was,' he replied. 'But there was no decorative or automatic lighting as such. They were all fixed.'

'What were those earlier lights like?'

'Simple bulbs or tube lights would be used to illuminate the streets. They would be placed in triangular or star-like patterns. But they were all fixed lights, either attached to the trees or on bamboo poles fixed along the streets.'

'And what about the procession?'

'The processions were interesting,' he replied with some interest. 'Initially people walked behind the idol with huge petromax lamps, like huge kerosene lamps, suspended from their shoulders. Before that they would march with lit torches in their hands.'

'Then it... it eventually evolved,' he continued, 'and tableaus were introduced. People dressed up as characters from history or Hindu mythology, at times from popular folk tales, and they acted out their parts on the moving tableaus.'

'So, it was basically like a moving theatre?'

'Precisely.'

I took down extensive notes.

'A long time ago something really interesting happened in one of the processions,' grandpa said. 'I don't remember which year exactly... but a puja committee had tried to portray the execution of the revolutionary Khudiram Bose. The guy who played the role of Bose got so excited that he went overboard with the part where he was supposed to hang himself from the poles and bars fixed on the tableau. He was just supposed to stand on a small stool for a minute with the halter round his neck for the execution scene, but in his enthusiasm, he kicked the stool and would have choked to death had he not been rescued in the nick of time. The entire procession was discontinued because the guy had to be rushed to the hospital immediately.'

'What?'

'I know what you're thinking,' smiled grandfather.

'Were you there when it happened?' I asked him. 'I mean, did it happen in front of your eyes?'

'Yes, I was there. It happened in Bidyalanka.'

I was convinced that this guy had somehow inspired my grandfather to be a daredevil himself when it came to taking risks.

'So, the second time you worked with the underwater lights, it was in the year 1969, am I right?' I enquired.

'Yes,' he nodded.

'And then came 1970, the year you met grandma!' I rubbed my hands excitedly.

'Yes, and then I married her in 1971,' said Grandpa. 'But before that, in... 1969, my father passed away.'

'Oh,' I sighed. 'What had happened to him?'

'We don't really know. He complained of chest pain and then he passed away at the hospital a few days later.'

'Was it a heart attack or something?'

'It might have been,' he replied. 'None of us were sure.'

'He wasn't that old, was he? That's so sad.'

'Yes, it was,' he replied. 'But I kept myself busy with work and soon your grandmother walked into my life.'

'Tell me all about it,' I grinned from ear to ear.

'I... I don't really remember much about those years.'

'How can that be true?' I asked him. 'You seem to remember most of the details from your past. You ought to remember something about your marriage!'

'You'd better ask your grandmother about it,' replied Grandpa, visibly uncomfortable. 'I'm sure she can give you more information.'

'Okay then,' I said, rather disappointed. 'I'll ask her.'

My grandfather, his feathers ruffled, now resorted to his pack of cigarettes for comfort. I suddenly remembered that I had never asked him how he got addicted to smoking.

'When did you start smoking?' I questioned him.

'Are you going to write all that in your book, too?' he looked guilty.

'If it's interesting, then definitely.'

'Okay, then listen,' my grandfather said. 'It all started after I left school. Parashuram and I used to visit the railway station to eat the delicious chickpeas and aloo kaabli *sold on the platforms and steal mangoes from the trees growing nearby. When the passenger trains used to pass us by, some of the passengers would discard their half-smoked cigarettes from the compartment windows and we would pick them up from the tracks and smoke the leftovers. That's how it all began.'*

I was horrified. 'You're kidding, right?'

He shook his head.

'What were you doing on the train tracks in the first place? It's dangerous to just walk around on the tracks like that!'

'We would occasionally hitch rides to the nearby stations that way too,' he responded.

'Were you never caught by the Ticket Collector?'

'A few times, yes,' he admitted. 'But it was all fun to us back then. Getting caught and scolded by the TC was thrilling. And we would wait for our chance to smoke. So, we prayed that the passengers in the approaching train would be generous.'

'Generous in littering the tracks with cigarette butts?'

'Now that you say it like that, I feel really guilty,' Grandpa replied.

'You should be!' I pretended to be cross. 'The train tracks

were not your playground. Most importantly, why on earth would you smoke cigarettes thrown around by strangers?'

My grandfather had a distant look in his eyes. 'People often forget that I am a human being too. They... they always expect me to be perfect, exemplary. But I was a kid once too, and then a young man. I made many mistakes in my life which I'm not proud of. So, don't be too shocked, my dear. It hurts me to see that look on your face. I feel like I've... like I've disappointed you with this story.'

'Well, I'm glad that you at least survived to tell the tale,' I told him. 'Because what you did was really dangerous. Playing around on the tracks like that and smoking leftover cigarettes discarded by strangers, both major health hazards.'

'What else could I have done? We didn't have m-money to buy cigarettes. So, the streets and railway tracks were the only places where we could get access to them.'

'Which brand of cigarettes did you smoke back then?' I said to lighten the mood a little bit.

'Charminar Cigarettes,' he remembered with a twinkle in his eyes. 'Those were the only cigarettes common people like us could afford back then. Gold Flake was way too expensive for my means.'

'Okay, that's quite a story, I must say,' I responded. 'But I don't know whether I should put it in the book.'

'On second thoughts,' said grandfather. 'I think you should definitely include it in the book. This is a flaw that I have, my oldest addiction. Without this, my character will be neither sincere nor complete. Besides, I... I don't want to be portrayed as this perfect man who never did anything wrong. I've had enough of that already and it exhausts me.'

I felt this sudden surge of admiration swelling inside my heart for the man in front of me but I didn't want to show it.

'Okay, we'll see about that,' I told him instead. 'But now let's get to the point we were discussing before that. About you and Grandma. I know it was a love marriage and neither of your families were supportive of it,' I toyed with the subject in a vain attempt to elicit some response from him. 'They didn't even attend the marriage ceremony.'

'They didn't,' he responded. 'Some of my friends stood by us at that time. We were married in Ramen Da's house.'

'Who was he?'

'An old acquaintance,' he replied. 'He was senior to me and... and loved me like his own brother.'

'I see,' I noted. 'So, why were your families not supportive of your marriage?'

'Because she was a Brahmin. And we belonged to a lower caste. We were Vaishyas.'

'That's it?'

'Inter-caste marriages were a taboo back in our time,' replied my grandfather. 'We weren't allowed to live in our Bidyalanka house after I married her against my family's will.'

'Wait, weren't you living with Vikash Kaka in Palpara?'

'No, I was allowed back in my house once I had started earning enough money after the success of the Bidyalanka panel lights,' he replied.

'Isn't that unfair?' I couldn't help but say.

'Of course, it was unfair,' agreed Grandpa. 'But I endured it all because they... they were the only family I had. I renovated our cottage to a pucca house with all

the money that I had earned to provide my mother and brothers with better living conditions. I provided for the family, and paid for most of the daily expenses. However, my mother was never affectionate to me. She wasn't proud of my accomplishments. She barely acknowledged them. She came to me only when she needed money and... and was very straightforward about it. As though I was somehow obliged to pay her. I made a separate room for myself with a permanent ceiling, tiles on the floor, plastered walls, a small aquarium, a radio and different kinds of lights. After I married your grandmother and was kicked out of the house the second time, my room was occupied by my brothers.'

'So, what did you and Grandma do? Where did you go?'

'We lived in one of Ramen's Da's houses, near Strand Road along the Ganga river. I paid him rent every month.'

'And what was life like there?'

'I hardly stayed at home. You'd better ask your grandmother all that. I barely got any time to spend with her.'

'At least tell me how you met her!' I insisted. 'I'll be writing a book on you, I absolutely need to know things from your viewpoint.'

'Okay, her father was very close to me,' he replied briefly. 'That's how I got to know her...'

'I know that,' I cut him off. 'I want to know how you met her, you know, the first time you saw her and all that. Try to understand, this is going to be a very important part of the book!'

'I... I don't really remember,' repeated my grandfather obstinately. 'Go ask your grandmother.'

My grandmother was in her prayer quarters when I went to look for her the next evening. She wasn't meditating so my conscience didn't prick me when I asked her for the interview.

'Why? What's the hurry?' She was a little irritated. She was always like that whenever someone interrupted her in the prayer room.

'I don't have time!' I told her. 'I've been meaning to speak to you for a very long time but whenever I look for you, you're either praying or watching TV.'

'Okay, fine, I'm coming,' she surrendered, blowing the conch three times and finally leaving her chair.

The numerous idols she worshipped seemed to look back at me with judgmental eyes since I had cut short the length of their worship.

My grandmother was short, plump and looked quite youthful but was bent with a problem in her spine that couldn't be fixed. In spite of surviving a multi-organ failure, she was quite active and tenacious for her age but the pain that affected her limbs often came in the way. She was still extremely beautiful, even though she looked nothing like what she did when she was young. I have encountered several people who've told me that I resemble my grandmother. She always thought they were joking but I couldn't help but feel a little proud every time someone said that.

'What do you want to know?' Now she was sitting comfortably on her bed all set with her little box of betel leaves, betel nuts and tobacco.

'Well, tell me all about your marriage with Grandpa.'

'Why don't you ask your grandfather about it?'

'Have you both sworn an oath of secrecy that you're never going to speak about your love life? He has buttoned his lips, which is why I'm here. It makes me wonder, what exactly happened in your marriage, huh? There must be something fishy.'

'Nothing, except it was the most awkward marriage ever. That's probably why your grandpa is embarrassed to talk about it.'

'Uh-huh? Why so?'

'First of all, it wasn't planned,' said Grandma, slicing the betel nuts with great precision. 'Neither of our families were involved in it.'

'I've heard all that a million times! Tell me something new!'

'Well, do you know that your grandfather left me in the middle of our marriage ceremony to go fix a bunch of lights that had stopped working in someone else's marriage banquet at Bagbazar?'

'Are you serious?'

'Ask your grandpa if you don't believe me,' she replied, chewing her paan. Her lips had acquired a permanent reddish tint over the decades due to the kattha *that she used to dress the leaves before consumption. 'He walked out on me right in the middle of our marriage rituals. Just before we were about to walk seven times around the holy fire.'*

'That must have been so embarrassing for you!'

'Of course it was! To make matters worse, all the people present at our marriage were absolute strangers to me, and most of them were men.'

'Oh my God!'

'Also, everything that I wore on the day of my marriage was borrowed. Starting from the saree to the ornaments, everything. And we got married in the house of a person whose mother-in-law had kicked my family out of another house she owned in Bidyalanka, in the middle of a stone-cold winter night.'

'Does this get any better? Or worse?'

'Well, my mother and I were pregnant at the same time.'

I was only glad that I wasn't drinking my tea at that time.

'Tell me everything, right from the very beginning,' I demanded, and then looking at my watch, said, 'You have the whole evening!'

What I didn't know was that right in the next room, separated from ours by just a flimsy partition wall, sat Grandfather who remembered it all. He remembered every single unsavoury detail. He just didn't know how to come to terms with them after having buried them for forty-eight years.

6

Summer of 1970

I really don't remember the day I first saw her but I do remember the curiosity and excitement in the neighbourhood that followed her arrival. She arrived with her parents, her three sisters and two brothers and rented the small single-room shack right next to our house which had a cheap asbestos roof and no electricity. They were all very good looking and the way they interacted with others was refreshingly different from what I was used to. Her name was Sumitra, she was the eldest of all her siblings and the most beautiful. I couldn't help but notice the striking resemblance between her and the famous Indian actress Vyjayanthimala. They were all high-caste Mukherjee Brahmins. Rumour had it that they had all arrived from Kolkata, and were all very well educated, refined and often spoke to each other in English, which I later learnt was actually true.

'So, why are they living in Ramen Da's tumbledown shack and not some nice pucca house?' my middle brother, who I called Mejda, asked one day.

'From what I've heard, their father seems to have suffered huge losses in business and they were kicked out of their ancestral house in Kolkata,' said another brother, Shejda, twirling his moustache.

'Whatever, they're all very good looking,' Kartik piped up with sparkling eyes.

'And they speak English,' added Krishna.

'They're all Brahmins,' our mother snapped from the kitchen. 'And that's all we should be bothered about. If I ever see any of you trying to fraternize with them, I won't let you set foot in this house again. Have some self-respect.'

In the year 1970, I was a man of twenty-eight, independent and free. My favourite haunt was the Manorama Medical Store which was owned by one of my Palpara friends. I used to spend most of my leisure hours there, drinking tea, reading newspapers and occasionally engaging in conversations with the other people who used to gather there. One of them was Sunil Babu, a medical representative. He was quite a bit older than me but that didn't prevent us from bonding.

In the course of our casual conversations, we discovered that we had similar tastes and several shared interests in food, music, films and football. We were both staunch supporters of Mohun Bagan, we loved to hum the tunes of Kishore Kumar, Mohammed Rafi and Hemanta Mukherjee, we were ardent admirers of Uttam Kumar and Suchitra Sen, we both regarded ourselves as unbeatable at chess and that's what cemented our friendship. I also discovered that Sumitra was Sunil Babu's daughter. On some subconscious level, I suppose, that was a major factor why I felt so drawn to Sunil Babu and wanted to be in his good books. He invited me over to his house for lunch one afternoon and that's when I had the opportunity to be formally introduced to his daughter.

'There are better houses in Palpara,' I told Sunil Da over my rice and daal. 'Why don't you move there?'

'I don't think I'd be able to afford them,' he replied humbly.

'You don't have to worry about that,' I assured him. 'I have friends in Palpara. I can get you a decent place to stay.'

'This place is decent enough for us, Sridhar,' he said. 'Besides, I'll get to the station faster from here.'

That didn't sound like a valid excuse. I couldn't understand how the eight of them lived in that single room. It was even smaller than the cottage we used to live in back in the 1940s and '50s. Sumitra's mother was in her mid-thirties, but looked unusually frail and ill. Her youngest brother, Gopal, was hardly a year old. She had three beautiful sisters nicknamed Mana, Nuna and Annie, all aged between fifteen and twenty and another brother, Proshanto, aged around twelve. Sumitra's immediate younger brother, Gedo, who was just twenty years old, was away in Kolkata, pursuing an MBBS in the National Medical College. Sumitra herself had just graduated from Lady Brabourne College with an Honours degree in Bengali. Sunil Babu often boasted that she was the best student in her batch.

'Mana will soon move in with one of our relatives in Kolkata,' said Sunil Da. 'And I won't be here every day. This place is decent enough for six people.'

'Why won't you be here?' I asked him.

'My company is in Kolkata,' he told me. 'So, I have to spend most of my time there.'

It was only later that I learnt that he had a second wife and three other children in Kolkata who he occasionally lived with. I didn't quite know what to think about that, so I had refrained from thinking about it altogether.

I was almost done with my lunch and about to leave when I saw her. She had just taken a bath, her saree was partially wet, and the thick sheet of long, black hair that covered most of her back smelled like jasmine. Her eyes were large, dark and dreamy, with a unibrow adorning them protectively like an eagle. With her translucent skin and her lips red from the juice of *paan*, she looked pristine, like a slender marble statue, the kind of beauty which was calm, serene and balm to the eyes but at the same time powerful enough to knock the wind out of my lungs. Never before had I felt that way around a woman.

The moment our eyes met, she flashed a curious smile, and without any trace of coyness, addressed me directly, 'Leaving already, Sridhar Babu?'

'Umm… yes,' I replied, taken aback. I hadn't expected her to be so forward. Besides, nobody had ever addressed me as 'Sridhar Babu' before. Had I been fair skinned she would certainly have noticed the blush on my cheeks. But I wasn't, so that saved me from a huge deal of embarrassment. It was during moments like these that my complexion proved advantageous.

'I've heard a lot about you from my father,' she added respectfully. 'It's an honour living beside your house.'

'No, no, it's nothing like that,' I waved my hand dismissively. 'It's a small town and only a handful of people know me. That's nothing to be proud of.'

'Will you be making the underwater lights this year?' she asked with genuine excitement in her eyes.

'Yes, but in Kolkata. Not here.'

'This is my eldest daughter, Sumitra,' Sunil Da proudly introduced her to me.

'I guessed so,' I answered, while she stood there with her bucket, her twinkling eyes, and her skin glowing in the sunlight that filtered in through the broken window, glowing brighter than any other light I'd ever seen before.

Autumn of 1970

As fate would have it, I fell head over heels in love with Sumitra. It wasn't love at first sight, no. It happened over time. Perhaps it was her selfless, nurturing nature that appealed to me. There was also an unshakeable sense of dignity and independence about her which I greatly admired. With all her scores and qualifications, she could easily get into one of the best universities in Kolkata for her master's degree and start her life afresh. But her siblings topped her list of priorities and for them she was ready to sacrifice everything. I wanted to help her continue her education so that she could be a lecturer someday. That was her dream. But she had made it very clear to me that she wouldn't be truly happy if she selfishly pursued her dream and left her helpless mother and siblings alone to fend for themselves.

Over time, we got to know each other as I often visited their house and Sunil Babu frequented mine whenever he was back in town. Such was their state of poverty that they often went without food. Sumitra never shared her toils with me. She always put on a brave and cheerful face whenever we ran into each other on the streets or at their place. But it was her brother Proshanto who found a confidante in me and kept me updated about whatever went on in their family. I never expressed my feelings to Sumitra but I had a feeling that she understood them. And whether she felt the same way about me or not was something I never thought about. Marriage was pretty much out of the question for me because my circumstances were still somewhat unstable. I wanted to think of marriage only when I could be sure that I could give my wife a good life.

Sunil Babu's wife had a lot of affection for me and regarded me like her younger brother. Even though they had little, she often invited me over for tea and meals, sacrificing her share and going without food herself. When I came to know about this, I offered to help them with buying groceries and supplying electricity to their house but they refused each time, owing to their sense of dignity and self-esteem. However, their impoverishment eventually outweighed every other sentiment, forced them to be practical, and they allowed me to help them make both ends meet. When Sunil Babu came back to town, I asked him to dine with me and stay over at my place so that the siblings could have the little house to themselves and spend their days comfortably.

My mother didn't like my association with the

Mukherjee family one bit. She could guess the feelings I had for Sumitra and decided to employ measures to stop me visiting her again. We had an acquaintance who was very wealthy. Without my knowledge, she fixed a match between me and his daughter and began planning my marriage well in advance to thwart any possibility of a relationship blossoming between Sumitra and me.

'Where have you been all this time?' my mother asked me one day, quite out of the blue.

'I was at Sunil Babu's house,' I replied honestly. 'Why?'

'You're going to visit Ramesh Babu's house tomorrow,' my mother dropped the bomb. 'I will accompany you.'

'What for?' I asked, completely unaware of the developments that had taken place without my knowledge.

'You're twenty-eight years old already, son,' she reminded me. 'It's time for you to get married and have a family of your own.'

'And what has Ramesh Babu got to do with any of this?'

'We have to keep our word to them, don't we?' my mother replied, not looking at me.

'Wait…' I was confused. 'What word?'

My brothers looked at me as though I was absolutely nuts.

'I'm completely at a loss here. Can anyone tell me what's going on?'

'The word of marriage, of course,' shrugged one of them.

'Marriage?'

'Yes, you are getting married to Ramesh Babu's daughter, Purnima,' another informed me.

'WHAT?' I exclaimed in disbelief. 'I don't even know her! I don't even remember the last time I spoke to Ramesh Babu. In fact, I don't even want to get married now.'

'We remember them,' replied my mother. 'We've known Purnima ever since she was born. She's perfect for you! She comes from a well-off family. We belong to the same caste. They are ready to offer you a rich dowry, a gold chain, gold buttons, furniture and also cash. Besides, Purnima would be a very good housekeeper. She is not like those educated, modern women who only think of themselves. They are so uncompromising that they cannot live in harmony with anyone. Maybe Purnima is not so good looking but beauty fades away with time. You will have a secure future with her and be happy in the long run. And don't be silly, you must get married some day or the other, and the sooner the better.'

'Well, *I* am the one who is supposed to get married, right?' I objected. 'I should be the one making these decisions.'

'That is exactly why we're going to visit them tomorrow,' said my mother, in a matter-of-fact manner. 'So that you get to know both her and her family well.'

I clutched my hair in despair.

'What's so wrong with this?' asked my mother, looking at me sharply. 'Your elder brothers are all married and well settled. Each one of them got married to the girl of my choice and look how happy they are. They never made such a fuss about it. They all got substantial dowry. Beds, cupboards, gold and cash. Sacks of rice, wheat and pulses are sent to us every year by Balaram's in-laws. They are all very decent people. What makes you different?'

'I don't think I'm ready for marriage, yet,' I told her bluntly. 'And when I marry, I'll make sure I marry the girl of my choice.'

There was a moment of silence after I said that.

'The girl of your choice, huh?' my mother asked me bitterly. 'Mukherjee Babu's eldest daughter, you mean?'

'What exactly makes you think that?' I tried to keep my calm.

'You think I'm blind, son?' she glared at me. 'Yes, I may not have studied in fancy colleges, I may be an unschooled, inexperienced, small-town woman, but I have been married for over thirty-five years now and have brought up eleven kids. I know the world and the people living in it better than you do. Your marriage with Purnima has been finalized. And you're going to visit her family tomorrow. That's the end of the matter.'

'I am NOT going to marry Purnima and nor am I going to visit her tomorrow,' I declared, and for the first time in my life I disobeyed my mother's orders to her face.

'What did you say?' she asked me, taken aback at my audacity.

'You heard it right, Maa,' I confirmed. 'I'm never going to marry her.'

My brothers looked enraged.

'Why?' my mother snarled.

'Because it's my life,' I told her. 'And I will make my own choices.'

'All for that Brahmin whore, is it?' she hissed. 'You think you are going to marry her and bring her to live under my roof? You think you're going to make me squirm every time she touches my feet?'

'She's not a whore,' my blood boiled. 'Don't you dare call her that!'

'Oh, so now you're going to dictate what I should do and what I shouldn't, huh?' my mother's eyes glowered. 'Who's teaching you all that, son? That slutty gold-digger? You need to be exorcized from that witch's spell to be able to think clearly again.'

'She's not a slut!' I shouted. 'Nor is she a gold-digger! If there's anyone here who's a gold digger it's you. The only time you even care to talk to me is when you want money. The only reason you got my brothers married is for the dowry. The more the dowry, the better the bride. Who cares about what they want? And don't tell me it's your roof when I am the one who mostly supports the family.'

'Well, we don't need your money, boy!' my mother retorted in a shrill voice. 'Keep your money to yourself. Your brothers are capable enough to provide for the family. And remember one thing, you're not the only one who runs the family, and this house hasn't been willed to you alone. As long as I'm alive, this is my roof and if you ever marry that Brahmin girl, you'll have no place under my roof.'

'I don't need a place under your wretched roof,' I hissed. 'I never belonged here, anyway. You can sit with your beloved sons under your beloved roof for the rest of your life, I don't care! But don't expect to suddenly play the role of a solicitous mother and have a say in my life after all these years that you've spent treating me like an outsider. I will never forget how you treated me, mother. As long as father was alive, you turned a blind eye to me when I needed you most. And now that he's gone, you've started talking exactly like him. Everything I ever did, I did without your love, your support. I've lived for years in Vikash's house and you never even cared whether I was dead or alive. And you know what? They never made me feel like an outsider. But you did. My own mother! Whenever I passed by this house, you turned your face away like I wasn't even your son. I shouldn't even be calling you my mother. I'll build my own house. I don't need to be a part of this contaminated cesspit that you call home. And you know what? I *am* going to marry Sumitra if she accepts me. Stop me if you can.'

I locked the door of my room and stormed out of the house, slamming the rusty iron gate behind me.

Winter of 1970

'Sridhar,' Parashuram touched my shoulder gently as I sat in my new factory welding two wires. It was the shabby front porch of a neighbour's house which he offered to me in exchange for rent every month. 'Mukherjee Babu's daughter is looking for you.'

'Who? Annie?' I asked, not looking up from my work.

'No, Sumitra,' he replied.

I looked up at him now, a trifle surprised. Sumitra usually never came in search of me. It was always either Proshanto or Annie who came to me whenever they needed to.

'Well, where is she?' I asked him.

'Right outside,' he replied. 'Should I bring her in?'

'Yes, of course.'

I stood up immediately, straightened my posture, rubbed the sweat off my forehead with one of my sweater sleeves and ran my fingers through my hair, trying to look presentable.

A few seconds later, Sumitra stepped inside my factory for the first time. And instead of the wind being knocked out of my lungs, a strange sense of fear crept into me when I saw her pallid, tear-streaked face.

'What's wrong, Sumitra?' I went over to her. 'Why are you crying?'

For a moment she couldn't speak a word. Tears simply rolled down her cheeks and she tried in vain to stifle her sobs with the loose end of her pale-yellow saree. The young boys, who I had hired to work in my factory and assist me in my projects, took the cue and left.

'I… I don't know how to tell you this, Sridhar Babu,' her lips quivered. 'But I have to.'

'You know you can tell me anything,' I had never been good at consoling people and at that moment I was clueless. 'Tell me what's bothering you.'

'Your brothers have made our lives a living hell,' she bit her lip, trying to choke back her tears. 'It's been a month, I didn't tell you anything because… because I didn't want to create any trouble. But after what they did today… I don't know how I'm going to show my face in the neighbourhood.'

I was definitely not prepared for something like this.

'What did they do?' I weakly asked.

'They've been throwing stones at our windows, shattering the glass. They've been messing with our asbestos, calling my sisters awful names in public. Last night they cut off the electricity line. Gopal's been extremely ill for the past couple of days. And t… today… while I was walking back home from the Manorama Medical with his fever medicines, they called my mother a… a prostitute and me, a slut. They told everyone in and around the neighbourhood that I've been seducing you for money.'

And then she burst into tears. Something inside me snapped.

'My mother's not a prostitute,' she was inconsolable. 'She's the most sacrificing woman I have ever known.'

'I know, Sumitra. I know. You don't need to tell me that.'

'She was married to my father when she was hardly over fifteen,' she continued. 'And since then she has dedicated her entire life to loving and serving him, never complaining, never demanding anything. Even when my father started seeing another woman and married her in less than a year, my mother didn't raise any objection. She was shattered but she endured it all and never questioned my father's activities. She never tried to stop him from doing what he wanted to do.'

'You really don't need to tell me any of that,' I told her again. 'I know how she is. And I know you. I apologize on behalf of my brothers, Sumitra. They have done something that deserves no pardon. I'm really ashamed of what they…'

'And just to let you know, Sridhar Babu, I… I haven't tried to seduce you,' she cut me off. 'I am not after your money. I never was. I have been good to you because you've been extremely generous to my family. I didn't know how to repay you with anything other than gratitude. But I'm trying to find some work now so that we don't have to depend on you for support all the time. However, nobody here wants to employ me or any of my sisters because they think we're... we're sluts. That's our identity now.'

When I went back home that afternoon to take my brothers to task, they pretended as if they didn't know what I was talking about. They even went to the extent of calling the Mukherjees 'a family of liars' and my mother participated in the conversation with supreme delight.

'Why don't you marry her?' one of my brothers taunted me. 'It's been over three months since you said you would.'

'Yeah. Besides, an extra room in the house would definitely be convenient for us, you know,' added another with a wicked smirk.

My mother encouraged them with her characteristic snicker.

'Say whatever you like,' I told them calmly. 'But if you dare trouble the sisters again or call them inappropriate names, I'm going to do to you what you did to them last night.'

'What did we do last night?' one of my older brothers feigned innocence. 'What are you talking about?'

'You know what you did,' I glared at him. 'Spare me the drama, please.'

'We didn't cut their electricity,' one of the younger ones blurted out and was immediately smacked on the head by another.

'Well, there you go!' I applauded. 'You just demonstrated what a family of liars actually looks like.'

'Why don't you leave the house, boy?' my mother intervened now. 'If we're all so bad, why bother living with us? You won't have to think twice about finding refuge. You're famous now! I know many people who would be overjoyed to offer you their room and more.'

Enough was enough. My mother had crossed all boundaries of civilized behaviour and gone out of her way to humiliate me in front of my brothers. My own blood had turned against me. I had no reason to live in that house anymore. So, I packed my belongings immediately and left for Vikash's place. His doors were always open for me. In fact, they had given me a separate room in their house where I could stay whenever I wanted to.

I worked late in my factory that night even after all my boys had left. It was biting cold, perhaps the coldest night of the year, and I wasn't in the best of moods. My work was the only thing that kept me going, the only thing I could employ as a distraction to keep my mind off the sneers of my own blood, my family. I was absolutely engrossed in my work when Parashuram burst in.

'What the hell's going on?' I asked him, shocked. 'It's 2 a.m.!'

'You have to go to your house immediately,' he told me.

'Did someone die?' I freaked out, instantly overwhelmed with guilt.

'No, but there's a possibility someone will, if you don't go right now.'

I rushed back home leaving my work undone and just when I had reached the gate, I noticed the Mukherjee family sitting in the dark on a parapet outside their house, shivering in the bitter cold. Little Gopal, sick with fever, was in Sumitra's trembling arms. Her pale face was flushed from crying and her mother and sisters, all huddled up in one blanket, wept.

'What is the matter?' I asked them, bewildered, looking at the padlock on their door.

'Ramen Babu's mother-in-law won't let us live in her house any more,' Annie's lips quivered. 'We implored her to let us stay for one night but she won't budge. Gopal's been vomiting all evening. He's going to die in the cold.'

'But the rent's been paid!' I cried. 'What's wrong with the lady?'

'She believes we've been having visitors over in the house.'

'So?' I asked, confused.

They looked at me as though I had asked the stupidest question.

'I don't think he understands,' Nuna whispered in Annie's ears.

'Clients,' said Sumitra with blank eyes. 'Say clients, Annie. Not visitors. She believes we've turned her place into a brothel.'

'What?' I was shocked.

'Yes,' she replied.

I immediately took them all into the warmth of my factory and, leaving Parashuram in charge, sat astride my scooter and sped off to Ramen Babu's mother-in-law's residence. Taming my anger, I knocked on the door four times. There was no response, and I had to shout. It was almost 3 a.m. with not a soul on the street except for the dogs and the jackals and there I stood in the cold and dark screaming for someone to answer the door. The door was finally opened by the bespectacled old widow who held a stick in one hand and a kerosene lamp in the other. Before she could ask me what I was doing there, I acquainted her with the purpose of my visit.

'What are you saying, Sridhar?' She looked surprised. 'It's your own brother who came to me this evening with three other young men complaining that those sisters have been using my house as a brothel.'

I tried my best to explain to her the truth of the situation, as calmly as I could.

Shocked and sorry after having learnt the whole story, the old woman handed me the keys to her shack and within half an hour I made sure that the Mukherjees were back inside their house, safe and warm.

Summer of 1971

The following year, in the month of April when Sunil Babu was back in town, I went up to him confidently and asked for Sumitra's hand in marriage. Quite contrary to my expectations, Sunil Babu disapproved of the match.

'But why?'

'I can't let my daughter marry into a family that doesn't have any place for her,' he said. 'Besides, I want her to study. To do her master's and be independent. She's too young for marriage. I'm extremely grateful for whatever you have done for my family, Sridhar, but I can't approve of this.'

However, later I learnt that one of the primary reasons why he disapproved of our marriage was my caste. He was of the opinion that being a Brahmin, Sumitra would never be able to adjust to life with a Vaishya, and it would also generate a contaminated bloodline. It felt like a punch in my gut. So, I did what I had to do, stubborn as I was. I went straight up to Sumitra a week later and proposed marriage to her.

'But I've never thought of you that way, Sridhar Babu,' she revealed. 'Besides, you know how things are between our families.'

'What if everything was alright between our families? Would you still refuse me?'

'I… I don't know,' she responded, and for the first time she couldn't meet my eyes.

She stared at the cold, hard ground, fiddling with the loose end of her saree and a few moments later when I asked her if she was alright, she answered in a broken voice, not looking up. That is when I realized that she was crying.

'What happened to you?' I questioned her, perplexed. 'Why are you crying again?'

'Nothing happened,' she replied, rubbing her tears. 'I'm sorry about my father. You did so much for us, and even after all that he…'

'That's not your fault. We can't change the way people think.'

'I… I just wish I wasn't born a Brahmin,' she replied with quivering lips. 'Then none of this would have been a problem.'

And in spite of the tense situation, I couldn't help but

break into a laugh. She glanced at me through her tears and was silent for a while. Then I saw the corners of her lips twitch a little bit.

'Not being a Brahmin wouldn't have solved it either,' I told her. 'As long as there's inequality, you will either be an oppressor, or oppressed, or both. There's no escaping the hierarchy.'

A tear trickled down her eye.

'Oh, Sridhar Babu, I've wrecked your life, haven't I?' she said. 'They don't let you stay in your own house because of me.'

'That's not a problem,' I told her. 'I've never been a part of that family.'

'Don't say that,' she cut me off. 'You were fine before I came here. You were getting along with them quite well.'

'Oh, you know nothing.'

'I feel terrible,' she sobbed. 'I've made a fool of myself, my family, as well as you. Everyone thinks I'm a slut and they talk ill about you because you're kind to me.'

'None of it is your fault,' I reassured her. 'You have absolutely nothing to do with this. Don't let anyone convince you otherwise. This is the fault of our society. They always blame the woman for whatever goes wrong. They are ready to believe in any rumour that they hear about a woman without even bothering to check the facts. It's solely my brothers who are at fault for this and I want to teach them a lesson. But you didn't answer my question, Sumitra.'

'Which question?'

'Would you still say no to me if everything was alright between our families?'

'I thought you weren't ready for marriage, Sridhar Babu,' she said.

'I am still not ready for marriage,' I told her. 'I don't want to marry anyone and make her suffer because of my struggles. I wanted to be sufficiently well-off before I thought about marriage.'

'Then what made you change your mind?'

'At this rate, I don't think I will ever be ready for marriage,' I replied honestly. 'I have been thinking of it purely in financial terms. But I cannot negate the fact that I'm deeply in love with you. I want to give you a comfortable life away from this mess. But I don't know how long it's going to take me to get there. All I know is that I love you, and I have for a while. I also know that I have to work tremendously hard to be able to give you that life. Instead of the two of us struggling alone, why can't we struggle together? But what's more important than any of that is how you feel about me. Have you really never thought of me as a man?'

A few moments of uncomfortable silence followed, at the end of which she shook her head from side to side, still not looking at me.

'Do you really not care for me? Not even a little bit?'

She shook her head again from side to side and I didn't quite know what to make of it.

'You do or you don't?' I asked her, confused. 'Tell me honestly, Sumitra. You don't need to be afraid of anyone or anything. But I want the truth. I haven't been able to focus on my work lately because these thoughts have been eating me up. Please tell me the truth. If you really don't feel that way for me, I will respect your decision and never bother you again.'

'I… I do,' she stammered. 'I do care about you.'

'Do you want to build a home with me?' I asked her, holding her hands earnestly.

After a long minute of silence, she coyly nodded her head and a large tear splattered on my wrist, 'Yes.'

My heart skipped a beat and for a moment I had no idea what I was going to say. And then these are the exact words that escaped my mouth.

'Then let's run away.'

'What?' she looked at me, shocked.

'Yes, let's run away and get married. We'll come back a couple of weeks later when things have settled down here.'

'I can't do that, no! I can't leave Gopal here alone.'

'We will come back for him,' I told her. 'Gopal will live with us. We'll bring him up. Is your mother against our marriage too?'

'No, she's not,' replied Sumitra. 'She's always liked you. But there's something else that you don't know.'

'What?' I asked.

She looked at me for a few seconds, deciding whether or not to disclose the secret and then she said, 'My mother is pregnant.'

'Again?'

'Yes, again,' she sighed. 'It's been nearly a month.'

'Does your father know?' I asked her.

'Yes, he does.'

'Well, then… then it's good news, I suppose.'

'I don't know how it seems like good news to you

at this moment,' she looked a little annoyed. 'We can hardly feed ourselves and now there's another baby coming. It's nothing but torture for the baby to be born in such an environment. Besides, my mother has already been suffering from ill health. I don't know if she can survive the strain of another childbirth.'

I didn't know what to say so I scratched my head.

'Running away from all of this seems like a great idea,' she sighed. 'But I can't do it. I have to talk to my mother. I have to make sure that she's alright with this. I have to talk to my sisters too. I want to run away with you, if only it were feasible.'

And feasible it was, for a few weeks later, on the 6th of May in the year 1971, Sumitra married me.

Interlude

'So, it was a happy ending!' I stretched my arms and legs. It was almost midnight. 'You finally got married and lived happily ever after.'

'It was far from a happy ending,' she replied, waving her hand dismissively. 'Because the real struggle began after that. Both for him and for me.'

'Tell me.'

'Now?' She looked tired. 'I thought I could finally watch the repeat telecast of my soaps.'

'Yes, now,' I folded my arms against my chest. 'Why? It's only 12 a.m.! I study all night during my exams!'

'Have you ever stayed up all night to soothe an ailing infant who died in your arms the next morning?'

'Fine,' I surrendered. 'I'm sorry.'

'I'll continue tomorrow,' declared my grandmother. 'I've spent an entire evening with you. Let me watch the soaps now.'

'NO!' I said vehemently. 'You are going to make a sacrifice tonight to help your granddaughter write a book. Cooperate with me and I will write good things about you in my book.'

My grandmother looked at me indignantly, annoyed and tired.

I gave up. 'We'll talk tomorrow morning. Right after you wake up.'

The next morning we sat down together over two mugs of tea.

'Last night, Mother told me something about Grandpa running away from the hospital with burns all over his limbs. Can you tell me more about that incident?'

'It happened when he was making the underwater lights for the Durga Puja at College Square in Kolkata,' replied my grandmother, sipping her tea. 'It was sometime around mid-1971. We were married. I was pregnant. He was in his factory working and there was a burning stove with a huge tumbler on it filled with hot, boiling compound.'

'What is this compound?' I asked.

'It's like... umm... a by-product of coal,' answered Grandma. 'It's solid at first and you need to melt it.'

'What is it used for?'

'Your grandfather used the thick molten tar to seal the holders of the 25-watt lamps against water.'

'I have always wondered how he made those lights waterproof. Now I have the answer. Thank you.'

'So, that tumbler full of boiling compound accidentally overturned on his limbs,' said Grandma. 'And when it happened, he instinctively tried to remove the compound with his bare hands before it solidified on his legs, and his hands too got burnt in the process. So much so that you could almost see his bones through the gaping flesh!'

I couldn't help but wince, visualizing the incident.

Sridhar Das as a young man

The light artist as he is today

Photo: Hiya Pal

Soulmates—Sridhar Das and his wife

Mayor of London with the peacock barge created for the Thames Festival, 2003

Photo: Martin Good, Courtesy LBB

Nandita Palchoudhuri, Cultural entrepreneur, in front of the barge

Magical lights—a creation by Sridhar Das

Image courtesy: 'In the Shadows: Unknown Craftsmen of Bengal' *by Payal Mohanka*

Masterpiece in the making

Image courtesy: 'In the Shadows'

Wheels of light—A worker with one of Sridhar Das' creations

Images courtesy: 'In the Shadows

A lifetime of achievement—Sridhar Das with his roomful of awards

Photo: Mayukh Banerjee

The maestro's helpers—some of the young men who worked with Sridhar Das

Penning a story—the author with her grandfather

Photo: Studio Deluxe, Chandannagar

'He was rushed to the hospital immediately,' continued my grandmother. 'And the doctors told him to avoid using his hands and legs for a week if he wanted to get better. They decided to keep him under strict supervision. But you know how stubborn he is. He escaped from the hospital that very night, limping on a stick.'

'What? In that condition?'

'Yes,' nodded Grandma. 'I was out of my mind when Parashuram came and told me that he was back in his factory, working again. Almost four months pregnant, I went running to him and implored him to stop what he was doing, afraid that his wounds might get infected. But he told me with a stern face to go back home. He was writhing in pain, but he wouldn't listen. With his hands and legs all bandaged, he sat there welding the wires painstakingly because his work was more important to him.'

'Why could he not stay in the hospital? What was the hurry?'

'The puja was in four days,' replied Grandma. 'This was his big break and he was working on several projects at the same time. He went to Kolkata four days later with all his wounds dressed, limping on that same stick. I have never seen blisters as bad as those in my entire life! But his work that year was a massive success. Soon most of the renowned puja committees in Kolkata hired him to provide illumination, not only for Durga Puja but also for Kali Puja.'

'Can you name some of the committees in Kolkata that he worked for?'

'Of course,' she remembered. 'He worked for Paikpara, and the Kali Puja in Keshab Chandra Street, started by the

famous Congress strongman Krishna Chandra Dutta. He was popularly known as "Fata Keshto".'

'He worked for Fata Keshto?'

'That's right,' replied Grandma. 'He even came to our house.'

'Wow!' I replied, fascinated. 'Who else did he work for?'

'He worked for the KNC Regiment in Barasat,' replied Grandma. 'That's another renowned committee that organizes Kali Puja every year. He also illuminated Amherst Street in Kolkata. For Durga Puja, he worked for committees like Mohammad Ali Park, Central Avenue, Bakul Bagan, Ekdalia Evergreen Club, Singhi Park, Dhakuria, Garia, Tollygunge, Ballygunge, Jodhpur Park…'

'From what you're saying, it seems like he worked everywhere in Kolkata.'

'He did,' replied my grandmother. 'He worked for most of the celebrated committees at least once in his lifetime.'

'I need a list of the committees,' I told her. 'You are going to talk to Grandfather and give me a list of all the names of the committees he's worked for. Because I need to be factually correct in my narrative.'

'Fine,' she agreed. 'He worked in several places outside West Bengal too. Almost the entire northern and north-eastern part of India including Delhi, Gujarat, Haryana, Bihar, Rajasthan, Uttar Pradesh, Chhattisgarh, Jharkhand, Orissa, Assam, Tripura, and so on. He also worked in Hyderabad. It was still a part of Andhra back then…'

'Please write that list for me, Grandma,' I said. 'There are too many places for me to remember.'

'Alright,' she said.

'Tell me more about the struggles.'

'Well, he's been struggling throughout his career,' Grandma replied in a matter of fact manner. 'First of all, he undertook several projects each year and all big ones. He hardly came back home. He practically lived in his damp, unhygienic factory. Even though he started earning quite a lot after he got the big projects, he used to starve most days because he either put all his money back into the business to finance the other projects or pay back his debts. His work kept him so busy that he just came home to sleep at night. Maybe three or four hours of sleep. And early in the morning, he was gone again.'

'Didn't you feel lonely?'

'Of course, I did,' she nodded. 'I felt very lonely. I grew up with so many brothers and sisters, I was always used to company. After marriage I felt absolutely alone. Your grandfather was hardly home, I wasn't allowed to live with my in-laws. We lived in a rented apartment at Mary Park, near Strand Road, far away from all the people I knew. I remember crying every day out of loneliness. I even regretted getting married. I was sick and pregnant and lonely. And I couldn't even blame your grandfather because I knew he was working so hard.'

'I understand.'

'Your Grandpa passed the first Jamai Shashthi *after our marriage in the police station,' she informed me. 'Did you know about that?'*

Jamai Shashti *is an annual Indian occasion where the mothers-in-law fast for their sons-in-law, invite them over to their place for sumptuous meals and shower them with gifts and delicacies.*

'Why?' I exclaimed.

'My mother had just arranged sweets on a plate and placed it in front of your grandfather when a jeep full of policemen forced their way into our shack and started ransacking it,' said Grandma. 'Your Grandpa's brothers, who were never up to any good, had informed them that we were secretly making explosives in the shack to aid the Naxalites. They found nothing, of course, yet they carried him away to the police station, depriving him of the opportunity to celebrate his first Jamai Shashti.*'*

'Were Grandpa's brothers temporarily deranged in their youth?' I was surprised, remembering all the faces who only ever smiled at me and made me feel extremely welcome whenever I was in their midst. 'They were always so good to me in my childhood. I have always liked them.'

'Oh, they were always creating troubles for us back then,' replied my grandmother. 'But then eventually they all changed after they got married and had kids. They became so much more mature and responsible. Their kids, your uncles, they all loved me so much. Your mother used to play with them all the time as long as we lived in that house.'

'They still love you.'

'Oh yes, they do. They have all grown up now and are well established. They have families of their own. I feel so happy when they visit.'

'So, there we have at least one happy ending,' I said.

'Yes, but the initial days after I got married were very hard for me,' Grandma said as she broke her second biscuit. 'On top of that, I had very difficult and painful pregnancies. I had a son before your mother was born. And a daughter

after her. Both of them died. All three of them were breech babies. So, I had to forgo normal delivery and have a C-section each time. And of course, Chandannagar back in the 1970s wasn't at all medically advanced. During the birth of my first child, I suffered from labour pain for two days and was then taken to the OT at the very last moment. My son was born alright but my belly was cut vertically, for the breech, and I was in severe pain for several weeks after my delivery. The only good thing was that, after my boy was born, my mother-in-law welcomed me home.'

'That was nice of her.'

'Well, you must also consider the fact that your grandfather was earning quite a lot those days. That was also a good reason. However, she was never nice to him. She was always sort of cold and formal in her interactions with your grandpa.'

'What was her problem? Why did she hate grandfather so much?'

'Mainly because he married me, a Brahmin,' she informed me. 'Besides, she hadn't received any dowry from my family.'

'So, dowry was another big reason!'

'Yes, it was. But she was never bad to me. In fact, she loved me more than her other daughters-in-law.'

'Wow, that's unexpected,' I said. 'But tell me something, why did your first child die? What had happened to him?'

'He was less than one and a half months old when he got diarrhoea,' she replied. 'At the same time, my baby sister, who was born a month before my son, was also suffering from diarrhoea. Annie was taking care of her since our mother was extremely ill and admitted at the National

Medical College, Kolkata. My brother Gedo, who was a doctor there, was looking after her.'

'Why was she ill?'

'She was suffering from puerperal sepsis,' she said. 'A kind of septicaemia.'

'That's what happened to Mary Wollstonecraft after she delivered Mary Godwin!' I cried out. 'That's exactly how she died too!'

'I don't know about Mary Wollstonecraft,' replied my grandmother. 'You keep your English Literature references to yourself. But yes, puerperal sepsis is lethal.'

'Okay, you continue,' I told her as I kept scribbling.

'So, I took my ailing son to a local doctor one evening,' continued Grandma. 'He gave a medicine that stopped both his loose motion and his urine. He kept crying in pain for hours. He cried all night. My mother-in-law had acquired some holy water from a Tantric woman in a neighbouring locality and she kept feeding it to my child, but nothing helped.' She paused, overcome by emotions and after a moment continued, 'He passed away in the wee hours of the morning. I had still not completely recovered from the pain of surgery when he died in my arms.'

I felt a lump in my throat and tried to swallow it, but I couldn't.

'After the cremation, your Grandpa sat me behind him on his scooter and we rode far away from town, far, far away till it was absolutely dark, and even then, he didn't stop,' Grandma said wistfully. 'We reached Digha, almost two hundred kilometres away from Chandannagar, and lodged in a cheap hotel for two nights. We didn't speak

much, we barely ate, trying in various ways to cope with our loss. I spent long hours staring aimlessly at the sea. Your grandfather, for the first time in his life, didn't think that his work was being jeopardized by his absence. Instead, he blamed himself for being neglectful towards me and our son. Neither of us could accept the idea of going back home, stepping into the same room that our child had lived and breathed, laughed and cried in for almost two months. We knew that his cradle, his oilcloth, the little pillows, the tiny aprons, the baby food and utensils were still strewn about in that room and that the air still smelled like him. And we couldn't think of going back there without him.'

It was getting increasingly hard for me to hold my tears back.

'How do you know that the holy water that your mother-in-law had brought from the Tantric wasn't poisonous or something?' I asked. 'It could have been the reason he died. He was just a new-born.'

'No, it was the deadly diarrhoea that took him away,' she replied with conviction. 'You'll know why soon.'

'Okay.'

'On the morning of the third day,' she continued, 'When your grandpa asked me if I was ready to go back home, I told him to take me to one of my aunts' places at Dakshineswar instead. He readily agreed. We had just reached there and my aunt had convinced us to have some food when…' and here she paused again.

Something tightened in my throat instantly because she didn't look good. I held my breath for the awful piece of information that was about to follow.

'When?' I prompted her.

'Your grandfather's friends Parashuram and Vikash arrived, asking us to come back home.'

'Why?' I enquired.

'When we asked why, they informed us that... that my little sister had died the previous night and my mother too had passed away in the hospital that very morning.'

My hands reached my mouth involuntarily as I tried to process that bit of shocking information.

'My sister didn't have the concoction, did she?' said Grandma. 'But she died too. It was the diarrhoea.'

I couldn't even imagine what she had gone through. So many deaths in such a short span of time was unthinkable!

'Two years later, in 1974, your mother was born to us,' my grandmother said. 'She didn't cry for two days. She couldn't breathe normally for some reason. We thought she wouldn't make it. But Gedo was in charge of her, and he tried his best, he stayed up all night and saved her life. He was pursuing his MD in the paediatric department back then and was doing quite well. On the third day she cried. That's when we named her Sanghamitra, after Emperor Ashoka's eldest daughter who was a messenger of peace. And then one year later another daughter was born to us while I was extremely sick. She had convulsions, turned red and blue and died in the hospital just a couple of days after her delivery. I had been delirious for two whole days after giving birth to her. The doctors didn't think they would be able to save me but three or four days later when I regained consciousness and asked the nurses to let me see my child, they said she was no more.'

I couldn't speak a word. I didn't know what to say.

'And just when I thought everything was finally alright,' my grandma recounted, 'in the year 1978, my closest brother Gedo, who was in fact the only hope of our family, was found hung to death on the very same day he finished his internship.'

'What?' My voice was hoarse. 'Why?'

'At that time, Kolkata colleges and universities were torn asunder by the Naxalite movement,' said Grandma. 'No one really knows the reason why he died. It has always been a mystery. Some were of the opinion that he was jilted in love and committed suicide, some believed he was murdered by his enemies since he was the leader of one of the most prominent student unions, some say that he was killed by one of the Naxalites. I had been very close to Gedo ever since he was born. We were born just a year apart. And I knew, better than anyone else, that he would be the last one to commit suicide for something as paltry as a love affair. He was the topper in his batch and had extremely bright prospects, he wouldn't give up his life for anything. When his body was found, his room was in disarray, but he was fully dressed in his robe and everything, wearing his spectacles and polished boots. His hands were tied behind him, which is what led to the belief that it wasn't suicide. We tried very hard to find out the cause behind his death, but we didn't receive much help from the police. So, after a point my father gave up trying.'

I got up from the chair I was sitting on, went over to my grandma and gave her a long, tight hug. I have never been one to hug people or show a lot of emotion. In fact,

I always shied away from such displays. But right there, at that moment, it was involuntary. I was flooded with emotions as I held her close, breathing in the sweet scent of her hair and the memories of nineteen eventful years of my life, most of which I spent with her.

My grandmother was the one who brought me up, who woke me every morning, bathed me, fed me, brushed my hair, put me to sleep and attended to all my needs. In fact, 'Dida-dima' was the first word I ever learnt to say. It comprised four syllables and sounded awkward but that's what I called her and I wouldn't have it any other way.

I was just three years old and attached inseparably to her when one evening she staggered out of the washroom and blacked out on the bed. She was rushed to the hospital immediately where the doctors looked at her and said words that sounded alien to me. I was too young to understand what 'Multi Organ Failure' meant, but somehow it felt like I was never going to see her again and that made me pee in my pants out of fear. My grandfather, as I still remember, had collapsed on the cold, white tiles of the hospital, crying his heart out. My mother, who was the only one standing, had also looked like she was about to collapse.

The next few months that I spent almost all alone at home with a caretaker were the darkest months of my life. I heard my grandfather talking to himself in his room like a lunatic almost every day and my mother spent days at the hospital devoid of any hope. My grandmother had eventually gone into a coma and doctors said there wasn't any hope left for her. Yet, I prayed for her every day. In fact, that's all I did. I prayed, I cried, I ate, I threw up and woke up howling in the middle of the night. She was the one I slept with, ever since I was a month old, and now she was not with me. I had terrible nightmares without her by my side, without her soft hands brushing through my baby hair, without her sweet voice that told me bedtime stories, without her gentle pats on my back that lulled me to sleep.

This time she had drifted off to sleep before me, and she had drifted far, far away to some unknown territory, lost perhaps, never to return. And our house, it seemed, had been submerged in absolute darkness.

But perhaps God had heard my prayers, and decided to grant my innocent wish, for my grandmother opened her eyes one day after several weeks. The doctors called it a miracle. I remember pinching myself to be sure I wasn't dreaming. That day it felt as though the light in our house returned although she didn't come home for several months. For almost a year, my grandmother wasn't the same and I often wondered if she ever would be.

'I can't believe how terrible your past has been!' I told her that morning.

'It's always been dark,' she replied. 'For both me and your grandfather. When you look at it from a distance, it seems all bright and sunny. But the closer you get the darker it becomes. We've gone through the worst possible experiences together. But whatever your grandfather is today is solely because he never gave up. He braved all the odds.'

'It's ironic,' I reflected. 'The man who illuminated the world with his lights has himself walked through the darkest alleys. Perhaps one needs to walk through darkness to be able to fully appreciate light.'

'Well, if you see it that way,' said my grandmother, 'he is the light himself.'

'How so?'

'If you think of his panels and figures, behind the light source it's always dark,' she explained. 'But placed before the light source, even the most commonplace object looks embellished and dazzling. If you think of your grandfather's life, especially his childhood and where he came from, it was all darkness. Nevertheless, he lit the road ahead of him, created new opportunities for future generations, a new art form, a unique culture...'

'Now everything shines brilliantly in the radiance he created.'

'That sums up his whole life and career.'

I nodded, in awe.

'Lights can shine only in the darkness, my dear,' said my grandmother.

'That's beautiful!' I told her.

'Well, don't forget to write good things about me!' my grandma's eyes twinkled.

'Of course not,' I replied. 'But there's something else that I want to know.'

'What is it?'

'From what I've heard from Mother, Grandfather and even you... it seems to me that he never had time for you. Didn't that affect your relationship in any way?'

My grandmother only smiled but it was quite a tell-tale smile.

'It seems like you've got a lot to say about this,' I commented. 'It's okay, we can do this later.'

She heaved an exaggerated sigh of relief.

7

My Grandmother's Recollections

Five years I had spent with this man, lived under the same roof, slept on the same bed. Five years. And he was still a stranger to me. I watched him every day as he woke up in the morning, took a hurried bath and left for work, never looking at me twice. My eyes followed him as he walked with long strides across the room. For five years I had applied bright red vermillion to the parting of my hair with pride and uttered silent prayers for his safety, security and wellbeing. I had woken up before sunrise, secretly wiping the dust off his feet. A woman I knew had once said, a woman's heart must worship in order to love. I think my mother had taken this advice a little too seriously, and for as long as she had been alive, she never failed to wipe the dust off my father's feet every morning even when she knew that he was leaving her alone to visit our stepmother. And I think I had taken after my mother even though I never wanted to, even though I had fiercely resisted the thought of ever becoming like her. I had seen her suffering endlessly right before my eyes and I had vowed that I would never let my life become like hers.

I would be my own woman. My stepmother was a modern woman. She had a job, a life of her own. She was willing to sacrifice everything for her job, make as many compromises as she could to keep her job at the ceramic glass factory intact. She was fiercely independent and headstrong. Perhaps that was why she was so irresistible to my father. People who love themselves are loved by everyone. And even though she was the reason behind my mother's heartache, I couldn't help but admire how empowered she was. Deep in my heart, I wanted to be like her. However, that was far from how I had turned out to be, and this is something I realized only after I was married. I wondered at times if I even deserved to call myself a modern woman.

My little girl, Mini, slept soundly next to me on my bed. It had been a week since I returned from the hospital after the birth and subsequent death of my third child. I lay awake, tears trickling from my eyes and wetting one side of my pillow. It was 5 a.m. and I was bleeding. My blouse was drenched with the milk from my swollen breasts. They throbbed with pain. Soon my husband would rise, follow the regular drill and be gone for another twenty hours. I wouldn't know what he did all day. I wouldn't know when he'd return. I would be half asleep by that time. So, I got up painstakingly, the flesh on my stomach tingling, the stitches threatening to tear open, and, like every morning, with the early birds chirping outside our window and the first rays of the dawn ushering in a new day, I took the dust off his feet and rubbed it on my head, my brow and my bosom, hoping he wouldn't wake up. I didn't need to do it at all, but I did it nevertheless.

'What… what is wrong?' he stirred.

'Nothing!' I answered, biting my lip, both from pain as well as embarrassment. 'Nothing is wrong. Your blanket was falling off.'

'Why did you get up?' he asked. 'I could have picked it up myself.'

'I… I didn't want you to catch a cold.'

'Please go back to sleep,' he said, sitting up on the bed. 'Do you need anything?'

'No,' I withheld the truth. 'I don't need anything.'

I was desperately in need of him. Every pore of my body and ounce of my soul tingled with the aching need to be desired once again by the man who I called my husband. For five years I had looked at his face longingly while he slept beside me. I had thirsted for his love and affection the way a desert thirsts for the rain. I had seen him devote every fibre of his being to the panels in his workshop, hoping against hope that one day he would look at me the way he looked at those lights. Oh, how I envied them! How I wanted to be those lights! If only he would bestow on me half the attention he bestowed on them, I would consider myself a blessed woman. Was I becoming like my mother? Would I share the same fate?

For five years, I had loved him and hated him. Many a time I had wanted to run away from his house and never look back. I never could. Often, I had regretted my marriage and also punished myself for feeling that way by fasting for days. I was grateful, and felt indebted. But I also felt neglected, forsaken and hurt. Was it love or indebtedness that I felt for him? I couldn't be sure. He hadn't done me any wrong. He took care of all my physical needs. Not only mine but also those of my brothers and sisters. But was it enough? How could I ignore the constant feeling of being unwanted, unimportant and unloved? He looked after me the way he looked after the plants in his garden. He sprinkled water on them every day, he nourished the soil with manure, and sprayed insecticides whenever necessary. He did everything that was necessary but nothing beyond that. But I wasn't a plant. I was his wife. Oh, how at times I wished I were a plant and not his wife! I wished I had no desires or volitions of my own. My life would have been so much easier that way. All these emotions and expectations would be the death of me someday.

I was, unfortunately, a living, breathing human being, with a cursed womb like they said, a cursed family, a dead mother, a dead sister, two dead children and an indifferent husband. How long could I expect to survive like this? What would I live for? And even if I did manage to survive, would it be a life worth living? A life without love was as good as a living death to me. Was it the sins of my father that made me suffer so much? Or was I looking for someone else to shift the blame on now that my husband had left my bed and was out of my sight? When did I become so nagging and complaining? When did I start indulging in such unfathomable self-pity? I was never this woman back in Kolkata. Would my friends from Lady Brabourne recognize me if they saw me now?

At times I trembled with an overwhelming desire to say really spiteful things to him. My fingers itched with fury while I prepared his meals and I wanted to make them as inedible as I possibly could. Once I added so much salt in his curry that I was sure he wouldn't be able to eat more than a spoonful. That was my way of taking revenge on him. But quite surprisingly, he ate it all as if there was nothing wrong with it. His mind was somewhere else, evidently. And it was me who ended up eating nothing that night. I couldn't deny him my body because that was the only time I felt needed. But soon afterwards, I felt absolutely barren as I gazed up at the ceiling in the discreet silence of the night knowing that he would soon return to the arms of Art, who I could never compete with, neither in beauty nor in grace. Art had him wrapped around her finger, trapped under her luminous wings. He was merely her bewitched slave. No amount of love or enticement on my part could break the spell that she had cast over him.

'Is something wrong with you?' he asked me before leaving for his factory.

'No,' I answered briefly.

'Why have you been crying?' he enquired. 'What happened? Are you in pain?'

'You will never understand,' I told him from my bed.

'I won't understand?'

'No,' I replied.

'Are you upset about the child?' he asked.

I didn't know what to say. Yes, I was upset about the child. But I was upset about so many other things as well, the primary reason being he, himself. I couldn't take it anymore. I burst into a deluge of tears, whimpering till the stitches across my abdomen hurt. He came over to me, slightly anxious, and sat on the bed right next to me, running his fingers through my hair. 'Please don't be so sad,' he implored me. But I was unable to acknowledge the affection in that gesture, just like the stomach loses its ability to digest food after a long spell of starvation. My heart felt ice cold, my body was broken and my soul exhausted. I felt nothing but pain.

'Tell me, what's wrong?' he insisted.

'Do you still love me?' I asked him after what felt like an eternity.

'What sort of a question is that? Of course, I do.'

'Then why don't you care for me?' my voice sounded unnatural to my own ears.

He looked at me, a little taken aback.

'Why did you marry me?' I sobbed. 'To leave me to rot alone in this house all day?'

'How can you say you're alone?' he asked. 'You have so many people around you all the time. You have my big family, Gopal and Annie. Who else do you need?'

'I… I need you. I married you. Not your family. I am your wife. I need you.'

'But I'm always around,' he said in a matter-of-fact way. 'My factory is nearby, you can reach me any time you like.'

Talking to him was a fruitless endeavour. It was like talking to a wall. At times I wondered if he genuinely failed to understand me or misunderstood me on purpose. All I knew is that I had no place in his scheme of things. I had no role to play in his life. I was a mere accessory, an ornament.

I was supposed to stay sequestered within the four walls of his house. I was supposed to smile and be respectful to people who treated me like dirt. I was supposed to cook and clean and conceive and deliver on and on for the rest of my life without any acknowledgement, appreciation or reward whatsoever. All because I was a woman and women were 'supposed' to do so. People were so much more liberal back in Kolkata. Where had I ended up? Why did my father ever bring us here? This was not the kind of life I had dreamt of living. But then again, I had a woman's heart, and no matter what we women were put through, we took pride in our ability to bear it all with a smile, to sacrifice all our happiness at the altar of love so that our husbands, fathers, brothers and sons could go out there and do what made them happy. What a doomed existence!

I spent the entire day in bed, crying, while my mother-in-law took care of my one-year-old Mini because she knew how sick I was. She sat by my bed, trying to console me with stories from her childhood, how she was married off at the age of eight in adherence to the ancient Indian custom known as '*Gouri-daan*', how she had lost several children to various illnesses too. She often referred to me as '*bamuner meye*' meaning 'Brahmin's girl' even amidst our conversations. And though she could be really sarcastic at times, she took more care of me than of any of her other daughters-in-law. She made me tea herself that day. And when I told her not to take so much trouble for me, she only asked me to be quiet.

'Don't say a word,' she told me firmly. 'If I can take care of my sons, why can't I take care of my daughters?'

'But Maa, you're not so well yourself…'

'Shush! I'm perfectly alright!' she retorted. 'These are the normal aches and pains of old age. We are made of steel, my dear. You are a *bamuner meye*, soft and delicate, you are different. You all get sick easily, you suffer so much for the smallest ailments. I really feel bad for you. But we are used to all this. Our mothers have prepared us for this life since we were born.'

'Thank you, Maa… for… for being so kind to me.'

'Keep all your "thank yous" to yourself,' she said as she placed a little glass of tea on the table next to my pillow. 'We don't understand all those English words. My beautiful little moon child is in pain, this is the least a Maa can do.'

Then she took Mini on her lap, and looked at her fondly for a few minutes. She told me 'Your child isn't going to be like you at all. She is going to be a warrior, mark my words. She's got our blood in her veins and your husband's colour in her skin. She won't have the easiest life either. But she is going to be a fierce woman.'

'I too wish for the same,' I replied. 'I want her to be strong.'

'She will be stronger than all your tribe combined,' she laughed while changing Mini's clothes. 'My little warrior child. You will be like your father, won't you, baby girl?'

Mini cooed unintelligibly in response.

Quite contrary to my expectations, my husband returned home a little early that night. He had brought for me a bunch of roses and a box of my favourite sweets from Surya Modak, one of the oldest and most reputed confectioneries in the town.

'I'm sorry if I've made you feel like I don't care for you enough,' he told me, sitting next to me on the bed holding my hand. 'It's not that you are not important to me. In fact, you are the most important person to me in this world.'

I turned my face away and cried.

'Look here, look at me,' he turned my face towards his and then, looking deeply into my eyes, said, 'All I'm doing right now is for our wellbeing. How long do you want to live like this? In a single room with a single toilet shared by the entire household. I want to give you and Mini a better life.'

He caressed my cheeks.

'I want to buy some land, build a house for us,' he continued. 'A big one, just like you always wanted, bigger than your Kolkata house. It will be two-storeyed with a garden, a separate room just for you, an office, a living space and I'll decorate it with nice wooden furniture. Gopal can also live there comfortably with us. It's too cramped here for so many of us, don't you think?'

I gently nodded.

'Now, don't cry, my dear!' he planted an affectionate kiss on my forehead. 'Please bear with me. I want to fulfil your dreams as well as mine. And if I don't work now, I won't be able to buy the land or build the house. You know how the price of land keeps increasing every year, don't you? So, I must work hard now. Because the more I earn, the sooner I can build the house for us.'

Tears rolled down my eyes.

'I didn't marry you to leave you alone,' he said. 'I want to spend time with you too. And that's precisely why I am working so hard now, so that one day I can be with you without any anxiety or guilt. I've built all that I have today from nothing. I was never at peace borrowing money from acquaintances or staying at Vikash's place indefinitely, but I was helpless back then. Now I have several debts to pay and only after I've paid them off will I be relieved. And then I can start saving for the property. You understand me, right?'

I nodded, cursing myself internally for being so insensitive to his struggles.

'Now, have this,' he said, as he opened the box of sweets. 'I have brought your favourite *jolbhora talshansh sandesh* from Surya Modak. You like the rose syrup inside these sweets, don't you? This box is entirely for you. You don't have to share it with anyone, not even me.'

But I wouldn't touch the sweets unless he had taken the first bite.

8

My Grandfather's Recollections

Looking back, the only regret I have is not being able to take care of my wife and children when they needed me most. I had done to them exactly what I had blamed my family for doing to me. I had inadvertently abandoned them when they needed me. I married Sumitra against the will of both our families, promised to give her a good life, but I couldn't fulfil my promise and I shall never be able to forgive myself for that. Perhaps her physical needs were all met but I was never able to reciprocate her emotions. My work was always my number one priority, and I couldn't be the loving husband she wanted me to be, nor an affectionate father. I always had a hard time expressing my emotions, and could not express what I felt for my family.

The death of my first child, the feel of his cold skin against my warm flesh and the smell of the deadly diarrhoea that took away his life are still fresh in my memory. I cremated my child with my own hands and I have never been able to get over that and never will. It was raining heavily that day as I carried my child in my cold, numb arms, heavy in the stillness of death, wrapped in a dull white cloth. With the winds howling and the rain battering against both our bodies, making my tears indistinguishable, I walked. I couldn't help looking down at him from time to time and holding him closer to my body for warmth, concerned out of habit that my child would catch a deadly cold if I wasn't careful. And then I remembered the grotesque truth, that it didn't matter anymore. He was long gone and the cold would never bother him again.

When it was finally time for me to let him go, I remember laying him down gently on the bier with a heart as heavy as stone. He looked peaceful, my little one, free from all his pain and woe, but his eyelids were pale and he looked a little blue. And the wet white cloth that covered him refused to burn. It was as though my little son was right there, resisting death with all his might, begging for another chance to live, while I, his father, stood by him with a burning torch in my hand, indifferent to all his pleas, preparing to turn him to dust in keeping with the rituals. Forty-eight long years have passed and this memory still haunts me.

After the death of our third child, Sumitra was absolutely shattered. The beautiful woman whose eyes once sparkled like the brightest lights had now become anxious, panic-stricken, pessimistic, always on the lookout for danger, disease and misery. We didn't have any mobile phones back in those days and I often used to be out of station working in various states all across the country. We wouldn't be in touch for days and my wife wouldn't eat or sleep a wink at night until I returned home. She would try her best to keep things in order at home. She fasted on several days of the week for my health and safety and prayed incessantly to God. But things changed for the better soon.

Throughout the 1970s, I worked for several puja committees in Kolkata and undertook more projects outside West Bengal. At the beginning of 1980, I invested my earnings in a large plot of land in Kalupukur. My wife never liked the idea because what I had purchased was actually a huge patch of dense bamboo forest where jackals were often said to prowl at night. However, I stood firmly by my decision because I always had an inkling that the piece of land would sell like gold someday because of its convenient location. It was situated on a main road, close to the station and also had a pond attached to it which was full of fish. The population was comparatively sparse in that area. Of course, I couldn't purchase the entire plot at one go and had to borrow money from my friends but I paid them back the full amount as and when I earned it, along with interest.

In 1982, I decided to build a house on that plot of land for myself, Sumitra and our only daughter, so that we could live there separately and in peace. But since most of my earnings went into the funding of my new projects, I had very little cash in those years. I could hardly pay for the construction of my own house. I had to dispense with the construction workers on several occasions and lay the bricks of the house myself. From a distance, people thought I was making a lot of money, but only the ones close to me knew the truth about my struggles. Later on, I constructed a new factory along the pond. It had a roof made of asbestos, but it was large, spacious and comparatively cooler than its surroundings.

My factory was like my place of worship. It was my source of livelihood, it was where I gave wings to my creative ideas and hence an extremely sacred and sanctified part of my property. I eventually adorned it with ornamental plants like one adorns a shrine, planting luxuriant passion vines on either side of the iron gateway. They climbed all along the rails of the gate bearing clusters of passion flowers which looked like exotic spiders. They were of a rich purple hue and emitted a sweet fragrance, so soothing to the senses! There was also an empty patch of land on the other side of the pond which I cleared so that I could display my panels for trial before installing them along the streets. And behind my house and close to the factory I constructed a few rooms and toilets so that my helpers could stay there at night if they wanted to.

Something interesting happened in the 1980s. I was made the Cultural Secretary of the Boys' Sporting Club in Chandannagar. I didn't know back then that I would hold that designation for seventeen long years. It was a renowned club which was extremely active in that decade, organizing excellent concerts without fail every single year with famous Bollywood celebrities, playback singers and dramatists as guest performers. And it goes without saying that most of the responsibility for the stage lights, the setting and sounds, the decoration of the club buildings and the massive boundary wall would fall to my lot. I had the once in a lifetime opportunity of meeting and being introduced to celebrities who I never expected I would meet beyond the black and white TV screen or the static of the radio.

It was here that I had the opportunity to see Kishore Kumar in all his glory, dancing on the stage with marigold garlands around his neck, keeping the audience on their toes with his vibrant attitude and hilarious antics. It was here, in the wee hours of the morning, just when the weary audience, tired of being out all night, were just about to retire to their dwellings, when Hemanta Mukherjee's heavenly melody, '*Jeona Darao Bondhu*', meaning 'Hold on, my friend,' found them sleepwalking back to the concert grounds as if under the influence of some spell. I also had the opportunity to see Hema Malini, the dream girl of Bollywood, and Helen, the first actress to introduce cabaret and belly dance in Indian films, sway their bodies gracefully as though to a snake charmer's flute. I witnessed the eminent Utpal Dutta set the stage on fire with his unparalleled theatrical abilities. Sumitra never failed to attend these concerts. And I never failed to realize time and again, while she stood there in the glowing lights, with her long hair open, falling down her back and her wide, mesmerized eyes twinkling like the stars in the sky, how my beloved's beauty surpassed that of those belonging to the glamour world.

In 1985, I got my first big break in the international sphere when Tapas Sen, one of India's most noted stage lighting designers, visited me with his son and a few other acquaintances. He offered me a very ambitious project and asked me if I was willing to have my lights displayed at the

Festival of India in Russia, for three months at Moscow, St Petersburg and Tashkent. According to Sen's directions and with the help of my boys, I prepared ten panels, each 10 feet long and 20 feet wide, with iconic Indian symbols like the peacock, the elephant, a conch, *alpana* designs and the like. The Russians were all so impressed with those lights that they wanted to know which computer software I had used to make the lights move. When they were shown my simple wooden rollers on which the enormous panels operated, they asked to keep one in their museum. My roller remains there till today.

The latter half of the 1980s I spent in Chandannagar, working for the various committee jubilees. The most notable of these was the Barabazar Jubilee in 1989. I illuminated the beautiful street of Barabazar with twenty figures of elephants, which sprayed rose water through their trunks. And so delighted were all the kids that they flocked to that area, running around the elephants, laughing and singing '*Chal Chal Chal Mere Haathi*' joyously till the wee hours of the morning! Parents carried their tiny tots on their shoulders just so that they could enjoy the fragrant spray of rose water on their faces. The atmosphere seemed enchanted by some strange, antiquarian magic with the people walking through the street as if in a stupor, the elephants glowing like gigantic constellations in the dark of the night, the mystic sound of the *dhaak* coupled with the sublime aromas of frankincense and myrrh and the hypnotizing melodies of Tagore that played through the speakers, inviting revellers from far and wide to come and be a part of our town's magnificence.

For the Bidyalanka Jubilee, I portrayed, on my 6.2 miniature panels, the various prerequisites and stages of Jagadhatri Puja in Chandannagar. I had made ten elaborate panels that year, two on each truck, and they were a grand success. Starting with the collection of *chanda*, then the making of the enormous idols of Maa Jagadhatri in all her glory and splendour, followed by the construction of the enormous puja pandals, the four-day worship of the flamboyant idols gorgeously bedecked with gold and silver ornaments and intricately embroidered and heavily sequined Banarasi sarees, to the marvellous skill of the *dhaakis* and the tantalizing *dhunachi* dance. Next came the panels on the grand puja procession where the idols, after being loaded on separate trucks, are taken around the town in an incandescent cavalcade with a fabulous procession of lights escorting them. Finally, the idols are immersed in the Ganga, the lights are taken down, the visitors say their teary goodbyes and leave for their homes by the earliest trains the next morning. I didn't forget to pay tribute to the people who cleaned the streets, picking up paper and making the town safe and habitable again. I made a separate panel of lights solely on their activities as a token of the town's love and gratitude for them.

The 1990s saw me working on bigger projects in Kolkata, not just Durga Puja or Kali Puja illuminations but decorating the Eden Gardens with my lights when Nelson Mandela paid a visit in 1990. Since there was a shortage of labour that year, my wife, her brother, my young nephew Haru and several other young boys from the neighbourhood joined me in wrapping the hundreds of 6.2 miniatures with colourful cellophane papers while I attached them onto the panels. I had the opportunity to illuminate the Eden Gardens once again at the Cricket Association of Bengal Jubilee. Fifty huge torches made of lights were used for this occasion. I also had the responsibility for illuminating the Vidyasagar Setu at its inauguration. Each letter of the word 'Vidyasagar Setu' that I had to create was 16 feet in height and made of high voltage lights. It was attached right at the top of the main span of the bridge, over 115 feet above the ground. Former Prime Minister of India Narasimha Rao was invited to inaugurate the occasion. When he shook his hands with me, I was on cloud nine! The inauguration of the imposing statue of Indira Gandhi in Kolkata was yet another important project I worked on. Former Chief Minister of Bengal, Buddhadeb Bhattacharya, unveiled the statue by pressing a button on a remote that made the curtain of flowers gradually descend, revealing the statue. I was in charge of making the remote as well as decorating the venue with my lights.

Soon, three-dimensional mechanical models made of Masonite boards and focus lights came into being and in 1996, I was hired to work for another committee using the new technology. The procession that year had been restricted to four lorries per committee and I managed to fit twelve mechanical sets of figures in them by constructing three stages in each lorry. And on those stages, I displayed the three-dimensional figures of the celebrated magician, P.C Sarkar, cutting up humans in boxes, making people disappear behind curtains, transforming humans into dancing skeletons, and making a plant grow out of a pot of soil the moment the light from his hand fell on it. Each and every model, no matter how big or small, was three-dimensional since I wanted to be as realistic as possible in my portrayal of the magic show. The Barasat Jagadhatri Puja Committee received twenty-three prizes that year and the people of my town said that they had never witnessed a magic light show before. A couple of years later, I portrayed a circus show in a similar manner and earned unparalleled recognition.

In the year 1998, when Amartya Sen won the Nobel Prize for Economics, he was invited to the Netaji Indoor Stadium in Kolkata and awarded a laminated panel of lights specially designed by me, a panel portraying the two great Nobel laureates, Tagore and Sen, two flowers on the same stalk. It was the proudest moment of my life and no words can ever express how I felt on that day.

Over the years my dear friend Amiya Das, the Mayor of Chandannagar, kept me engaged in several projects of public utility, the decoration of the Rabindra Bhavan, the Strand Road, even the Water Plant. He remained the Mayor for twenty-one years and was a constant source of encouragement and support for me. I was even entrusted with the introduction of the first traffic lights in Chandannagar at important junctions.

A few years later, I worked for an ad company in Malaysia. I had constructed for them a three-dimensional mechanical dragon that released actual fire from its mouth, a mechanical tube well that ejaculated water and a mechanical train, all made of 6.2 miniatures planted over perforated Masonite boards. They wanted to offer me lifelong employment and were even ready to pay me three times more than what I received from my projects in India. However, the very prospect of leaving my country, especially my dear town, seemed impossible for me and I politely declined their offer.

And then came the millennium and with it, a new era in my life began. An era which had its fair share of ups and downs. On one hand, I was busy with illuminating projects in London, Ireland, Los Angeles and Malaysia and my name and fame was splashed across foreign newspapers. On the other hand, the familiar faces of my own town, especially my contemporary light artists, had reduced me to a laughing-stock, their criticisms and mockery dripping through the pages of local and regional newspapers. It felt as if they had geared up to pull me down from the heights I had scaled.

I had simply tried to usher in much-needed change. They responded with bitter rebellion.

Interlude

'And just a year later, the rebellion fell through when the very people who had conspired against your grandfather and criticized him most bitterly found themselves following his lead,' my mother told me.

I laughed out loud, finding this knowledge wickedly satisfying.

'Read any article on Chandannagar lights now, you'll see several light artists talking about the introduction of LED lights as a positive and welcome change. None of them ever touches the subject of how your grandfather was ridiculed and humiliated by them when he first tried to popularize the idea. And today, wherever you look, you'll find LEDs,' added Mother. 'Nobody here works with 6.2 miniatures or 25-watt lamps anymore.'

'I can't understand why Grandpa never told me any of this,' I wondered.

'He's always been that way,' replied Mother. 'I find it strange sometimes how immune he is to any kind of enmity, negativity, controversy, or ridicule. He never acknowledges them. It's almost as if he can't even see what's happening!'

'Do you think he remembers these things?'

'Of course, he does,' said my mother. 'Who wouldn't? But at the same time, he's always been strangely indifferent to these things. It's like nothing negative could ever touch him.'

'I remember you telling me that he had many enemies who tried to sabotage his major projects,' I reminded her. 'But he hasn't told me about any of them.'

'I'll tell you,' she replied. 'Oh, there are so many incidents! I knew he would never open up about them because he always wants to talk about the good things. I often wondered how my father was able to put up with them and continue with his work. Anybody else in his place would have given up.'

'Tell me everything!'

'Once,' began my mother, 'just a day before the grand procession, your grandfather went to give his panels a final trial and discovered that some traitor had poured bleaching powder over several of them, damaging most of his lights. He had just one day to fix them. The panels were huge, there wasn't sufficient time and he was so stressed that he blacked out and had to be rushed to the hospital.'

'What? Who was the traitor? Did he find out?'

'Yes, he did. It was one of his own helpers, who was bribed by one of his rivals to destroy the panels before the procession so that he wouldn't win any prizes that year. And just a year later maybe, on one of his most important processions, one for which he had worked extremely hard, another fellow light artist bribed one of his other helpers to shut down an entire panel of lights just before it was about to pass by the panel of judges.'

'I feel so sorry for Grandpa. What did he do when he came to know about this?'

'There was nothing he could do,' said Mother. 'They disappeared after doing the damage. He had to face all the humiliation and the mockery. And it didn't just affect him, it affected all of us.'

'I understand.'

'Once in the late nineties or perhaps in the early two-thousands, he created an enormous rolling ball of lights that was an introduction piece followed by several procession panels. The ball was so mesmerizing that when it came rolling through the street in the dark of the night, it looked like a hot, blazing ball of fire! He had probably used white and golden miniatures to make it. And it was a three-dimensional figure, a real rolling ball like the sun. People stood up from their chairs and roared in amazement as it passed! His procession that year was hands down the best one... but the judges disqualified it.'

'Disqualified it? On what grounds?'

'They considered the ball as an "extra" item,' replied Mother.

'No!' I cried in frustration, putting myself in Grandpa's shoes. 'How could that ball be an extra item when almost all the processions nowadays begin with separate introduction pieces? Either a peacock displaying its feathers or a dancing doll or a clown or a dragon! All of them have introduction pieces! How could they have disqualified him?'

'It definitely was unfair.'

'How did you feel when it all happened?' I asked her.

'Terrible,' she replied without even having to think. 'I felt terrible. I don't know about your Grandpa but I personally have still not been able to forgive those people. The committee

for whom he made the ball didn't even pay him because they had been disqualified from the competition. The older people in the committee supported him but the hot-headed younger men believed that your grandfather had broken the rules and so it was his fault. But it was so well received by the public that from the next year, several other light artists started making introduction pieces for their processions.'

'And were they disqualified too?'

'No.' replied my mother. 'That is what was actually unfair. If there are rules, the rules should apply to all, isn't it? Not just one person. The next year all the renowned puja committees had introduction pieces. How many processions would they disqualify? Hence, from the following year, introduction pieces were considered to be a part of the procession. It became a trend. And the puja committees who made them had an edge over the other committees who didn't.'

'I don't know what to say, really. They ridiculed him for introducing the trend and then just went along with it?'

'That's how it was,' she shrugged.

'How strange!'

'Besides, several aspiring light artists came to your grandfather every year to learn the trade and he would be extremely happy to teach them,' continued Mother. 'He taught them everything right from scratch, how the panels were made, how the designs were drawn, how the connections worked. He even used to demonstrate in their presence how the rollers operated. Having learnt everything from him, they started their own business which was exactly what your grandfather wanted them to do. But only a few

acknowledged him. Some of them spoke ill of him behind his back, spread rumours about him deliberately so that they could bring him disrepute. But to your Grandpa it never mattered because he had reached a certain level of recognition by then. He was already famous. And whenever he was asked how he felt about the criticisms, he would say that it didn't matter as long as they were doing their work well and earning their livelihood. He believed they were keeping the business alive and was happy because he didn't want this industry to begin and end with him. He wanted successors who would carry forward the baton and generate more employment. So, he didn't really pay any heed to what they were saying.'

'How could he be so unaffected by all of this?' I asked my mother.

'I don't think he was unaffected,' replied mother. 'He just didn't want to show it. Besides, he didn't want to fritter away his time and energy thinking about what other people said. He knew he had greater heights to scale and was extremely focussed on his work.'

'Anyway,' I moved on to the next question. 'Which of Grandpa's works were your favourite?'

'All of them! But there were few that really amazed me. One of them was a mechanical rocket. I was angry when I came back home from school one day and my mother offered me two slices of bread and a bowl of puffed rice for lunch. But when I entered the kitchen, I saw the half-cooked meal sitting on the stove. Apparently, my father had carried away both the cylinders to use the gas as a propellant for his rocket.'

'He made a flying rocket?'

'It didn't just fly,' replied Mother proudly. 'It released fire when it was launched into the sky, it encircled a moon made of lights, which was recorded by a mechanical satellite. Then there was this mechanical TV set fixed at a distance from the rocket with a moving antenna on top that caught signals from the satellite and broadcasted the whole rocket show on the screen of the TV. And a couple sat on a couch in front of the TV watching it.'

'Wow! And all of these were made of lights? This whole elaborate set?' I couldn't keep the astonishment off my face.

'Everything,' replied my mother. 'It was all made of lights and the figures were all three dimensional, not flat. The rocket looked almost real!'

'That is amazing!' I replied, spellbound. 'What else did our old man make?'

'A mechanical, three-dimensional submarine,' said Mother, 'which operated exactly like a real submarine.'

'It travelled underwater?'

'Oh yes, it did!' said Mother. 'It dived into the pond, travelled underwater and then resurfaced again at a different part of the pond.'

'And it was also made of lights?'

'Everything I'm talking about was made of lights,' replied Mother. 'Your grandfather was a light artist, for heaven's sake!'

'And I missed all of that,' I sighed. 'I have never seen these figures which is why it all sounds so incredible to me. Was he the first one to make these mechanical figures?'

'There were a number of people who made mechanical

figures in Chandannagar back then, but your grandfather took it one step ahead by decorating those figures with lights. And then later he even introduced sounds. Like a roaring mechanical tiger, a whistling train, figures from Indian mythology and so on.'

'He made a train too?'

'Yes, he made a mechanical train with a number of compartments, brightly lit. He made the tracks of the train, the signals with red, yellow and green lights and even small figures of people inside the compartments. He was that accurate when it came to the detailing. The train operated on those tracks like a real train does. It stopped at the platforms, halted at the red signal, left again at the green one, whistled and released smoke. The figures were all enormous and the tracks went all around the Bidyalanka pond.'

I gaped at her, wide-eyed.

'A few years later, for one of the puja processions, he made three-dimensional mechanical models of Spiderman, climbing skyscrapers, jumping from one building to another, and fighting with the villains from the show. Back then Spiderman was a hit TV show which we used to watch religiously. He used the background music from that show to create the whole vibe. That one is at the top of my list of favourites.'

'I wish I had seen them!' I exclaimed. 'Where did he get his ideas from?'

'You should definitely ask him about that,' said Mother.

'I have one last question for you,' I told her. 'What was your childhood like? How did you feel when you were little, being the daughter of a local celebrity?'

'Well, my father always used to be busy,' Mother replied honestly. 'I didn't get to spend much time with him. Besides, I was extremely afraid of him. He was very strict, you know. He wasn't one to tolerate any nonsense. Absolute silence prevailed in our house whenever we heard the sound of his scooter in the garage. He wanted me to study, got me admitted to St Joseph's Convent which was the best school in Chandannagar back in the seventies.'

'It still is,' I replied, feeling a little nostalgic for my school.

'It was the most expensive, too. He wanted me to study, since he didn't do so himself. So, naturally, he scolded me a lot if I didn't study or remained absent from school. Besides, my father didn't raise me to be someone who crumbles under the slightest pressure. He raised me to be my own woman. When my friends were hanging out and going shopping together, my father was teaching me how to drive a four-wheeler. He taught me how to swim, how to do gymnastics, how to ride a bike, how to drive a car and always impressed upon me the importance of being self-sufficient and financially independent, a strong woman who is in no way dependent on a man. He constantly told me not to depend on anyone in the future, neither him, nor my husband.'

'If you ask me, I'd say he was way ahead of his time!' my mother added. 'He had two helpers, Rustom and Mustafa, who had worked for him ever since they were ten or eleven years old. Their father used to be a ragpicker and those two kids were extremely malnourished. They used to accompany their father every day, helping him with his work. One day your grandfather asked their father if he was willing to let

his sons study. But he wasn't in favour of that and since their family was badly in need of money, he asked your grandfather if they could work for him instead. Up until they were fourteen, your grandfather let them perform simple tasks like bringing tea, wrapping cellophane paper around tiny lamps, counting the miniatures, and so on. He paid them both in cash and kind, gave them food to eat, proper clothes to wear. Eventually he taught them the illumination work and they worked with him on all his projects till the day he retired.'

'I remember them well,' I told her.

'They even went to London with him, all four times. Your grandfather loved them so dearly that when he retired from the business, he gave them almost all of his equipment so that they could set up their own independent businesses and they have become big names in the industry today.'

'Yes, they are famous,' I recalled with happiness. 'They work on some of the most wonderful projects every year. Also, they still remember me and talk to me like I'm a five-year-old. I miss those days.'

'You should visit them,' my mother suggested. 'I'm sure they will have many stories to tell.'

'That sounds like a great idea, but tell me something…'

'What?'

'Is there anything you disliked about Grandpa?' I asked her.

'I thought you were done questioning me.'

'Okay, this is the last one, I promise!'

'Your grandfather never thought much about family, except when one of us was dying,' she replied with a straight

face. 'I never saw my mother wear anything nice till I got a job of my own and started earning. Your grandfather had once bought her a pair of gold bangles but then he pawned them for money when there was a shortage of funds and she never saw those bangles again. With my first salary, I bought her two beautiful silk sarees. Once during the puja, I bought her ten gorgeous sarees, two for each day till Dashami. And I saved up a part of my income every month to buy her gold jewellery because I knew how she had always secretly craved some.'

'Is that why she's always wearing jewellery now?'

'Yes,' smiled my mother. 'I've asked her to do so. She never got to wear any when she was young. But better late than never, right?'

'Yes,' I replied.

'Besides,' my mother continued. 'Your grandfather was never sociable. He always kept to himself and mixed with a limited number of people. His old friends, his clients and his helpers. He's also always been a poor judge of character. He trusts people very easily and is often blind to the faults of the people he likes.'

'Like the helpers who betrayed him?'

'Yes,' she said. 'And no matter what someone did or said behind his back, if he showed up in the guise of a well-wisher and flattered him a little, he could easily be won over. He hungered for admiration. People have often taken advantage of him that way. He was often short-tempered and has almost always prioritized his work over his family. We never went out on any family trips, he never went to my school for any of the parent-teacher meetings or the

functions in which I performed. He never spoke to me like an affectionate father. He was always a strict disciplinarian. More than loving him, I was afraid of him. Well, I already said that before, didn't I?'

'You did.'

'Yes, and that's perhaps because of the neglect he faced as a child. He had never seen what it was to be a loving husband or a loving father. He didn't have any examples that he could follow. Or perhaps he was simply not wired to function that way. '

'But he's so affectionate now.'

'Only to you,' replied my mother. 'He's been that way only to you. Yes, he has changed a lot over the years as a person but you are the only one who's enjoyed all his love and affection. He's good to us nowadays, but he goes overboard when it comes to you.'

'I wonder why,' I muttered. 'He wasn't always like this though. I remember being extremely afraid of him when I was a kid myself. It's only after he stopped working that he actually started opening up.'

'Some people change a lot over time, I guess,' she responded. 'Some for better, some for worse.'

'Yes, true. Anyway, thank you, Maa! You've helped me a lot today.'

9

My Mother's Recollections

The Moral Science class was in full swing that morning and Sister Andrea was reading out the ten commandments from the Bible when one of the senior section teachers knocked on the seventh-grade classroom door. She was an Anglo Indian and ever since I had known her, I couldn't help but stop and stare every time she passed by. Her skin was porcelain, with a smooth, buttery texture, and a rich and healthy glow. Her long and wavy hair extended to her hips and was of a shade lighter than brown but darker than orange. And her green eyes! They looked like two little emeralds. How lucky some people are to be born with features like that! I wonder how they feel every time they look in the mirror. Could they see how blessed they were? Or had their eyes got accustomed to their beauty? I wish I had been born with even an iota of that perfection. I didn't want green eyes, bronze hair or porcelain skin. A medium skin tone would be enough for me. Why hadn't I taken after my mother? She wasn't ivory skinned, she had dark eyes, dark hair, yet she was so beautiful. I felt like a misfit next to her at times. I felt like a misfit everywhere.

Sister Andrea stopped reading and answered the door.

'Come in, Miss Leticia,' she said pleasantly.

'Thank you, Sister,' Miss Leticia replied and walked into our class with a bunch of notices in her hand and an air of confidence.

'Good afternoon, Miss!' we said in chorus, standing up all together.

'Good afternoon, girls,' she responded. 'Please sit down.'

We sat down on our respective seats as noiselessly as possible.

'Is Sanghamitra Das present today?' she asked, looking around.

I could feel something sinking within me as I stood up, confused and a little bit scared.

'Yes, Miss,' I said meekly, raising my hand.

She looked at me with what I could perceive was disappointment and I gulped down the ball of anxiety that had started to form in my throat, waiting for her to speak.

'Your fees haven't been paid,' she said strictly, her voice curt and dry. 'It's been over four months, and it's the second time this year. Show this notice to your parents and tell them that if the fees aren't cleared by the fifteenth of next month, you won't be allowed to sit for the second term exams.'

Thoroughly embarrassed, I almost felt the ground beneath my feet give way when I saw several of my classmates exchanging glances and smiling surreptitiously at each other. Even the Chinese hostel students made fun of me. I didn't know why I still felt bad. I should have gotten used to this by now. What else could I expect, being what I was? I stepped away from my bench somehow and walked the walk of shame in front of all of them to collect the notice from Miss Leticia. And while I did so I could barely look at her perfect face. How could my father forget about my school fees every month? Did he not understand how humiliating it was for me to be singled out like this in front of all my classmates? It would be fine if it happened once or twice but it happened regularly. This is what I had to experience every single year.

We received our Maths class test papers after recess and I had managed to score only an eight out of twenty. Our teacher looked at me disapprovingly as she handed me my paper. I couldn't look her in the eye. Thank heavens that she didn't call out our marks loudly for the whole class to hear! So, when my bench partner asked me how much I had scored, I told her 'sixteen' and I couldn't look into her eyes either. I kept the paper deep inside my bag, buried under all my books and notebooks. My classmates couldn't be trusted. Once while I was away, they had opened my bag and ransacked it for one of my test papers to verify if I had indeed scored the marks that I had told them I did, and then when they discovered that I had scored five marks less than what I had said, they taunted me for the rest of the day, calling me horrible names. 'Blackie is a liar! Blackie is a liar!' And I cried all the way back home in the rickshaw.

I had told my mother repeatedly that I couldn't understand Mensuration, and that Exponents made no sense to me, that I needed someone to guide me. After a lot of persuasion, my father brought home a tutor, who was one of his old friends from school. He wouldn't take any fees. Now my teacher was a very good man, but the problem was that he didn't understand English at all. And all the sums in our Maths book were in English. So, he explained everything to me in Bengali and I inevitably got a zero out of three in each of the four long problem sums because even though I was good at English, I couldn't make head or tail of anything when it came to Maths problems. My mother knew English but she was not an expert when it came to Maths.

'Hey, why don't you hang out with us at lunch today?' my friend Anindita asked me when she noticed me sitting alone in class after the lunch bell. 'We're having a picnic.' She was the only person in school who was nice to me, perhaps because her mother was friends with my mother.

'It's okay,' I replied. 'I've got to do my science homework, you know. Sister Agnes will be really angry if I don't submit my notebook today.'

'Okay, then,' she chirped. 'But you'll be all alone. That's not very nice, is it?'

'I won't be alone,' I said. 'I'm sure there will be others too. The class is never empty at lunch. Besides, the homework is really important. I have to finish it by hook or by crook. I don't want to get another demerit slip.'

It wasn't the truth. I had finished my science homework ages ago. It's just that I didn't want to go out there and be humiliated once again for the two slices of bread and a banana that I had been carrying to school as my standard tiffin every single day for the last seven years. A picnic involved sharing food with one another. It was mandatory. And next to those tempting boxes of egg noodles, fried rice, chilli chicken, fish cutlets and pastries, my bread and bananas would stand out like a joke. Nobody would want to have them. So, after Anindita had left, I stuffed the slices of bread quickly into my mouth and downed them with water. The banana, I saved for Parameshwar Kaku, the rickshaw puller, for he gladly accepted whatever I offered to him and never ratted me out to my mother.

However, I didn't dislike everything about the school. Deep down in my heart, I was really attached to it. I liked the yellow and green buildings, the lush green fields, the notes of the piano, the chirps of the kindergarteners, the austere corridors, the smart white shirts and the navy-blue skirts, the enormous chapel, dark, solemn, and awe-inspiring where I knelt before the holy cross and prayed every single day and even cried when things became too much for me to endure. I always went to the chapel alone. Somehow it helped me connect better with God. I liked the daily prayers, the calls for silence, the chiming of the bells, even the rules and regulations. It wouldn't be wrong if I said I liked everything about my school, except the people. I wondered why there was never any rule that prohibited bullying, name calling and treating your classmates like dirt. We got demerit slips for not finishing our homework, forgetting to bring a book, being rude to the sisters and teachers, not cutting our nails or wearing clean uniforms. But there were no measures taken against students who were rude to other students, who made their lives a living hell in school.

If I ever had any sense of belonging for my school, it lay in the inanimate—the feel of the place, the smell of the grass, the silence, the serenity, the calm, the antiquarian buildings, the sound of the bells, the unnoticed nooks and corners where wild blue flowers bloomed. They didn't always grow out in the open, exposed to the sunlight and rain but if one looked at them closely, one couldn't help but notice how intricate the patterns on their petals were. They survived even in adverse conditions without anyone attending to or even noticing them, unlike the fancy roses and orchids which dwindled under the slightest lack of attention and care. They knew how to survive on their own under any conditions. They were wild and free and independent.

I was right about one thing though. The class was never empty at lunch. Around fifteen minutes later, my batchmates started pouring in one after another, tired of being out in the sun for too long. They sat in groups on desks with their feet on the benches and hardly shut their mouths. They liked nothing better than interesting gossip and I liked nothing better than to put my head down on the desk and take a short power nap. But today somehow I couldn't. I couldn't help overhearing some of their conversations, especially that of the group that occupied the last two benches right behind mine.

'You should have seen Taniya's trip photos from last year!' exclaimed Sara. 'They are all so pretty! She brought the whole album today.'

'Where did she go?' asked Shreya.

'They went to Darjeeling,' replied Sara. 'I wish my

parents would take me to Agra this year. I really want to see the Taj Mahal! It's one of the seven wonders of the world! But since my father suddenly got busy with office work, we had to cancel all our trip plans. We go for a trip every year without fail. Last year we went to Shimla. This is the first time we had to cancel.'

'That's so sad!' sighed Ananya. 'We go for a trip every year too. This year we are going to Kerala. We will be leaving the day after tomorrow.'

'Bon Voyage!' responded Sara sadly. 'I wish I could say the same to myself. But never mind, we went to Kolkata for a week right after the exams and lodged at a cousin's place. My mother and I went to the New Market and she bought me three pairs of jeans, five tops and two new stockings for the pujas. We also had our lunch at the famous restaurant, Aminia…'

'Oh! I went there too!' cried Shreya. 'In fact, quite a number of times. The Biryani they make is just amazing! It melts in the mouth!'

'Totally,' Sara agreed.

'Where else did you go?' asked Ananya.

'We went to the Globe Cinema!' Sara proudly said. 'To watch *The Adventures of Tarzan*!'

Such lucky people! Forget about family trips, I had never even gone to Kolkata. It was the city of my dreams, a city that seemed to call out to me every time the school closed for a vacation. I had heard so much about Kolkata that I felt I could freely navigate through its lanes and bylanes without even having to consult a map.

My mother had lived in Kolkata for almost twenty

years. She often talked about it. She talked about the grand Durga Puja and reminisced how when they were little, their grandfather took them to Wellington Park every evening to ride on the swings and have sugar candies and crushed ice. The Victoria Memorial was like the Taj Mahal to me. If only I could see it someday! She had once told me that a few days after her wedding, my father had taken her to visit the Victoria Memorial. And then when he learnt that she had already been there a number of times, he lay down in a corner of the sprawling garden and asked her to give him a foot massage. My mother complied. I didn't know how to feel about that. It was funny but at the same time a little frustrating. Would I ever be able to do that for somebody? I didn't think so.

The school closed for our puja vacation that day and I was as happy as I was sad. I was happy because I wouldn't have to come to school every single day and look at all the faces I detested. I could sleep a little more, play with the neighbourhood boys at the Gul factory and take things easy as there would be no class tests to study for every other day. But on the other hand, I would have to sit and rot at home all day while my cousins and neighbours all went for trips, dressed in new clothes and went pandal hopping in Kolkata. They would come back with marvellous stories about everything they had seen and done and eaten and drunk and I would be looking blankly at their glowing faces with nothing of my own to share.

'Mother, I'm home,' I announced as I slumped on the divan all exhausted.

'Go take a shower quickly, don't be lazy,' my mother replied from the kitchen.

'Can I take it tomorrow? I'm extremely tired today.'

'Absolutely not! We should bathe daily. You go to the Gul factory every day and return home looking all black. And then you don't even wash yourself before you go to school. You don't want to let the coal dust sit on your skin and make you look darker, do you?'

'Don't call me that!' I shouted, hurt.

'What?' my mother's voice was drowned out by the loud whistle of the pressure cooker. 'What did I call you?'

'You said I am black!'

'Did I say anything wrong?' she replied over a boiling pot. 'Then why do you come crying to me all the time when your friends tease you? I'm trying to give you good advice. Take it or leave it, it's up to you. But you must shower every day.'

She hadn't said anything wrong. I knew I was dark. People reminded me of that every single day, yet her words stung me. I wished she wasn't so straightforward about the thing that hurt me most. I felt helpless when she said things like that to me. I was extremely tired that day, and sad too. The weather was already cloudy and the very thought of having to pour cold water all over my body made me wince. Besides, I didn't know how to tell her about the Maths paper. I knew she wouldn't be too upset. She wasn't the one to throw a fit if I scored poorly. But she wouldn't be proud of me either. I wanted to make her happy. So, I took my towel and a set of fresh clothes and went quietly to the bathroom.

That evening, my friend Soma came to visit me wearing a new frock and looking like a rose. She always had my back and we played together every day with some other kids in the neighbourhood. She was a little shy and timid by nature. I was brave and aggressive as long as I wasn't in school. We made a great duo. The boys all liked her a lot because she was very pretty but they never bothered her because they were afraid of getting beaten up by me. I had beaten up boys before who had tried to make fun of my appearance. They were all a little afraid of me. Besides, my father was very popular around these areas, both for his light shows and for his fiery temper. Hence, they treated me with a lot of respect. I was the group leader. They obeyed all my orders and never bothered my best friend. That was the only good thing in my life because I felt like a warrior queen in their midst, unlike how I felt in the presence of the haughty girls who bullied me at school.

'Your dress is so pretty!' I told her that evening while I walked with long strides towards the Gul factory.

'Yes, it's a new dress,' she replied as she struggled to keep up with my pace. 'My aunt gave it to me for the puja.'

'And you've worn it already! What a greedy girl you are! What will you wear during the puja now?'

'Why? I will wear all the other dresses I got.'

'How many dresses have you got this year?' I asked her curiously.

'I got eight!' she replied happily.

'Eight new dresses!' I was amazed and a little jealous at the same time. 'You're really lucky. Not everyone has such generous relatives.'

'Actually, I got only four from my relatives,' she confessed with a grin. 'The four other dresses are the ones that my father bought me.'

'Ah, I see.'

'How many dresses did you get this year?' she asked.

'None yet,' I replied honestly. 'But Baba said he will take me to the shop today in the evening after he's done with work and get me a new dress. So, I'm looking forward to that.'

'But the puja is in two days!' said Soma. 'All the nice ones will be gone by now.'

'What can I do?' I responded sadly. 'He's always so busy. But I'm glad that he's at least going to take me out today.'

'He's really busy, huh, your Baba?' she ruminated.

'He is the busiest person I have ever seen.'

'Quite natural, no?' said Soma. 'Everyone looks up to him so much and expects him to always come up with something new. It's sad that you barely get to spend any time with him.'

'That's okay,' I told her. 'To be honest, everything is fine as long as Baba is not home. The moment he comes back, we can't talk loudly, we can't turn up the volume of the TV, we can't laugh or have fun. He always wants to see me sitting with books. Studying. So, we have to be extra careful and quiet when he's around. It's like being in school. No, worse, it's like being in prison. It's such a relief when he leaves for work!'

'Hey, don't talk like that about your father!' She slapped my arm. 'He's a good person. A little scary, that's true, but nevertheless he's a good man.'

I made a face at her. What did she know?

But later that evening as I was dressing up to go out with

him, I felt a little guilty for having bad mouthed my father before. I knew that he was a good man, that he worked very hard, that he was extremely loyal to my mother and always gave one hundred percent to whatever project he undertook. I just wished that he wasn't so intimidating all the time. But that's how he was with everyone. I was not an exception. Everyone was afraid of him. Starting with my mother, my aunts and uncles, the neighbourhood boys, even his clients and the puja committee people who he worked for. The only people he was nice to were Vikash Kaka and Parashuram Kaka and his helpers. With them he was a completely different person.

I wondered if he would be nice to me if I could live up to his standards of perfection. He was a perfectionist in his sphere of activities. But I wasn't great at anything in particular. I could do a few things moderately well. I could swim, I usually participated actively in sports, I could perform gymnastics, play the sitar, sing and dance, but I didn't take any of these too seriously so I wasn't exceptionally talented in any way. I wished I could change my appearance, too. All my cousins were immensely fair and pretty, just like my aunts, and I looked out of place in their midst in every family gathering. They would sit all around me in their beautiful dresses, with pretty little ornaments glittering on their rosy skin, smiling, laughing, talking, basking in the radiant warmth of the compliments that the other guests generously showered on them. Whereas all they ever said to me was, 'Oh my, you look exactly like your father!'

I hated myself in all the group photographs. I didn't

think I deserved to be there, like I was somehow spoiling the overall aesthetic by simply being in the frame. The only place where I wouldn't stand out was next to my father since I had taken after him in every way. But even he didn't like having me around. I did nothing to give him an opportunity to boast about me at these gatherings. I felt I was a huge disappointment to him which is why he always looked so dissatisfied with me. If I worked harder and scored better marks, maybe then he would look up, take notice of me, listen to me with interest and talk to me affectionately at times. It's not as though I didn't like my father. I loved him and I was extremely proud of his achievements. But he upset me a lot too.

'Why did you put so much powder on your face?' laughed Gopal Mama uncontrollably when I came out of my room all dressed up that evening. 'You look like someone slapped you with a bag of flour.'

'Stop it,' I told him. 'I look fine.'

'Okay, as you wish,' he whistled nonchalantly. 'I was just being honest.'

I made a face at him. He was the most popular boy in the neighbourhood because of his handsome looks and charming manners. But what most people didn't know about him was that he was a master manipulator who could turn on his easy charm effortlessly to get whatever he wanted. He was just a few years older than me, and we were almost like siblings. When he was much younger and I was in primary school, he used to buy me ribbons, hair clips and glass bangles from local fairs, give me piggyback rides to Laxmiganj Bazaar from where we would both see the majestic Rath Yatra and eat jalebis from tiny paper bags. But the older he grew, the prouder he became. Being sought after by young women, he was always conscious of the way he appeared in public and spent hours before the mirror every single day grooming himself. Some of my friends had their eyes on him too and it annoyed me. We had grown distant over time but I knew he still cared for me. Both he and my cousin, Haru Da, would put their heads together and play practical pranks on the people who teased me. They always had my back whenever I was in serious trouble. That was their way of showing that they cared for me. But at the same time, they didn't know how to behave like young adults. They were still immature. I knew that they were not inherently bad people. They had just changed a lot over the years. Perhaps that's what coming of age does to one. How I wished at times that we could have the old days back when things were all good, when I was child and I never had to worry about my looks.

'Why have you suddenly dressed up like a clown?' asked Haru Da, my cousin and Mama's partner-in-crime, coming out of the washroom. 'Going somewhere?'

'Baba said he will take me to Upahar today to buy me a dress for the puja,' I said proudly.

'I see,' he replied, hanging his towel on the railing.

'Also, you have no right to call me a clown,' I told him as he ransacked the kitchen cupboard.

'Have you looked at your face in the mirror?' he muttered. 'It's all white.'

'Have you ever looked at yours?' I retorted. 'It's all black.'

'Sorry to burst your bubble, dear cousin, but I don't think your father is coming home anytime soon,' he grinned with a mouth full of *chanachur*, completely unaffected. 'I was just at the factory with the boys and I think some generator has gone out of order. They are all busy with that now. Kaka looked really upset.'

'What?' I wanted to cry. 'Are you sure about that?'

'One hundred percent,' he nodded, munching and savouring his snack. 'But then again don't give up hope. Hope's all we've got.'

And then the two of them went out happily to enjoy the evening and live their carefree lives. How I envied them! They never invited me to go out with them. They had their own gangs and they continuously played pranks on various people in the neighbourhood and entered into brawls every day. And while everyone else would get beaten up, Gopal Mama, who was usually the mastermind, would escape unscathed because no one believed that a boy with such an angelic face could do anything wrong. Haru Da, on the other hand, would easily get into trouble because, being my father's nephew, he looked just like me. We had the same complexion, and very similar features. However, that didn't make him one bit empathetic towards me. Since he was a boy, people never really teased him about his appearance unless they were looking for someone to blame. Very early on in life I had learnt that dark-skinned people who didn't look pleasing were usually the scapegoats of society. And dark-skinned women always underwent additional humiliation.

My cousin, however, was right about one thing. My

father didn't come looking for me that evening. I waited for hours on the front porch hoping to see him turn the bend from the factory any moment and come towards the house, but he never turned up. When it was around 9 p.m. and all the shops were on the verge of closing for the day, Vikash Kaka, who was passing by our house, found me sitting on the porch with tears in my eyes and asked me what was wrong.

'Baba didn't come back from the factory,' I told him, sobbing.

'What's the problem, dear?' he asked me. 'Is anyone sick in the house?'

'No,' I replied. 'He promised that he would… he would buy me a puja dress today from Upahar.'

'So, that's the matter.'

And then he took me to Upahar himself. But just like my friend Soma had predicted, all the good dresses were already gone. All that was left was the stock of dresses that people had not found appealing enough to buy.

'Do you want to go to some other shop?' Vikash Kaka asked me.

'No, it's alright,' I told him sadly. 'They will all be closed by now.'

So, he bought me two of the best dresses from the rejected stock and took me back home.

'I'm so sorry, little one,' he told me as we walked back. 'I had no idea that your father was so busy. I didn't buy you a dress this year because I thought I should let you choose what you wanted to buy. I gave some money to your mother last week and asked her to buy you something nice.'

'But Mother didn't give me anything,' I complained to him. 'I didn't know about this at all. She never told me.'

'Really?' he looked a little surprised. 'That's quite unexpected. But perhaps she forgot about it. Bhabi has a lot to take care of too. Your father is quite a handful himself.'

Later I came to know that my mother had given that money to Gopal Mama and Haru Da so that they could buy something for themselves. That angered me a lot. Why would she give away something that was meant for me? It wasn't fair to Vikash Kaka either. She could at least have told me about it. But then she too was helpless. She knew I wouldn't be too pleased with her decision so she had kept me in the dark. Having no income of her own, she had nothing to give to anyone. Baba bought everything that was necessary for the household and never left idle cash lying round. So, this was the only option my mother had to make sure that none of us were deprived. But at what cost? At the cost of depriving her own child.

As much as I appreciated my mother for her selflessness and self-righteousness, I wanted to take a road quite different from the one she had taken. I would never be a submissive housewife and deprive my own children to make others happy because I had no income of my own, because all my ceaseless efforts at home would never be truly valued or compensated. I would work hard to earn my own money and never depend on my future husband for anything. As long as I was in school, dependent on my father, I knew there was nothing I could do. But once I got a job of my own, I would live my life on my own terms. I would travel the world, I would buy whatever I wanted to buy, I would give my children a comfortable life so that they'd never have to feel deprived or small next to their cousins or batchmates. Most importantly, I would bring them up so that they could speak their minds with me and confide in me like they would confide in a friend.

I would teach them to value what's really important in life, and that is financial independence. And I wouldn't care if anyone called me 'materialistic' because in a material world, only the materialistic can actually survive. Not everyone can afford to be philosophical and occupy the moral high ground unless they already had enough in their bank accounts to fall back on. I would build my own house and my own business. I would earn my own money, spend it the way I liked and be answerable to none. And most importantly, I would strive to reach a point where it wouldn't matter to me whether I could make anyone proud of me or not as long as I was proud of myself.

I would never bow down before any man, neither for love nor for money. Not even my own father.

I would be my own hero.

Interlude

That evening I went to my grandfather's room and asked him straightforwardly, 'Will you tell me something about your rivals?'

'What do you want to know?' was his reply.

'Mother told me that they often tried to come in your way, even bribed your workers to wreck your projects.'

'Nothing like that ever happened,' he replied dismissively.

'Never?'

'Never.'

'But Mother told me otherwise.'

'She must have been mistaken,' he was resolute. 'Nobody ever tried to... to do me any harm.'

'Mother told me about someone pouring bleaching powder over your panels, destroying the lights.'

'It wasn't his mistake,' said Grandpa promptly. It became immediately clear to me that he remembered the incident. 'The godown was infested with rats, he did that to prevent the rats from spoiling the panels.'

'By pouring bleaching powder over all the lamps and the wires?' I asked. 'Why would anyone do that?'

'Ah! He wasn't aware of the consequences! It... it wasn't intentionally done. They were all little boys.'

'Now I really don't know who to believe,' I told him. 'If you don't want to share these things with me or give me the correct information, I'll have to find some other way. I'm definitely not going to exclude all that from my narrative.'

'Why do you want to write about these things?'

'Because I want my narrative to be true to your story,' I said. 'I don't want it to read like a glossary of all your achievements, like you said. Your setbacks are important too and they equally deserve mention.'

'But there were no setbacks,' he told me obstinately. 'People have umm... always been supportive of me. Whatever setbacks I experienced were during my initial years when I was just starting out.'

'What about the time people ridiculed you when you introduced LED?'

'What? I didn't introduce LED!' he replied with a laugh. 'A younger light artist named Asim Dey did.'

I looked at him dubiously.

'You can ask anyone around,' he added. 'They'll all tell you the same thing.'

I found that hard to believe. 'But all the articles I read on the internet, they mention only you when they write about how LED panels came into existence in Chandannagar.'

'Well, that's wrong then,' he said. 'The people who wrote those articles probably misunderstood the situation. I... I wasn't the first person to use LED in Chandannagar. I only tried to popularize the idea because it was the only alternative available to us back then.'

'So, nobody ever tried to tamper with your work?' I asked him.

'No,' he declared, watching a shampoo commercial on TV with unusual attention.

I got up from the chair I was sitting on. 'I think I'm going to have to take my mother's help here.'

'Don't write about these things,' he told me.

'That's for me to decide,' I declared, a little annoyed. 'I'm not a journalist and this is not a blog post or a newspaper article. And you don't need to worry because I'm not going to use any names. I'm not trying to cause any controversy. I just want to write the truth. And I think these incidents need to be mentioned.'

'I don't think it's a... a good idea. Why beat a dead horse? So many decades have passed and... and... they have moved on with their lives. I don't want to stir things up again.'

'I told you, I won't be taking any names. What's the problem?'

'They really meant no harm.'

'Yes, I've heard that before,' I told him. 'I mean no harm to them either. Trust me.'

'Whatever you say, I don't think this is a good idea.'

'Okay,' I gave up. 'I understand your perspective. Fine. Since this is your story, your consent is important too. But from a writer's perspective as well as from a reader's perspective, I believe these are some of the most vital parts of your journey. But I respect your decision. If you don't want me to write about these things, I won't. However, do think about this a little bit. And let me know if you change your mind.'

'Okay,' he replied indifferently, tugging at his hearing aids.

I had a feeling that it was the end of the conversation.

10

The Late 1990s

He walked into my life one fine day like a bolt from the blue, begging to work for me though he knew nothing of the trade. He had just got married, his wife was expecting a baby. He told me that his mother was ailing and his family had been undergoing a severe financial crisis. Even though he didn't live in town and hadn't been in touch with us for a very long time, he was one of my own. So, without any second thought I took him under my wing and gladly taught him everything right from scratch. He dined at my place almost every day and was close to all my family members. My daughter looked up to him as a brother. And even though he wasn't one of my immediate nephews, I considered him my very own son.

'Your hands are exactly like mine,' I remember telling him one day and decided in my heart of hearts that I would entrust him with the responsibility of carrying forward my legacy after I retired.

He was polite, respectful and soft spoken. With his dark

skin and tall, lanky stature he reminded me of my own self back in the sixties. He got along well with my helpers and did his work sincerely and cheerfully. I helped him meet most of his financial obligations whenever he came to me asking for help.

Two years later, I was hired to create panels for the Jagadhatri Puja procession of one of the most prestigious puja committees in Chandannagar. We worked day in and day out and came up with something unique. On the day of the rehearsals, the members of the puja committee were so elated that they booked me in advance for the next two years and said that no one could have illuminated the panels half as well as we had. All my helpers waited with bated breath for the procession day, certain that we would bag all the awards. Surprisingly, on the day of immersion, the truck loaded with my very best panels blacked out completely just a few minutes before it was supposed to pass by the panel of judges. At first, I thought perhaps the generator had run out of fuel and rushed to the scene with several barrels of diesel. But my helpers told me a very different story.

'The generator won't work,' one of them said.

'How did this happen?' I was bewildered, not knowing how to face the members of the puja committee who had trusted me blindly.

'It was him,' they told me. 'Your nephew.'

'What?' I asked them, shocked.

'It happened right in front of our eyes!'

'What do you mean it happened right in front of your eyes?'

'He was working on the generator,' they said. 'We saw him meddling with the wires.'

'Then why did you not stop him?'

'We thought he was fixing some glitch.'

I still remember what followed. I did the best thing I could possibly do in that situation and that was to let the other trucks go ahead and hold back the one in which the damage had been done. That obviously caused some delay and held up the other trucks that followed mine. Nevertheless, I tried to be optimistic in that situation and held onto the hope that the judges would like my other panels. However, the panel that had blacked out was the one that displayed my theme, and without it the other panels would not make any sense.

My procession panels didn't win a single award that year and it was not only a disgrace to me but also extremely disappointing to the puja committee members who had entrusted me with the responsibility of their procession lights with sky-high expectations. They had, in fact, paid me in advance for the next year too.

'How did this happen?' I questioned my nephew. 'How did you mess up?'

'It was a mistake!' he said with a meek face. 'I really didn't mean to do this. I was in a hurry and… and I messed up!'

'Do you know the implications of it?' I questioned. 'Can you even understand the magnitude of damage you have caused?'

'I didn't mean to…'

'I had assigned you the generators solely because you

were good at it,' I told him sternly. 'You had handled generators for five years before you came to work for me. Moreover, you yourself asked me to give you that responsibility, promising me that nothing would go wrong.'

'I'm extremely sorry,' he cried. 'I really didn't know how it all happened. Please give me another chance, Mama!'

So, it was a mistake. It wasn't done intentionally. Or was it? It happened before the entire crew. However, it was me who had to face the humiliation when the puja committee members walked up to me demanding a refund of the advance they had paid to me, saying that they had changed their minds. A part of my payment was also withheld and I was no longer the most sought-after light artist in my town. Everything changed overnight.

'It was just a mistake,' I told myself. 'And everyone makes mistakes.'

I forgave him but I could not trust him completely after that. I could have fired him but, thinking of his family, I retained him as supporting staff. It's only later that one of my helpers came to me and said that it wasn't really a mistake, it had all been perpetrated by one of my rivals and my nephew was picked for the job because everyone knew I had a soft spot for him.

'How do you know if that's true?' I asked the helper.

'I have seen him talking to that fellow,' he replied. 'Several times!'

'And why do you think he did this?'

'For money, of course! And to sabotage your work.'

It goes without saying that I was shocked. And in my shock, I yelled at my helper. I didn't know who to believe.

My nephew was seen just talking to my rival. How did that matter? How could that possibly prove that he was bribed to sabotage me? And yet a part of me could not completely deny what I had just heard. I didn't have the time to investigate the matter. I had several projects lined up and I was too tired to think about whether it was merely a blunder or a premeditated, well-executed sabotage. And at that point of time, the thing I needed most was mental peace. I wouldn't be able to function otherwise. Hence, I put this issue on the backseat and focused on my upcoming projects. I let him work for me even after that incident and never raised that issue again.

A year later, one of my generators was tampered with once again on the day of immersion, this time by a little boy who had been sent up on one of the lorries in the dark of the night by the same adversary. The procession that year had cost me an arm and a leg. But this time too I pulled myself together and let it go. It was no use crying over spilt milk. Next time I'd be more careful. For three consecutive years, either my panels or my generators were targeted and tampered with. Once with bleaching powder, once with the generator suddenly running out of fuel. I realized that I was losing the trust of the committee members of my own town because over the next few years, none of the famous puja committees approached me with contracts.

My nephew soon left my employment to go work for my adversary. And that was in itself too difficult for me to come to terms with, let alone acknowledging it or acting upon it.

While I was being hailed all across the country as a

successful light artist, I was made to look like a joke in my own town. And the very people who had learnt the fundamentals of the trade from me were taking immense pleasure in sabotaging all my local projects and then celebrating my failures.

My Grandfather's Recollections from the 1980s

'Are you aware of what's happening in the house?' I asked my wife.

'What are you talking about?' She looked at me quizzically.

'About your sister,' I said.

'What about her?'

'Is she involved with my manager?' I asked. 'Are they interested in each other?'

'Who told you that?' Sumitra's eyes widened.

'That's what everyone is talking about,' I replied. 'Is it true? Do you know anything about this?'

'I don't think it's true,' she replied, busily folding the clothes.

'But I have seen them talking to each other very cordially.'

'So, what?' asked Sumitra coldly. 'Can two people belonging to the opposite sexes not even be cordial to each other?'

'Well, I don't know,' I replied. 'The only woman I've ever been so cordial to is the one I married.'

'You can't expect everyone to be like you,' my wife replied, tucking a thick lock of hair behind her ear, not looking at me. 'I don't think there's anything going on between the two of them. Your manager is an extremely good-humoured man and he's cordial to everyone. My sister is no exception.'

'Okay, fine,' I replied. 'But I'd like you to keep an eye on them, alright? I don't want your sister to get involved with my manager.'

'Why? Will it be bad for your reputation?'

'No, why would it be bad for my reputation? But I'm afraid the fellow doesn't really come from a very good family. She will never be able to adjust to life with those people. They are very quarrelsome.'

My wife gave me a hard, frozen look and I knew exactly what she was thinking. So, I hurriedly took my lunch and left for my factory that afternoon in an attempt to avoid being called a hypocrite by my own wife.

It was the second time that the Tata Company wanted to work with Chandannagar light artists for the decoration of the Jubilee Park at Jamshedpur, and I was their first preference since I had worked with them the previous year too and it had been a roaring success. I knew that if I got that year's contract it would be extremely beneficial for my business since I had kept several lucrative projects on hold for lack of capital and had also had to pay back several of my creditors. Almost all the other light artists and contractors in town were contending for this offer since the money was huge. As a result, all of them were eager to submit their quotations for consideration.

Since I was always busy in my factory, I had employed my manager to perform activities like going to the company headquarters, submitting my quotations and dealing with the contracts on my behalf. We had to travel a lot, visit all the big companies who wanted to employ us, depend on other people, submit the quotations, a document that contained all the details regarding the project plan, the design, the cost of various items including manpower, transportation charges and the like. It was based on these quotations that the artists were selected, negotiations were carried out and finally the contracts were signed. Hence, a considerable amount of secrecy had to be maintained where a quotation was concerned because it contained the whole idea.

However, about a week after I had submitted my quotation, I received a call from the Tata Company saying that they had found better quotations from a few other Chandannagar light artists that year and would work with one of them instead. That came as a blow to me because I was so sure of securing the Tata Company contract that I had agreed to several other contracts based on the assumption that I would be able to finance them from the remuneration I received from this project. Now I realized that I had committed the major blunder of counting my chickens before they hatched. Cancelling all those other contracts would be damaging both for my reputation as well as my business. The committees were starting to lose their trust in me and I was in turn losing the goodwill I had worked hard for years to build. I also had to postpone my payments to my creditors who came knocking at my door. And each time they left muttering curses under their breath, I couldn't help but kick myself for having banked on uncertainty. How could I have been so sure about the contract? How could I have assumed that they would hire me again just because they had hired me once? Had my growing popularity started to make me overconfident? Or was I becoming too complacent about my work? Were my rates really so high that a company as renowned as Tata would choose the less expensive alternative without even bothering to negotiate with me? My rates might be a little higher than the other contractors, but that was solely because I never compromised on the standard of my service, the quality of my lights and panels, the intricacies that went into the designs, the thought and effort that I put into each project. But who cared about quality any more? I had lost the contract and that was the end of the matter.

It's only later that I learnt from a few of my friends and associates that my manager had gone around leaking my quotation to the other contractors who had had their eyes on this project right from the very start. And they had all cut down on their cost prices, set their rates lower than mine, changed their ideas, modified their own quotations and sent them to the company a couple of days later. My friends also told me that my manager had been earning thousands of rupees from other contractors by leaking ideas to them and indulging in other underhand dealings. He had also gone around spreading untrue rumours about me, telling everyone that he was the mastermind behind all my projects and I merely received all the laurels and enjoyed the credit. He had also tried to brainwash my most trusted helpers into leaving their jobs and joining other artists, though without any success.

When I asked him why he had done it, of course he had no answer. I was still willing to give him another chance because I didn't like firing people and depriving them of their livelihood, but he quit the job of his own accord and soon opened his own electrical business. And a few months later I learnt that he had spoken to my father-in-law asking for my sister-in-law's hand in marriage and they had readily agreed to his proposal on the grounds that he was a Brahmin and he had his own business now. When I first learnt about all this, I didn't quite know how to process the whole thing for several days. Never in my life had I imagined that the only people who I had called 'family' and who I had gone out of my way to help in their hour of need would be embracing the person who had walked every mile to bring me disgrace just because he was a Brahmin.

'Are you people out of your mind?' I asked my wife as soon as I came to know about it. 'That man deceived me! He has gone around spoiling my reputation, profiting from my endeavours and bluffing all along! You know everything! How could you have tolerated this?'

'My sister is in love with him!' she replied. 'What could I have possibly done? How long will you keep paying for her expenses?'

'We could have looked for a better match!' I said. 'There is no dearth of eligible bachelors in this town! We could have at least looked for a decent person who comes from a respectable family and earns his living by honest means.'

'What's wrong with his family?' My sister-in-law, who had been eavesdropping on our conversation all this time, now boldly entered the scene.

'Have you spoken to his family?' I questioned her. 'Have you ever seen them?'

'Yes, I have,' she replied coldly. 'And I don't think there's any problem with them.'

'You're saying that because you're blinded by love,' I told her. 'You won't be able to adjust to life there at all. They are different from us in every way! He has five sisters, several brothers and a huge extended family…'

'So did you!' She cut me off.

'But they quarrel with each other for the slightest reasons! It's a very nasty environment. You will be sick of it soon.'

'You are not my father, Sridhar Babu,' she snapped. 'You don't have a say in any of this. What I do with my life is none of your business!'

'I know I'm not your father, but I personally know the man as well as his family. Your father doesn't.'

'Well, I know him personally too,' she retorted. 'And I will be marrying the man, not his family. What do I care for their fights? And when my father has no objection to our match, why should you interfere? Just because you've been generous to us, do you think you've bought us?'

'What?' I asked, shocked. 'I'm only saying this for your own good.'

'I think I'm mature enough to decide what's good for me and what isn't,' she replied stiffly. 'I don't need you to patronize me. Besides, have you thought about your own roots, your caste, your family and culture? Have you forgotten the kind of torture your brothers put us through? My sister married you, nevertheless. You think she couldn't have found a better match?'

I was stunned at what she had said, completely bereft of words.

'I don't see why I shouldn't marry the man of my choice just because of his roots,' she continued. 'At least he comes from a Brahmin family, unlike you.'

'So that's what it is!'

'And he has his own business, too!' she added.

'A business built on fraud, you mean?'

'What evidence do you have of him doing all those things that you've accused him of?' she flared up at this, her voice loud and shrill. 'You've just blindly believed your sycophants, haven't you? Did you see him leaking your quotation? Did you see it with your own eyes?'

And there, the question of evidence arose, once again. And once again, I had no solid proof though it was an open secret and there were several eyewitnesses.

'You've got nothing to say now, have you?' she said sarcastically. 'I'm not surprised.'

'All I can tell you is that you're committing a major mistake.'

I stood there that afternoon listening to her hurling one insult after another at me, and my wife only tried to placate me instead of defending me. I couldn't believe that they were the ones I stood by when no one else did. They were the ones I gave shelter to and went against my family to support. Time and again I was reminded by them that I was an illiterate lower caste person and they had condescended to accept me as a part of their family even though Sunil Babu had himself requested me to take care of his children and get his other daughters married because he was bankrupt. And that is exactly what I had been trying to do. But after hearing my sister-in-law speak blatantly about my caste and qualifications, all I felt for them was pure, unadulterated hatred. My tongue stuck in my throat. My heart felt like a stone. Perhaps my mother was right. This marriage was a big mistake. Perhaps I should have listened to her and married someone of my own caste.

I didn't talk to my wife for weeks after that incident. And when I did, it was she who came to me to inform me with tears in her eyes that my manager and her sister were getting married soon and they had invited everyone they knew apart from the two of us.

'Is that why you're crying?' I asked her, not looking up from my design. 'Hadn't you foreseen it already?'

'She is my closest sister and… and she is getting married now,' she replied. 'And I can't believe that I won't even be a part of it.'

'Yes, that's rather strange,' I responded. 'I understand why she didn't invite me but she should have invited you at least. You supported her so much through all of this.'

'I didn't support her!' she cried, stung. 'You are wrong if you think I supported her for my sake. My sister has always been too picky about men which is precisely why she has been unmarried for so many years. In fact, she told me just last year that she was never going to marry anyone. She doesn't even want to work. I have tried for years to persuade her to get married to somebody. I couldn't let you bear her expenses for the rest of your life. You've already got so much on your plate. You're paying for Gopal, you helped my other sisters get married, you're there for

Proshanto whenever he needs you. And on top of that, we have Mini's expenses, her school fees, you have your own business and so many creditors to pay back. Don't you think I can see how hard you're working? Why would you keep paying indefinitely for my family? You are not responsible for my father's mistakes.'

'I think I told you already that we could have at least looked for a suitable man for her,' I told her calmly. 'I would have helped her to get married.'

'Yes, I am coming to that,' my wife said impatiently. 'She fell in love with him before he leaked your quotation. She thought he was a good man. She knew nothing about the things he had been doing behind your back.'

'And what about after she knew about those things?' I asked her. 'Did that change anything at all?'

She stood there, silent, tears rolling down her eyes. It disgusted me how easily she could cry about everything in order to avoid taking a side. She had always been blind to the errors of her siblings. No matter what they did, she would invariably refuse to take action against them. Rather she would sympathize with them and badmouth whoever tried to rectify their mistakes.

'Why are you not saying anything now?' I questioned.

She looked at me indignantly and replied with palpable discomfort, 'Because by then, they had already gone too far.'

'What do you mean?'

'They had already gone too far in their relationship,' my wife repeated. 'Who would marry her after that?'

Things were a little clearer to me now. But that didn't solve anything.

'And what about the vile things she said to me?' I asked her. 'How can you justify that?'

'She shouldn't have said all that,' my wife replied. 'It was extremely ungrateful on her part to have said all that to you, especially after all that you have done for us. I never expected her to say all those things to you, trust me.'

'You didn't say anything, Sumitra. You just stood there, listening. She belittled me for my caste, the fact that I didn't finish school, the way I look, my family members, everything.'

'I didn't know what to say, I was so shocked...'

'Please stop,' I requested. 'Please... don't say all that to me... I don't want to listen to any excuses. Your neutrality disgusts me!'

'I'll never allow her in this house again,' she cut me off. 'I have made up my mind. She's... she's not my sister anymore.'

I was a little surprised at what my wife had said to me. I wanted to believe her but I decided to wait to see how things turned out and exactly eight months later, my wife came to me once again, her eyes brimming with tears.

'What now?' I asked her.

'Have you heard about the baby?' her lips quivered.

'Whose baby?'

'My sister's,' she replied. 'The little girl is so sick. The doctors said she needs surgery.'

'And how do you know about all this?'

'She came with the new-born this morning,' my wife answered after a very long pause. 'There's something wrong with the baby's neck. She cannot even move her head...

the poor little girl is in so much pain! I couldn't even look at her.'

And saying so she burst into tears.

'Why don't they get the surgery done?' I asked, a little touched.

'It's too risky to be done on a new-born,' she replied. 'The doctors have asked her to wait for a year.'

'But she will get cured, won't she?'

'They cannot guarantee that,' she sobbed. 'If the operation fails, she might die or survive with a distorted neck for her entire life. But that's not what is torturing me right now. It's the child's pain. She's in tremendous pain! And she's just a new-born. What if her heart gives way?'

'But there is nothing you can do about this, is there? You cannot cure her.'

She shook her head.

'I'm sure her parents and your father will know how to handle the situation best,' I further said.

She didn't respond to that.

'And how is your sister nowadays?' I asked her, hesitatingly. 'Although I know I shouldn't be asking this since it's none of my business.'

'Not good,' she replied after what seemed an eternity. 'She's not doing well at all.'

'Really?' I pretended to be surprised. 'Why so?'

'I don't know,' said my wife. 'She's just not happy there. She says there's no one willing to help. She isn't getting along with her in-laws because they are very abusive. And her husband is always busy…'

'I see.'

'I wish she had taken your advice,' she muttered.

'Ah, I'm sure she'll figure things out soon,' I said with biting sarcasm, 'since she is mature enough to make her own decisions. And I don't think it really matters how her in-laws are treating her as long as they are Brahmins.'

The next morning, when I came back home from the factory to take a shower, I saw an extra pair of lady's slippers at the front door. I planned on making my way quickly upstairs to my room without being noticed because if it was one of the mothers my wife had befriended at Mini's school, I sincerely wished to escape the perfunctory introduction followed by a long session of small talk, unwilling head-nodding and smiling till my cheeks felt stiff. So, I sneaked into my own house and was just about to take the stairs when my wife summoned me. And turning around, I saw her sister standing right behind me, holding the baby in her arms wrapped in white cloth. It came as a shock to me at first, but when the shock subsided, I noticed that my sister-in-law looked pale and thin with dark circles under her exhausted eyes as though she had been made to starve for weeks.

'Won't you bless my daughter?' she asked with tears in her eyes.

'But I'm not a Brahmin,' I wanted to say, but I somehow restrained myself. 'Why would you condescend to something like that?'

'I know I told you some really terrible things, but that's not my child's fault, is it? So, hold her once at least,' she said with quivering lips and came over to me with the child. 'And be careful... she cannot turn her head to the right.'

I took the little girl from her involuntarily. She stirred a little in my arms but then fell asleep again, her tiny hands closed tightly into fists. She looked smaller than an average new-born, or perhaps I had forgotten how tiny a new-born could be. She was a little too pale with a stiff neck and a blue knot of veins so clearly visible through her translucent skin. And wrapped in a white *kantha*, as I looked at her face, the memory of my dead son, unmoving in my arms, came alive once again. I couldn't help noticing the striking resemblance between the corpse of my dead son and this helpless, living child who lay weakly in my arms.

A shiver ran down my spine. I knew I had to save this child somehow.

Interlude

'It was a failed marriage,' said my mother. 'She couldn't live in that house with her in-laws. It was a madhouse. It was all good for a few months, you know, the honeymoon phase. But soon the inevitable happened exactly like your grandfather had predicted. She fell out with her husband and they fought with each other every day like cats and dogs. She kept complaining to my mother that she had to live in a single room, living, dining, kitchen, all rolled into one. She had to cook for herself separately since she couldn't eat the kind of meals they took. Her husband's business had suffered huge losses and she had a sick child to look after all alone. So, she started spending most of her time in our house with your grandmother after her daughter was born and here's where my cousin mostly grew up.'

'But Grandma too faced all of these things and worse after her marriage, didn't she?' I asked. 'Grandfather used to be extremely busy back then too. She lost two children and so many of her loved ones. She had to cook and clean and do all the chores in spite of being sick and pregnant herself.'

'Yes, she did,' replied my mother. 'But she was accepted

by my father's family after my brother was born and my grandma cooperated with her as much as she could thereafter. But it was very different at my aunt's place. She had no one to stand by her or help her manage things. Besides, my mother and my aunt are two very different people. My mother has always kept quiet and tried to adapt and adjust to different situations. My aunt couldn't. And my mother, unlike my aunt, has always been extremely kind to people. She is very soft spoken and pleasant to all. Which is why everyone loved her. She always had a smile for people, even people who had wronged her. No matter what she felt inside, she never let it show on her face, which is why even all your grandfather's troublesome siblings warmed to her very soon after she shifted to the Bidyalanka house.'

I said, 'I can understand from whatever you told me that my grandmother was submissive and docile which is why people liked her. They could walk all over her. She put up with whatever hardship she was put through and was still warm to everyone. It's easy to like people who are like that because they don't hold you accountable for any of your errors. On the other hand, her sister was a loud and opinionated woman. She didn't want to put up with things and was quite honest about her feelings. She could stand up for herself and fight for what she believed was right. Which is quite admirable for a woman of her time, if you ask me.'

'But she was also extremely casteist and quite ungrateful. She was arrogant too because she was well-educated and could speak in English. She found it acceptable to look down on your grandfather who had dropped out of school very young.'

I replied, 'In fact, I have a feeling that had my grandfather not been so successful and popular, had he not saved them from financial doom, their family would never even have bothered to look at him twice. It's only because of his fame and money that they treated him differently. Otherwise, he would just be another dark-skinned, lower caste, uneducated person of no significance to them.'

'That's a pretty accurate assessment,' said my mother.

'But what angers me a lot is the fact that even after he was rich and famous and successful, even after he went out of his way to help them, stand by them in their hour of need, broke off all relations with his own family, his caste was still important to them,' I continued. 'Your grandfather didn't want a contaminated bloodline but he was okay with indefinitely receiving help and financial support from a lower caste person without any scruples. Your high caste aunt was happy to be provided for by a lower caste person, living in the house that he built, and then coming back to the same house after her marriage failed, but she had no reservations in ridiculing Grandfather with her casteist remarks when he tried to offer her advice. No matter what you did, or how successful you were, you would still be ridiculed by people if you belonged to a lower caste. And this continues even today.'

'Your grandfather was still a Vaishya,' my mother added. 'Think of the kind of torture the Dalits went through back then, especially the Dalit women. In fact, there was a Dalit family living across the street from your grandfather's house and your grandfather was friends with their sons since they were of the same age. They often played together, but my

grandmother wasn't too pleased if she ever heard that he ate or drank water at their place. She would make him wash himself after he had played with them. Only after that would he be allowed to enter his own house.'

'So, even the people who themselves faced discrimination from the higher castes, freely indulged in discriminating against others.'

'Yes,' my mother replied. 'That's how it has always been.'

'Did you face something like that, too?' I asked her.

'Not to that extent,' said my mother. 'But there's a sort of instant profiling that happens when people from higher castes look at you. They look at your skin colour, your physical features and they've already categorized you. Then when they hear your surname, the look on their faces, no matter how subtle, tells you enough. My classmates who came from affluent families always made me feel like I wasn't one of them, that I could never be one of them.'

'I understand,' I nodded sadly. 'I'm really sorry that you had to go through all that.'

'That's okay,' my mother smiled. 'It's made me what I am today. If you're pretty and you come from a supportive, well-to-do family that helps you grow, you're already above others who don't have these things. That's a bitter truth. Family is the strongest backup one can have. And pretty privilege is a real thing, too. I didn't have either of those things. So, I had to work a lot harder to stand out and make a name for myself. But it helped build my character.'

'I have everything,' I muttered, realizing that I would never have to go through what she had. But it didn't fill me with a sense of relief. On the contrary, it filled me with a deep

sense of sadness. 'I don't know what to say, Mother. My life is so different. Do you ever think of me as one of you? Or do you think I will never truly be able to empathize because I've never lived through any of the things that you, Father, Grandpa and Grandma did? Should I even be writing this book? I don't know.'

'What are you saying, silly?' my mother laughed in response. 'We are all so happy for you! I'm happy I could give you the life I wanted. I wouldn't want you to go through what I did. Nobody wants that for their child.'

'It's not about being happy for me, Mother,' I replied. 'I feel like I'm not good enough to be writing this story. Perhaps I don't have the depth or the understanding that is required to properly delve into all your lives… or to comprehend all the nuances that went into building your characters. We occupy such starkly different worlds.'

'I do understand what you're saying,' my mother said. 'You're afraid of misrepresentation. You're probably also afraid of being biased in your accounts because you're so close to us. But I believe, and so does your grandfather, that you're the best person to be writing this book.'

'How?' I asked her. 'What makes you think so?'

'Don't ask me how,' she said. 'We just know. You've always been a very sensitive child. You have a sharp eye and a kind of critical insight which even I don't have. You've seen us all up close for two decades. You are worthy! You're worthy because your grandfather has entrusted you with the story of his life, not someone else. You cannot back out of this now.'

'I won't back out,' I told her. But I wasn't convinced of

all that she had said. Now more than ever, after listening to all their stories, I could understand how privileged I had always been. My own issues had started to seem so small to me. I wanted to give back to this world so much more than I had received.

But time was running out, so I decided to snap back my attention to where we were before I had digressed, 'Tell me something, how did my grandfather react when your aunt came back after her daughter was born?'

'He didn't react at all,' replied my mother. 'He said nothing. Perhaps he was touched by my cousin's helpless state. But at the same time, he could never again be warm to my aunt. His warmth was reserved only for my growing cousin. His manager, of course, didn't succeed in his electrical business. He came back here too, requesting your grandmother for money for my cousin's surgery and your grandmother went running to your grandfather asking for help each time. The medical expenses were exorbitant but your grandfather paid most of them.'

'And as far as I know he still helps them, doesn't he? Pays for most of their medical and day-to-day expenses.'

'Yes,' replied my mother. 'Almost thirty years have passed since my aunt got married and it's the same even now. But they have also realized their mistake and made amends. They are always there for us now whenever we need them. My aunt's husband has gone out of his way to stand by us through difficult times. However, his relationship with my aunt has never been fulfilling. She says she is the unhappiest woman on the planet and that her life has been nothing but a vale of tears. She hardly speaks to her husband even

though they live under the same roof and whenever they do, they end up fighting. Their house is dilapidated, the few surviving members of that family are never at peace with each other. And the one who has been worst affected due to all of this is my cousin. Not her fault, of course. That's how you would have grown up to be too if you always saw your parents fighting tooth and nail every day.'

'I feel so sorry about all this,' I told her. 'She certainly didn't deserve a life like that. But why did Grandma never object to her sister's misbehaviour?'

'She didn't know whom to defend,' replied my mother. 'She wanted her sister to get married so as to remove some of the burden from your grandfather's shoulders.'

'Why couldn't she, with the same enthusiasm, persuade her to get a job instead? Marriage was not the only solution and women did have jobs back then. Their stepmother too was a working woman, as far as I know. Your aunt had graduated from Lady Brabourne, right?'

'No, my mother graduated from Lady Brabourne,' she rectified. 'My aunt graduated from Bethune.'

'Then why did she not look for a job?'

'She did have jobs, but that was after she got married,' replied my mother. 'Also remember that things were very different back in their time. It wasn't so easy for women to get jobs in small towns. Getting a job in Kolkata was comparatively easier. And my aunt was way past the ideal age of marriage. She was just a few years younger than my mother who had been married for over ten years. Two of their other sisters had also gotten married years ago and had kids. But she was still unmarried. Soon she got seriously involved

with my father's manager. And people back then usually looked down upon such relationships before marriage. My mother was extremely concerned about her. She was sure that her sister didn't stand a chance of getting married anymore. At the same time, she was also heavily dependent on your grandfather. She didn't know whose side to take.'

'I understand.'

'She did a lot for our family,' my mother changed the subject. 'Your grandmother, I mean. She had all the necessary qualifications but she sacrificed several job offers because she needed to look after her family . She was well aware of the fact that my father was extremely busy and like most of the women of her time, she believed that only a man who has a secure family could go out and give wings to his dreams. If she hadn't helped me in bringing you up, I'd never have been able to build my own career. But she did it all at the cost of her own life and career. When I was young I couldn't understand her at all, but when I grew up and especially after you were born, I understood how important a role she played in all our lives.'

'Yes, I know. She's always been there for me too. Whenever I needed her, she was there, willing to do whatever it took to fulfil my needs. I don't know what I'll do without her or Grandpa.' The lump in my throat throbbed. 'I see them every day getting older and weaker. And it constantly reminds me of the fact that they won't be here with us forever. I don't know what my life will be like after they are gone. This house won't feel like home anymore.'

'Don't think of all that, dear,' said my mother, lovingly. 'Cherish the present. You can never be certain about the future.'

'Mother, do you believe in the afterlife?' I asked her, a moment later.

'I don't really know,' replied my mother. 'Who knows what's out there? But one thing that I strongly believe in is karma. As you sow, so shall you reap.'

'There's something else I want to know.'

'Yes, what do you want to know?'

'All these things... I mean, these sabotages and deceptions, these family squabbles, they had an impact on Grandpa's health, right?'

'Definitely,' replied my mother. 'Before his pacemaker was installed, he often blacked out while working. The stress was tremendous and he couldn't take it. When he went to the doctor, he took certain tests and discovered that he was suffering from a blockage in the left bundle of his heart. The doctor suggested that he should get a pacemaker installed but he also said that your grandfather wouldn't be able to work with high voltage electricity with a pacemaker inside him. So, your grandfather kept postponing it for years till he was on the verge of a heart attack and had to be taken to B.M. Birla hospital immediately.'

'And then the pacemaker was installed.'

'Yes,' replied my mother. 'But he didn't listen to the doctor's advice. He continued working with high voltage electricity. In fact, the very day he was released from the hospital after the installation of the pacemaker, he went out to work in the Boys' Sporting Club as he had an important assignment going on there.'

'Are you sure he's a human and not a cyborg?'

My mother chuckled.

'He's a human alright' she replied. 'He just has what it takes. Your grandfather has always been freakishly ambitious. His rates have always been higher compared to the other light artists. He thus lost several contracts to them but he never compromised on the price or the quality of his work or the originality of his ideas. He told me never to settle for anything less than what I believed I deserved. As a result, he always found people who were keener on quality and thus never lacked projects. This helped him to be both a quality artist as well as a successful businessman.'

'I see. But there were other light artists who learnt the work he started and set up their own businesses, right? The industry grew quite rapidly. But why was it always Grandfather who received most of the contracts even though later on there were several other people doing the same kind of work?'

'That was because most of the other artists and contractors used cheaper raw materials, fewer miniatures so that they could cut down on their costs. They never quite hit the mark. Your grandfather's work on the other hand was very artistic, his ideas were socially relevant. So, he always received critical acclaim. Besides, the panels that your grandfather made were based on a variety of themes which could be used anywhere for any occasion. On the other hand, the other contractors, in order to outshine him, made huge panels during the puja based chiefly on regional themes with the effect that people outside our town or state had no use for those panels. Their themes would stand out as irrelevant to the context and the power consumption would be massive considering the size of their panels.'

'So, would they destroy those panels after they were displayed and create new ones all over again?'

'Yes, they would have to dismantle most of their panels completely to take up new orders, and because of this they incurred enormous losses. Some of them even had to close down their business due to lack of funds. They also had massive labour problems as they were unable to pay salaries at the right time. Your grandpa never had such problems. The helpers doing long hours of work during the festival season were paid in advance so that their families did not suffer as they were required to stay away from them for weeks. He also arranged four square meals for them per day and set up a separate kitchen running for them during the peak season.'

'He took care of everything, didn't he?'

'He did. He cared more for his helpers than he cared for himself or his family. He often forgot his meals but always made sure his helpers didn't go hungry. Now they are all well established.'

'I wish I were half the person he was,' I sighed.

'You have to be willing to work for it.'

'I know,' I muttered. 'I know.'

11

The Early 2000s

'SRIDHAR DAS IS FINISHED!' the headlines of a local periodical read.

'IT'S THE END OF THE ERA OF CHANDANNAGAR LIGHTS!' another proclaimed.

I didn't have to read the articles. I knew what was written in them. Word spreads fast in a small town.

Two years ago, a journalist had asked me a question which I had failed to answer satisfactorily, and it had been tormenting me ever since.

'Sir, don't you think the excessive heat that the panels give off and the massive amounts of electricity they consume are detrimental to the environment? Do you have any eco-friendly ideas to counter that sort of thing?'

I hadn't been able to answer him. So, he had left that question out of the pubished interview. However, to me it seemed like a big defeat. The journalist had made a valid point and I was surprised at myself for not having thought of it before. There were over a hundred puja committees in Chandannagar who spent lavishly on their processions. Each of the committees were allowed four to five lorries to display their panels of lights, which, if taken together, came to around five hundred trucks of lights alone and only for the procession, excluding the four nights of continuously glowing street lights. If the traditional method posed such massive threats to the environment, it would certainly need to be replaced with something else soon. Several cottage industries had been shut down before for the very same reason. I couldn't let my art die. The thousands of people engaged in the industry would all lose their livelihood if I didn't think of some alternative soon. It gave me sleepless nights!

A year later, an artist named Asim Dey had made simple panels using LED lights. And the people of my town jeered when they saw his panels pass and it weren't even considered as a part of the competition. However, I was curious and I called him up that very night wanting to know more about the LED lights. New innovations in the field of lighting always fascinated me.

'They consume much less power,' he had told me. 'They are extremely safe. You can touch the lights on panels while they are running and nothing will happen to you. These lights are comparatively cheaper and you don't have to use coloured cellophane paper because they are available in various colours and they give off negligible heat.'

'That's excellent!' I had told him, almost leaping in joy. 'That's exactly what we need right now!'

'Well, then you are the only one who thinks so,' he had replied sadly, his face pale and distressed.

When I went back home that night, I was in such a bright mood that my wife looked at me suspiciously.

'What is the matter?' she questioned me over dinner.

'You won't believe what happened today,' I told her. 'All my anxieties have finally come to an end. I have finally found an alternative to the 6.2 miniatures, one that is absolutely safe for the environment!'

'Where did you find it?'

'Asim worked with them this year,' I informed her. 'Those lights are called LED. They look like stars! I'm going to shift to LED immediately.'

'Don't make that mistake,' my wife warned me instead of encouraging me and that came as a surprise.

'Why?' I asked her.

'The people here love the 6.2 miniatures,' she said. 'Those lights are the essence of our Jagadhatri Puja! I don't think they will ever be able to accept LED. Besides, I heard about Asim's panels. Haru and Gopal were laughing at them earlier this evening. I don't want people to laugh at you too.'

'That's because they don't know how harmful the miniatures are,' I told her. 'We must tell everyone.'

'Look,' she said. 'You are almost sixty years old and you have achieved everything you have ever wanted in life. Why don't you take a break now and diversify your business?'

'Are you asking me to give up?' I asked her, surprised.

'No, I am not asking you to give up,' she replied, exasperated. 'But I don't want you to lose your reputation at the end of your successful career. If you don't want to work with miniatures, don't. Do something else. But don't shift to LED. I don't want you to be a laughingstock.'

'That's an extremely selfish way of thinking, Sumitra,' I couldn't help but say. 'You are only thinking about my reputation. What about the others? What about the thousands of people who are engaged in this industry? They will all lose their jobs if the Pollution Control Board issues an order against the use of miniatures. I might have achieved enough to be able to live lavishly even if I stop working now but what about those people? This is their only source of livelihood.'

She didn't respond but from her expression I could understand that she was not very happy.

'Whatever you say, I am going to shift to LED,' I declared. 'And once I explain the reason for the shift, I am sure people will understand. And if they don't, it won't be long before they don't get to see any lights at all during the pujas.'

I was soon invited to Rabindra Bhavan to be a part of the grand annual award function organized by Morton Dairy and present the awards for street lights and procession lights to the budding light artists who had made it to the top that year. It was a matter of great pride and honour to me when they touched my feet as I handed over to them their well-deserved awards. However, just before the winner's name was announced, a group of men occupying the front rows hooted Asim's name, laughing amongst themselves, distracting everyone around. Asim's dejected face immediately flashed before my eyes and in the heat of the moment, I couldn't help but make a speech that night in his defence, a speech that had unimaginable consequences.

'I would like to congratulate all the winners tonight,' I began. 'May you keep up the excellent work and strive towards immortalizing the name of our town. But there's something else that I would like to mention. And it's about my friend, Asim Dey, the one who introduced the beautiful LED panels this year in Chandannagar…'

My speech was greeted by an outburst of laughter from the electrical contractors and light artists who occupied the front rows. They thought I was cracking a joke at Asim's expense just like they had been doing.

'For all I know,' I continued. 'There are thousands of visitors who come to our town each year from far and wide to witness the Jagadhatri Puja. In the late 1900s there were only five or six light artists who were engaged in the illumination work and not all puja committees in Chandannagar participated in the procession or opted for street lighting. Nowadays you won't find a puja committee which doesn't do either of these. The situation is different now. So, in this changed scenario, it is not safe to expose the multitudes of visitors to the risks of the 6.2 miniatures. We've had several accidents each year where people have received electric shocks from the street lights because of being shoved against the panels by the bustling crowd. Many have lost their lives in an attempt to install the heavy panels at precarious locations. Besides, we must think about the environment too. The amount of heat that the miniatures give off is not at all safe for the environment. Hence, I personally feel that all of us light artists should follow Asim's lead and switch to LED for a safer and healthier puja environment.'

'IS THAT MAN CRAZY?' I heard someone scream from one of the front rows.

And pandemonium followed, with people expressing contrary opinions fleshed out with a whole lot of sneering and jeering.

'You may laugh now,' I added, caught off-guard by the sudden turn of events. 'But one day, LED is all that is going to reign in Chandannagar!'

And since that day my new reputation was, Sridhar Das, the once celebrated but now demented electrician.

Deciding to be the change in order to bring about the change, I started working with LED and soon I noticed a conspicuous change in the attitude of some of my helpers. Somehow, they seemed a little defiant. They looked at my designs with noticeable indifference. I often found them grouped together whispering among themselves. They were not prepared to forgo their old habits and learn anything new. Whenever I issued any order, they often pretended not to have heard me well. When they talked to me, they couldn't look into my eyes. It was all about money now. As long as they were paid their salaries on time, they were fine. Many of them eventually left my employment and joined the other artists and contractors who still worked with the tried and tested methods of street illumination.

My neighbours looked through me. My old friends didn't wave at me in the streets anymore. It seemed like the people who had previously called themselves my well-wishers and thronged my house all day devouring tons of snacks and gallons of tea, the people I went out of my way to help, be it with money or advice, and never expected anything in return but friendship and love, had suddenly changed their minds. They hardly recognized me anymore. Some of my brothers were delighted. My mother was cold in her grave. Had she been alive, I'm sure she would have taken great pleasure in contributing a few lines to the derogatory columns in the newspapers herself. The only people who stood by me throughout were my bosom friends Vikash and Parashuram, and my dearest boys Rustom and Mustafa. Funny how it's only during moments of crisis that true colours are revealed.

I had gone to the Chandannagar Municipal Corporation one day to meet my dear friend, Amiya, and there I faced the kind of treatment I never imagined the good corporation people were capable of. The people who would jump out of their seats upon seeing me were now too engrossed in their work and tea to take notice of me. All were extremely intent on the red-taped files on their tables and offered me a chair, and a cup of tea, unwillingly. They were too busy to talk to me or answer any of my questions. My friend, the Mayor, however, greeted me warmly and was extremely hospitable, like always.

One day while I was on my way to my factory with some cake and snacks for my workers, I saw my own self painted on the outer walls of my house, reduced to a ridiculous cartoon with a bald head, an exceptionally long and blunt nose, and other exaggerated physical features, wearing strings of LED instead of clothes. Next to it, written in a careless manner, was a vicious rhyme that declared I was mentally unstable. My friend Vikash, along with a few of my boys, scrubbed the stubborn paint all morning. I bore it all at that moment but the tears I shed all alone in my room that afternoon were enough to have washed the entire wall clean.

'Listen,' Vikash told me one day, looking deep into my eyes. 'You give your all to an LED procession next year. Do something different, something revolutionary with LED. Something they have never seen before. I know you can do it. You don't have to worry about what's going on at home. We'll manage it.'

'I'm really finished, aren't I?' was all I could say.

'You're not!' he gave my shoulders a good shake 'You are not over! You can never be. You are the pioneer, my friend!'

'Hah! Pioneer!' I sighed, laughing at my own self.

'They know lights because you have taught them what lights are and what they can do!' Vikash continued. 'They wouldn't have cared about any of this if you hadn't begun this phenomenon in the first place. They would have still been stuck in the 1960s with their tube lights and bulbs. Now you want to introduce a change, a positive change, thinking about their safety and the environment. They don't like it because they don't yet know what it is. There's a famous saying that a prophet is never honoured in his own land. You have to show them, Sridhar! You have to open their eyes to the wonders one can do with LED.'

'You think I can do that?' I asked him, doubtfully.

'Who else can?' he laughed. 'You didn't ask this question before you made those lights glow under water, did you? You didn't even listen to me back then! You did whatever you wanted to do irrespective of what people thought or said about you.'

'It was different back then, Vikash,' I told him. 'I was a nobody back then. No one took me or whatever I did seriously. I was still in the experimental stage where I could go wrong, I could make mistakes and nobody really cared. But I can't do that anymore. Everyone knows me now. They've all got their eyes on me. It's like I'm always in the spotlight and everything I do is subject to relentless scrutiny. There are people out there waiting for an opportunity to catch me at a disadvantage so that they can spew all their bitterness.'

'Uneasy lies the head that wears the crown, my friend,' said Vikash. 'You must accept it. Hold your head high and do what you want to do. Don't care what people say! If you think you're on the right track, you stay on that track. Mark my words, there will come a day when they'll have to abandon their ways to follow yours.'

I decided to take Vikash's advice and do something innovative with LED. And weird though it might seem, my course of action was revealed to me partly in a dream and partly by one of the books my granddaughter loved to read, a book of nursery rhymes, replete with bright, colourful pictures and funny stories in the form of catchy little poems.

I went to bed one night, and dreamt of a procession. I stood by the side of the road preoccupied with my thoughts as one lorry after another bedecked with marvellously illuminated 6.2 miniature panels passed before my eyes. I gazed at them fondly for a while but soon things started going awry. Suddenly, out of nowhere, an enormous clown made of miniatures advanced towards me. Just as it was about to pass me by, the truck screeched to a halt right in front of me with a terrible noise that made my ears ring. And the clown which had been fixed all this time, slowly and eerily turned its head towards me…

The people around remained mute as the large, yellow eyes looked directly into mine, glaring with a ghastly light. Soon it erupted into a fit of unearthly laughter, revealing a set of exceptionally large front teeth, and making me shiver uncontrollably from head to toe. The people who had been watching the procession all this time now followed the clown's lead as though under the influence of magic. They laughed at me too, mocking me, ridiculing me, uttering spiteful remarks and obscene profanities. A shower of disembodied voices soon buzzed around my head like a swarm of locusts and as I tried to plug my ears with my fingers and close my eyes, they battered my body like a stream of bullets from a shotgun.

But then they all came to a standstill and silence was restored once again. I opened my eyes half-afraid, half-curious to see what it was that had silenced all those voices, and I was blown off guard by the mesmerizing figure of a fairy with silver hair that sparkled like diamonds and an oddly designed magic wand in her hand. There was something different about this figure. It was not made of miniatures. It was made of lights that had a pristine star-like quality and were mellow, calm and balmy to the eyes. The silver fairy glowed so radiantly that the spiteful clown dwindled under the aura of her light until it eventually disappeared and then, with a swish of her wand, she made all the people kneel down before her, bewitched.

Then she turned and bowed to me respectfully. And this is when I woke up with a start.

I found myself on my bed, my granddaughter seated right next to me, looking at her favourite book of rhymes and reciting a few of them loudly in English. 'I'm a fairy doll on the Christmas tree. Boys and girls come look at me... Come look at me, see what I can do! If I can do it, you can too.'

'When did you wake up?' I asked her, a little surprised.

'Long time ago,' she replied, her eyes large, dark and glittery. 'It's almost 12 o' clock. You've been sleeping all morning! Dida's been so worried about you.'

'I was up till 4 a.m. last night,' I told her.

'Ah, I see,' she responded. 'That's why your room was all smoky when I entered. Now I understand.'

Then she turned the page she was reading and began to hum, 'Little Miss Muffet... sat on a tuffet... eating her curd and whey...'

'You're still reading that book?' I interrupted her 'Don't you think you're too big for nursery rhymes?'

'I'm just practising,' she replied, flicking the glossy sheet of dark brown hair off her shoulder. 'I'm practising them for my baby sister who's hiding in my mother's tummy right now. Mother said I have to teach her all these rhymes before she turns one. So, you see? I have a huge responsibility.'

'You want a sister?' I asked her, affectionately. 'What if you get a brother?'

'Umm... then I guess I just have to accept it,' she shrugged. 'Even if I get a brother, I will be thankful to

God. At least I don't have to be alone, right? And I think I can bring him up to be a less noisy brother for sure. I will make him read some good books. My brother's going to be different from other boys. I'll name him Bonny.'

And then she resumed her rhyme. 'There came a big spider, who sat down beside her… and frightened Miss Muffet away…'

A peal of laughter followed.

'Why are you laughing?' I asked her, amused.

'Miss Muffet is just like me!' she said.

'Why so?'

'Because I'm terrified of spiders too! And look, Dadu, she looks a lot like me too! Doesn't she?'

And then she pressed the little book of rhymes against my nose for me to notice and acknowledge the resemblance between her and Little Miss Muffet. That's when the figures on the old pages of the book intrigued me.

'Doesn't she look like me, Dadu?' she was impatient to know. 'Doesn't she?'

'Indeed!' I replied enthusiastically. 'You almost look like twins!'

I failed to notice the happiness on her face because that's when I had another brainwave.

'But the book's gotten too old,' she replied wistfully a moment later. 'The pages are almost coming off. I'm not sure how long I'll be able to preserve it. Can you do something about it?'

'Hmm… let me think,' My mind was working at a pace it never had before. 'What if I bring these figures out of the book for you, huh?'

'That's impossible!'

'Nothing is impossible,' I told her.

'Then that would be great, Dadu! I no longer need to worry about the pages!'

'And what if I make them move?'

'Is that why they call you the magician?' she asked me, her voice shrill with excitement.

'And what if I make them with lights so that they can glow even at night?'

'Can I keep them in my room?' she wanted to know.

'I don't think you can, because I'm going to make them really big! And if I am to make Miss Muffet, I would have to make the spider too. Would you like to keep a big, glowing spider in your room?'

'Oh no! I can't! I would die of fright! I wouldn't be able to sleep a wink at night!' she hugged me out of imagined fear, her hair tickling my neck. 'How big is the spider going to be?'

'About triple your size,' I replied and watched her gasp with horror. 'But don't worry, it won't do you any harm! I'll make sure of that.'

'Please do it!'

'Would you let me borrow your book for a while, little one?' I asked her tenderly.

'Of course! Of course!' She was extremely eager and handed me the book over immediately. 'Anything for you, Dadu!'

I was not finished. Not yet.

It wasn't the end. Just another beginning.

Interlude

They were the best light models I had ever seen! I had never seen anything so beautiful in my entire life. I squealed with delight as the lorries passed by me, unable to believe my eyes. He had breathed life into the characters from my old book of rhymes! And he had done it in a way I never could have imagined. A candle nearly six feet tall, studded with gold and silver LED was displayed on one of the trucks. The sheer brilliance of its fluttering flame was almost blinding as the old nursery rhyme 'Jack, be nimble, Jack, be quick! Jack, jump over the candlestick!' played on the sound box. There was the life-like shadow of jumping Jack depicted beautifully on a panel positioned right behind the three-dimensional candle.

Then came the giant shoe-house from the rhyme 'There was an old woman who lived in a shoe,' and it had these little windows and doors which had looked so real when my grandfather worked on its intricate structure in the factory that I had fantasized about living in there for a day or two. I had detached myself from the rhyme and liked to believe there was a kitchen inside the house with a cute little table, a baking oven, a tiny fridge and endless jars of cookies, donuts and rainbow sprinkles. 'A perfect place to play "house"!' I had told my mother. I also liked to imagine that elves lived there at night, secretly making shoes of every hue and every shape just like in the marvellous story, 'The Shoemaker and the Elves.'

It was awesome!

My grandfather had portrayed separate nursery rhymes in separate trucks. Not just isolated characters, but complete nursery rhymes with their separate settings, separate characters, all moving around and acting out the stories. There was Miss Muffet, eating her curd and whey and a giant moving spider which frightened her out of her wits. There was a beautiful silver star from 'Twinkle, Twinkle Little Star,' and rows of pretty houses portrayed in the panels with a brilliant blue night sky glittering above them. And in the background, the rhymes played loud and clear.

I remember my grandfather borrowing from me the old cassette of nursery rhymes that my mother had bought from Music World. He then recorded each of the tracks on separate cassettes. Each truck had a different track playing and the lights depicted the story from the track. I thought them better than the Disneyland light and sound shows! One particular show in Disneyland, 'The Flights of Fantasy' which I had myself witnessed, just had focus lights and people dressed up like characters from fairy tales and dancing to the music. But what Grandpa did was different. He had used both panels as well as enormous mechanical structures entirely made of lights, like huge, fluorescent, glow-in-the-dark figures from some strange, enchanted land.

'Do you remember what you did when you saw the spider in his factory?' my mother reminded me.

'I do, I do,' I nodded. 'It looked like a giant tarantula moving its tentacles and I've never screamed so loud in all these twenty years the way I screamed the first time I saw it. Not even when an actual spider landed on me.'

'He received several awards that year,' my mother reminisced. 'That was the first time a procession made entirely of LED lights received so many prizes.'

'Yes, but he didn't receive the most coveted ones.'

'No, those awards went to the artists who had done it in the traditional way,' replied my mother. 'Most of them had no specific theme but were gigantic structures decorated entirely with 6.2 miniatures, the same old story.'

'And by the same time next year so many light artists had switched over to LED. Now LED is all we have.'

'That was his exact prediction. That one day, LED would reign in Chandannagar. He was humiliated when he said that. They called him the "demented" electrician. Look who's demented now!'

That's when my noisy brother announced his entry into our peaceful household by kicking the door open so forcefully that the windows rattled.

'I had a horrible day at school!' Bonny complained as he dropped his bag with a thud on the floor.

'Oh, why?' Mother asked him.

'It was too hot and I had a bad headache! I went to the Nurse's room and she gave me some medicine but it didn't work at all.'

'You should go take a shower immediately,' my mother

told him. 'I will give you medicine as soon as you have your lunch and you can rest for the whole afternoon.'

He did as he was told but he was incredibly slow and nagged my mother to cancel his Maths tuition that evening. I looked at him suspiciously. Did he really have a headache? Or was it just one of his consummate sick-boy impersonations? I couldn't tell.

'One last question, Mother, before I go,' I said. 'I haven't been able to figure out one thing. Where did Grandpa get the ideas for his mechanical figures from? How did he learn how to make them?'

'You should ask your grandpa that question,' my mother suggested.

When I asked my grandfather later that evening where he got the ideas for his mechanical figures from, his reply was fascinating.

'From toys,' he told me.

'Toys?'

'Yes,' he nodded. 'Whenever I came across a toy I liked, I... I bought it from the market and opened it with my screwdrivers to see how it functioned. I took note of all the miniature parts that went into the making of the toy and constructed similar mechanical figures with bigger parts. I made the bodies with masonite, drilled holes in them and attached the lights through the holes, just like I did with the panels initially, remember?'

'Yes, I do,' I smiled. 'So, that's it? You got all these wonderful ideas from toys?'

'Yes,' he replied. 'The mechanical train that I made was based on a toy train set that I saw one of my friends' sons playing with. I made several other mechanical figures which

were replicas of toys. Besides, there were other people in Chandannagar who used to make such figures. Kashinath Neogi was one such person who inspired me. I used to spend hours in his factory and he was ever so welcoming.'

'I think I've heard that name before.'

'He is an extremely qualified man!' replied my grandfather. 'He got an MTech degree back in our time, which was not very common back then. The mechanical figures he used to make were extraordinary. When he worked, he allowed nobody inside his factory, tolerated no interruption. But I was an exception. He loved me like his own and called me whenever he made something new. He asked for my opinions and welcomed my suggestions. I, in turn, asked for his views on the projects I'd been working on. We had an extremely affectionate camaraderie where we helped each other grow by learning from each other.'

'And nowadays it's all about competition.'

'It's not that we didn't have competition back in our time,' said Grandpa. 'But we had incredibly loyal friends and well-wishers too.'

'Speaking of well-wishers, tell me about London, Dadu. Didn't someone help you get there to exhibit your lights'

'Nandita,' he replied with a sparkle in his eyes. 'Nandita Palchoudhuri.'

The name brought to my mind a host of foggy memories, extremely pleasant ones.

'I remember her!' I exclaimed. 'I was just three years old when she used to come to our house but I remember her perfectly.'

'She's the kindest woman I've ever come across!' said Grandpa. 'I'll give you her number. You must contact her.'

12

Summer of 2001

The project in Ireland was my second international project after the one in Russia, but it was my first international trip. I was extremely nervous and disconcerted at the thought of having to interact with foreigners. I wasn't familiar with English, let alone the Irish language! I could hardly even make sense in Hindi. Bengali was the only language I was fluent in. Also, I was sure that my lights wouldn't stand a chance of standing out in a foreign land. Surely they would be accustomed to finer, more sophisticated technology, next to which my paltry Ramayana and Diwali panels, operating on simple wooden rollers, would look laughable.

I was to display twelve panels in the opulent gallery of the Queen's University at Belfast. Nandita accompanied me on this project. In fact, she was the one who had offered it to me at a time when my life was pretty stagnant and I was tired of doing the same thing over and over again. I had jumped at the prospect of an international project.

Nandita sat beside me in the plane, constantly reassuring

me. 'Sridhar Da, it's going to be absolutely fine! You don't need to worry at all. All they want is to see your lights!'

Even in that air-conditioned flying machine, I had to rub the sweat off my forehead from time to time. My boys, on the other hand, looked completely at ease and a little too excited as they inspected the glossy magazines, the headphones, the TV remotes with their various buttons, and summoned the air hostesses every ten minutes to ask for water and other things.

'Look how they are enjoying themselves!' Nandita whispered to me with a gentle laugh. 'You ought to loosen up a bit too.'

I was so nervous that I could barely even respond with a smile.

However, when we landed at Dublin Airport, something quite contrary to my expectations happened. A group of young Irish students from the Queen's University stood at the bottom of the stairs with large trays in their hands. At first, I didn't even imagine they were there for us but when I reached the bottom step, I was caught off guard as they advanced towards me with those trays. On those trays, they had everything we would require—sweaters, jackets, socks and shoes, handkerchiefs, small grooming kits and the like, for each one of us.

'What's happening?' I asked Nandita, bewildered, as all my other co-passengers stared at me. 'Why are they coming towards me?'

'That's because they are here for you!' her eyes twinkled with laughter. 'To welcome you with gifts and greetings!'

'But I haven't even worked for them yet!'

‘That doesn’t matter,’ she replied. ‘You’ve come here all the way from India. This is how they want to express their gratitude.’

They welcomed our team warmly with gifts and bouquets of flowers and led us to their private vans which would take us to the University. I kept smiling all the way. I had no idea what they were saying to Nandita. But they all looked cheerful and that cheered me up too, and when they laughed, I laughed too. I never expected the Irish people to be so warm and welcoming because I had always harboured the belief that the whites looked down upon us. But I was proven wrong and that made me exceptionally happy.

The gallery in Queen’s University where I was supposed to display my lights was nothing like I had ever seen before. There were several kinds of lights installed all over the auditorium. There were a number of entries and exits, a central air-conditioning system and infinite rows of gleaming seats stretched all around me. For a moment I was absolutely spellbound!

‘What happened, Sridhar Da?’ Nandita asked me. ‘Aren’t you feeling well?’

‘Yes, I am,’ I managed to reply. ‘I have never seen an auditorium like this before!’

She smiled and nodded.

‘This auditorium is going to look a lot better once you put your panels on display,’ she encouraged me.

‘I really hope it does.’

And she was right. For after we had put up our panels the appearance of the gallery transformed completely and the students were all awestruck. I could almost have cried in happiness when I saw the look of sheer amazement on their faces.

'They've never seen anything like this before either,' said Nandita, once the programme began.

A team of students stood in a group at some distance from my panels and began their recitation about the Indian festival of Diwali and the stories from the Ramayana that were recreated and depicted on my panels.

Once the light show was over, we were offered refreshments, coffee, cookies, sandwiches, tiny bottles of mineral water like the ones we were offered in the plane and various other quaint-looking delicacies that I never knew existed. A few students came over to me and asked me questions. Nandita explained all the questions to me in Bengali and translated my replies into English for them to understand. She was completely at home in this foreign land and I couldn't help but admire how fluently and confidently she spoke with them. What surprised me about the Irish people was their curiosity, their tireless desire to know more about the technical aspects of my work, their never-ending questions about how I had made lights glow under the water, and I was amazed at how easily they could make nervous foreigners like me feel at home with their warm, affable manners. They all shook hands with me and clicked several pictures of my panels. Many of them had their photos taken with me and asked for my signature on small pieces of paper and tiny notebooks. Oh, it was such a delightful experience!

Something funny and quite unlooked for happened a week later. I had to return to India urgently owing to some unfinished business which demanded my immediate attention. Nandita had to stay back for the rest of the event because she was the one in charge of it. There were twelve enormous panels and a whole lot of other electrical apparatus that had to be brought back. So, I couldn't ask any of my three boys to accompany me back to India either before the completion of the event. I decided to go back home all by myself.

Now, given the short notice, I couldn't get a direct flight back to India. I had to break journey via Heathrow. And this is where I found myself in a pickle because I could neither speak English, nor did I understand the language much. I couldn't comprehend anything after I landed in Heathrow. Which way to go, what to do, who to speak to, which flight to take next, how to get to the aircraft, I had absolutely no idea! I wondered why I had even thought of doing something like this in the first place. But I didn't have any alternative either. It was impossible for Nandita to leave the event midway just because I had some unfinished business to attend to. And even if one of my boys had accompanied me, it wouldn't have been of much help because none of them knew English either. There would have been two clueless people running from pillar to post in Heathrow airport instead of one.

However, just when I had almost given up hope, I noticed a person wearing a turban at one of the counters and rushed to him for help. In broken Hindi, I explained my plight to him and he patiently told me in broken Bengali what I had to do. He pointed to a certain location and asked me to go and sit there in front of the display board, watch out for my flight number and the gate number next to it and then take that gate when called upon to do so. I obeyed him to the letter and soon found myself on the correct flight flying back home. It was altogether a very memorable experience and I felt quite proud of myself when I finally landed in Kolkata.

Autumn of 2003

The environment in London was strikingly different from that of Ireland. When Nandita next offered me the project for the Mayor's Thames Festival in London, I jumped at the possibility, expecting an experience similar to the one we had had in Ireland. But I found Londoners far from friendly or hospitable and they lacked the vibrant curiosity of the Irish people. London was more formal and less warm. I didn't know their language, yet I could perceive the difference in their attitude. The contrast was palpable.

For the festival, we constructed an illuminated three-dimensional peacock boat of 6.2 miniatures. It was all Nandita's idea and it was supposed to symbolize the arrival of the East India Trading Company in India. This imposing barge was 25 feet tall with a massive sail, almost 12 feet wide and used 1,56,000 lamps. It was to travel through London along the banks of the river Thames on a flatbed truck with open sides. The then British High Commissioner, Sir Michael Arthur, paid a visit to my house in Kalupukur, Chandannagar, to have a glimpse of the peacock barge that was to be displayed in London two months later, while the entire neighbourhood flocked around my house for a glimpse of the European. Talk about priorities!

I wasn't nervous this time. My involvement in the Queen's University project had been an eye opener for me and had loosened me up a bit. Besides, I had both experience and skill backing me up this time.

One of the best things about London was that I made a friend there. A fellow electrician named George, around fifty-five years old, pink of skin and blonde, who often broke into fits of laughter and had a huge grin permanently on his lips. He owned a huge jeep in which one could find almost every kind of instrument and electrical spare part that has ever been made by humans! Always ready to help us in whatever way he could, he was like one of our own teammates, so warm and good humoured that the very sight of him could cheer my heart.

On the day the Thames Festival was about to take place, Nandita looked at the peacock boat critically and expressed her opinion with her eyebrows furrowed. 'Sridhar Da, it's beautiful! But there's one major flaw which we have overlooked.'

'What?' My heart seemed to come to a standstill.

'I'm afraid the sail won't pass under the bridges. It's too tall! And there are too many bridges on the route.'

She was right! It was a major oversight. And I just had a few hours to set it right.

I was so tense that I had to pee. I rushed to a public restroom, brainstorming all along the way, and that's when my eyes caught sight of the lifesaver. It was an instrument that resembled a car jack and had a long pole with a handle which could be rotated clockwise and anticlockwise to increase and decrease the length of the pole. No sooner had I spotted it from a distance in the hands of some construction site workers than I hurried to Nandita, showed her what I'd seen and told her that if we had to save the day, that's precisely what we needed, that blessed jack!

'We have to find that jack,' I told her. 'And we might need more than one.'

'Okay, let me see what I can do!'

Of course, we couldn't take that one, but George came to the rescue. He listened to our plight and within half an hour he arrived at the scene, with a couple of those jacks in his jeep.

I immediately set about working, first separating the sail from the barge and then fixing it to the jack. And then came the final stroke which was again a major game changer. Employing my common sense, I started thinking of my Indian Peacock as the Trojan Horse, put two of my boys inside the hollow belly of the peacock, with one of them assigned the responsibility of holding the jack and the other, of rotating the handle anti-clockwise whenever the truck was about to pass under any bridge, so that the sail came down by about five feet, and then rotating the handle clockwise so that the sail popped out again once the truck came out from under the bridge.

The banks of the river Thames were exploding with Londoners that evening. Several Indians stood in the crowd too and cheered till their voices were hoarse for my peacock barge as it passed them by. My work was the centrepiece of that pageant and became the talk of the whole city. Never in my life had I felt so proud of myself and my boys! Unable to control their emotions, they all came over to me, hugged me and cried when they looked down from the bridge on which we stood and saw our countrymen saluting our work. We didn't understand a word of what was being announced. We only looked at the jubilant faces of our people and let the sublime feeling of happiness wash away all the stress and anxiety we had felt up to that moment.

My peacock boat was such a hit that it was kept in London for two years, and displayed again at the Mayor's Thames Festival next year with some changes. It was also displayed in Blackpool, in the Winter Gardens auditorium for almost a month in the following year. And our names made their way to the headlines of *The Guardian* newspaper.

After my return from London, my house became a den of journalists and the media. Almost all the major national newspapers, *The Telegraph*, *The Times of India*, *The Statesman*, et cetera, flaunted my name in their headlines. My interviews were featured on the various news channels, and several documentaries were made on me. Celebrities visiting Chandannagar during the pujas would almost always drop in at my house for a chat.

My days were spent quite differently now. I was invited to most of the major cultural events and fairs hosted in and around Chandannagar either as a chief guest or as a judge. Prestigious corporate houses and organizers in Kolkata wanted me to judge the street lights of the various puja committees during the Durga Puja. I was flooded with new projects from the bigger metropolitan cities like Mumbai, Delhi and Chennai. My lights went overseas once again to Los Angeles and unlike the traditional methods that I had been asked to use for my projects in London and

Ireland, the people of Los Angeles preferred the modern, environment-friendly LED. I couldn't accompany Nandita this time because I had a number of important projects to take care of in the country. Besides, I had been forbidden by the doctors to undertake the long 23-hour flight since I had recently been diagnosed with a blockage in my heart. My boys had a great time and they couldn't stop bragging about their experience when they came back.

Some of the things about London I liked most were the streets. They were absolutely spick and span! The punctuality of the people amazed me. The way they took care of the environment and maintained the cleanliness of their surroundings was praiseworthy. I even saw the Mayor of London, Ken Livingstone, sweeping the street outside his house one day. The poor people in London never asked for alms. Some of them were really talented people who stood on the pavements or outside some monument, painting brilliant pictures or playing wonderful melodies on their violins or mouth organs. They usually had a contribution box close to them in which people dropped currency notes and coins of their own accord. In fact, 'artists' would be a more appropriate term for them because they earned their livelihood through their art, which is exactly what I did, too.

I still miss my old friend, George. Fifteen years have passed since we met and we haven't been in touch. He was one of the most good-humoured men I have ever come across in my life. We didn't understand each other's language, yet we travelled through the immaculate London streets, ate at different restaurants, smoked cigars and worked together with such camaraderie. We had a weird way of speaking with the help of signs and gestures. Whenever I wanted something to eat, I would rub my hands on my stomach and then point to a restaurant. He'd take me to that restaurant immediately and together we would examine the food. He would make his suggestions, pointing out various dishes that he thought I might like and I would think about it for a minute and then point at one of his recommendations. He'd order it for me and then we would eat it together, sometimes inside the restaurant, sometimes outside in his jeep. We had a lot of fun together. He is the one who made London feel like home to me.

On our parting day, George gifted me a pack of cigarettes, a brand that I had grown to like and which he knew wouldn't be easily available in India. I still remember how I treasured that pack of cigarettes, not consuming more than one or two each week and smoking each cigarette ever so slowly to savour it. It reminded me of the day when I was first allowed to have one full egg, the excitement, the thrill and how I had savoured every bite. I hadn't known back then that I would never have to pine for eggs again. Similarly, I have had several packs of Dunhill cigarettes later on in my life but I shall forever remember the day George introduced them to me inside a tiny shop along one of the many London streets.

The peacock barge at the Thames Festival was one of my most successful and celebrated projects, one for which I gained worldwide fame. Hence, London shall always occupy a special place in my heart.

Interlude

Nandita Palchoudhuri, for me, was the human embodiment of the word 'sophistication'. I had first met her when I was barely three years old and one of the main reasons why I still remembered her was because she had brought back a box of chocolates for me from London, the Toblerone bars being the ones I cherished the most.

She was and still is a cultural entrepreneur curating and consulting internationally in the field of Indian folk art, craft and performance practices. Tall and slender with straight, long black hair, dark, deep set eyes and dusky skin, she is perhaps the most dignified and elegant woman I have ever met, her knowledge and intellect surpassing that of everyone I have ever known.

I didn't know how to establish contact with her after almost seventeen years. I knew she was always extremely busy, constantly travelling abroad. Would she even remember me? Would she have the time to spare for me? My hands shook as I typed her a WhatsApp text.

The two gray ticks made my heart pound. She had definitely received my message. Now all I had to do was wait for her reply. Quite contrary to my expectations, the ticks turned blue in the very next minute, and prompt came her reply:

'Samragngi, I am the happiest person today! Please come over to Kolkata. Let's meet up, have lunch together and I'll help you in whatever way I can. I have the greatest respect for your grandfather and your family. You, I know since you did not know how to talk! And now you are writing a book!'

Her reply was so heart-warming that I almost did a little jig in my bedroom out of happiness! However, my college wouldn't open for another month, which meant that I wouldn't be traveling to Kolkata anytime soon. So, I had to talk to her over the telephone. I explained my plight to her. She seemed fine with it, promising to call me the next morning.

'How are you, ma'am?' I asked her when we had finally established contact. 'It's been such a long time!'

'I'm good, sweetheart! How are you?' she replied cheerfully.

'I'm great! But I hope it's convenient for you to talk right now?'

'Absolutely,' she said. 'So, how do you want this conversation to go? Do you want to ask me questions? Or do you want an overall opinion?'

'I have some questions that I would like to ask you,' I said. 'But I would like to know anything and everything you'd like to tell me about your experience with Grandpa.'

'Okay then, let's begin.'

I asked my first question. 'How did you get to know Grandpa?'

'Well, my work is to use traditional skills in a contemporary way,' she informed me. 'When I thought of doing something abroad with Chandannagar lights, I had some ideas in my mind. But then I didn't know who would make them. I started asking around in Kolkata, and the people there in the different Kolkata puja committees told me that the maximum illumination work was done by someone called Sridhar Das. I got your grandfather's telephone number from one of them and tried calling him but your grandfather never picked up the phone. So, I went to Chandannagar directly. I met him and told him about my idea. And what was fantastic was, even though the whole atmosphere of Chandannagar was very non-dynamic and unprofessional, he was refreshingly different.'

'How was he different?' I wanted to know.

'When I first met him, I expected he would tell me that he's a very busy person,' she laughed. 'I thought he would have no time for me and would probably find my plans and suggestions outrageous, being the celebrity he was. Because the kind of idea I had was completely different from what was being done in Chandannagar at that time.'

'You mean, your ideas for the Ireland Project?'

'Yes, for the Ireland Project,' she confirmed 'I wanted to organize a storytelling exhibition based on four or five events from the Ramayana and this was to take place in a huge gallery.'

'The Queen's University gallery?' I rechecked.

'Absolutely,' she stated. 'You know the lights I often used for story telling purposes were merely ornamental but this time I wanted to make the lights the primary attraction

of the event, something that people would come to see for themselves. So, I basically shifted the focus from lights being used for mere decoration to them being the primary attraction. This was to be a light exhibition where people would come and hear a story that would be told through your grandfather's lights.'

'Okay.'

'So, when I told Sridhar Da about this idea, he was so receptive that his eyes became bright and he smoked his cigarette even faster,' she laughed. 'He was so excited and happy! It was just the opposite of what I had expected. He said, "Of course, I'll do it! Tell me how you want me to go about it. I'll do whatever you ask me to." It was almost like I was giving him oxygen to breathe!'

I responded with a laugh.

'You know what, actually he was very bored at that time,' she explained. 'There was nothing new for him to do. His workers, Sujit and all, were running the show with Rustom, Mustafa and all those chaps. They were extremely efficient. He just had to supervise their work and give them the ideas. Do you remember those guys?'

'Yes, of course! I remember all of them.'

'They all knew what to do. He had made them experts. Your grandpa didn't have to do much except, you know, get the contracts, give them the ideas, and advise them on technical issues. So, when I approached him, he really rose to the occasion like I never imagined, to make all the designs and everything. We also had to consider that this whole structure would be out in the sea for two months and the simple miniatures would probably not be able to withstand the influence of saline water for so long.'

'Yes.'

'So, I had to do a lot of planning and thinking but I could do it only because Sridhar Da was always willing to listen to and approve of whatever mad idea I came up with. He was hugely receptive. And more than being receptive, he would come up with newer ideas than what I had told him. He was really in his element doing new things!'

'Yes, he's always liked experimenting with new ideas.'

'You know, one of the funniest things that happened as soon as we landed in Belfast was that the workers noticed how scarcely populated it was and I remember one of the chaps asking, "Is there some bandh going on here today?" And the way he said that had me in stitches!' she chortled, remembering the old times. 'However, the programme was a great success and it was broadcast on the television, it came out in the newspapers and the visitors wrote excellent reviews about the light show.'

'So, these were the Ramayana panels?'

'Not just Ramayana panels but also panels on Diwali, the different firecrackers and how Diwali came into being. "What is Diwali in India?" was the topic we were looking at. How Diwali is celebrated and why it is celebrated. Also, the panels were free standing, they were not stuck on the walls. You could move the panels anywhere as per your convenience.'

'And what about the peacock barge?'

'That was placed on a flatbed truck and it went through the centre of London,' she explained. 'We made the whole design in Chandannagar and the British High Commissioner even went to see it.'

'Grandfather told me about that.'

'The barge that we did in London was taken to Blackpool too. Blackpool is actually the place where the 6.2 miniatures and all the other kinds of lamps originated but they worked with fixed lamps. Chandannagar has taken it all light years ahead by animating the lamps. Which is why your grandfather is called the pioneer. He's the first one who came up with the idea of moving lights and taught the world how they could be used for elaborate designs and themes. However, Blackpool hadn't been able to make much progress on that front. The barge was taken to Blackpool to mark the 125th year of lights in Blackpool. It was displayed in the Winter Gardens auditorium.'

'So, Grandpa worked in London, Belfast and Blackpool.'

'And Durham,' she added.

'What did he do in Durham?'

'There's a huge seventeenth century heritage bridge in Durham known as the Elvet Bridge,' she informed me. 'We worked there for the Enlightenment Festival. Your grandfather decorated the two enormous gates on either end of that bridge.'

'And what was done in Los Angeles?'

'It was a huge three-dimensional figure of the doll Bula Di,' she told me. 'It was part of my project with UCLA when the HIV awareness campaigns were going on. Bula Di was a doll who appeared in television and radio commercials to educate the people in West Bengal about HIV transmission and prevention. Sridhar Da made a three-dimensional figure of Bula Di and decorated it with LED lights.'

'What was your experience of working with my grandfather?' I asked my final question.

'He is the most interesting, innovative and intelligent man I have ever come across,' she said. 'He should have been a scientist! Once, in London, when the truck was loaded with the peacock barge, we discovered that the sail of the barge was too high. And because London is full of bridges, the height of the sail had to be very low to go under the bridge. When I told him about it, in just a few hours' time, he did something that made the sail go down under the bridge and come back up again when the bridge was crossed.'

'Yes, I have heard about that.'

'Then there was this man, this British electrician who befriended Sridhar Da. I don't remember his name. Together they used to ride in his jeep, puffing companionably on their cigarettes. They didn't understand each other's language, but they didn't require translation either. They were almost like long-lost brothers!'

I didn't think talking to Nandita ma'am would be so smooth and effortless. She had so much to say and so much that she still remembered that I hardly had to ask any questions. I invited her over to our place at the end of the conversation which she readily agreed to and at the same time expressed her disappointment for not visiting us sooner.

'I should have gone to Chandannagar months ago,' she sighed. 'I would get to eat the mangoes from your orchard! I never had to yearn for mangoes back then. Your grandfather used to send me loads of them.'

A Month Later

'What are you doing?' my father asked me as I sat on the living room couch staring at my laptop screen. He had just returned home from one of his business tours.

'I'm thinking of how to begin Grandpa's story,' I replied, without looking up. 'I don't know where to start.'

'Ah, the book? Your mother told me about it. I'm really glad that you're doing it.'

'How was your tour?' I looked up at him now and smiled. 'Did you have fun?'

'You know I can't have fun without you all. If anything at all, it was very hectic. You look a lot happier than before.'

'Yeah, I am happier, Dad,' I smiled. 'I've finally found a purpose.'

'Well, if you need any help,' he said. 'I'm here.'

'If you have any information about Grandfather which you think would be interesting, please tell me. That would be a great help.'

He thought about it for a while and replied. 'Well, there are a few things. But I'm afraid they're not about his struggles or achievements. Do you think that will be of any help?'

'What are they about?' I asked curiously.

'They're about certain peculiar traits that I have noticed in him,' he said. 'Certain things he's done which I've never been able to figure out why.'

'Are they good or bad?'

'Eccentric,' he stated in one word. 'You can never pin that man down.'

'What do you mean?'

'Well, let me give you a simple example,' said my dad, sitting beside me on the couch, still in his suit and tie.

'Wait a second,' I stopped him, fishing for my phone. 'Let me switch on my recorder first.'

'Now that's going to be weird.'

'Absolutely not. This is how I have interviewed everyone.'

'I feel like some University lecturer now,' laughed Dad.

'Now let's begin,' I said excitedly.

'I'd heard a lot about your grandfather before I met him,' said my dad. 'Everyone knew him and spoke highly of him. Naturally, I had formed my opinion based on what people said. But when I saw him for the very first time, I was shocked.'

'Why?'

'Because he didn't seem like he was such a renowned person at all!' replied my father. 'I had imagined it all very differently in my head and was nervous to meet him. But when I finally did, I was as surprised as I was relieved. He was wearing a very old and simple button-down shirt and a loose pair of threadbare trousers which, I was certain, were over a decade old. He had this careless appearance of a starving artist that just didn't fit the image of a successful man. I never saw him wearing anything formal unless he had some big event to attend. And even for those events, he had this one royal blue blazer which he wore everywhere. If you look at his old photos, you'll see him wearing the same blazer to every event.'

'Well, he's still that way, isn't he?'

'Yes, but he stays at home now,' he replied. 'You can

wear anything at home, nobody will raise any objection. But when I first met him, he used to be extremely busy, always out and about. He was hardly home. And that's how he always dressed, wherever he went.'

'Even now he wears the same blue cotton shirt to every interview,' I added. 'And when a journalist comes home, he sits in his office, amidst all his awards, wearing that old, discoloured blue shirt and a lungi *below. I've told him many times to wear something nice, at least a pair of trousers. But he says it's of no use because only his top half will be visible above the table and he feels more confident answering questions in his* lungi*.'*

My father laughed uncontrollably at that. 'I know that famous blue shirt. His brother, Ganesh Kaka, gifted him that on his seventieth birthday.'

'Yes, it's been so many years but he just won't let go of it.'

'Back then, he also rode a very old Bajaj scooter which you could hear approaching from five kilometres away,' my father added, chuckling. 'It was quite legendary around these areas. In other words, if you didn't know him and just randomly ran into him on the streets, you would never believe that he was such a big shot. He looked so ordinary and down-to-earth.'

I nodded.

'Yet he had a very strong personality and I could instantly get a whiff of that when I finally got an opportunity to speak to him,' said my father. 'He seemed like a very straightforward, no-nonsense sort of a person. He didn't like people who beat around the bush and he had absolutely no problem speaking his mind. One thing I have always admired in him is that he never tried to be anything he wasn't.'

'That's right.'

'You know, one day he caught a young boy stealing a box of lamps from his store. Do you know what your grandfather did?'

'You said he's eccentric,' I told him, scratching my head with the butt of my pencil. 'Mom said he was indifferent to whoever tried to do him any wrong. She said that he barely even acknowledged it. So, I think maybe... he just ignored him and continued whatever he was doing.'

'No, he went up to him and caught his hand,' said my father. 'And then he told him not to sell those lamps but to rent them to people instead, because that way he could earn more money from the lamps, and over a longer period of time. He then gave him a few extra lamps too, the spare ones that he had lying around in his factory.'

'What?' The shock was evident on my face.

'Yes,' my father laughed. 'Can you believe it? He didn't just let the thief get away but also advised him as to how he could profit from what he had stolen.'

'That is hilarious!'

'Whenever someone came to him asking for help, he bought them food and groceries and whatever else they needed besides giving them money. Once during the puja season, he came back home late in the afternoon and had just sat down to lunch after a very exhausting morning. He had barely even touched his plate when an old man came knocking at the door asking for some food. Guess what he did?'

'He offered his share of food to the old man. I think I have heard that from Grandma before.'

'Exactly!' said my father, 'People often came to him for help. Some had ailing family members, some wanted money for their children's education, some simply belonged to rackets. Your grandfather was very generous to those that came saying they needed money for their children's education. That was one soft spot that he had. Perhaps because he realized the importance of a formal education later in his life. Had your grandfather received a formal education he would definitely have made significant scientific discoveries by now.'

'That's true,' I reflected.

'Those that came to him asking for money for ailing family members, he went after them or sent one of his boys after them to investigate whether there was really an ailing family member or not. And more than often, in such situations, his boys would be deserted in the middle of the streets by those men. But if they really found an ailing person, your grandfather would do everything he could to get them proper treatment and buy them the prescribed medicines.'

'That was so nice of him.'

'Your grandfather was very selective about who he gave alms to,' replied my father. 'Mostly he offered to buy them food, clothes, medicines, and tried to fulfil their needs. But when he came across able-bodied people, he offered to employ them to work for him. He separately arranged for their food and lodging, and stood by them if there was any crisis in their families. Many such people are in the industry now. They have all learnt the work and are now very successful.'

'Yes, I think I know some of them too.'

'There's something funny which I just remembered,' said my dad and smiled a little at the recollection. 'You see the debdaru trees planted on either side of the street outside?'

'Those that are planted along the street till Jhapantala?'

'Yes, those were planted by your grandfather with the Mayor's consent. Eighty beautiful debdaru trees, forty of them planted on either side of the street. They were supposed to enhance both the look of the street as well as keep the air clean around here. So, once there was this unruly neighbour who expressed his disapproval and chopped off a tree planted near his house. When your grandfather went to enquire why he had done that, the man misbehaved and questioned his authority. Your grandfather went straight to the Mayor, lodged a complaint against him, and then he along with his boys went to that neighbour's place, slammed the Mayor's notice on his table, and planted another, larger tree on the same spot.'

I couldn't help but double up with laughter on the couch.

'What are you two laughing about?' my mother, who had stepped out to fetch my dad a cup of tea from the kitchen, demanded to know.

'Daddy was telling me about how quirky Grandpa was,' I told her, still chuckling.

'What kind of quirks?'

I told her in brief about the incidents that my father had just narrated to me.

'Oh, there are many more!' said my mother, settling on one of the chairs. 'Did you know that once your grandfather, acting on a bet that he had entered into with his friends, spent an entire night alone in a graveyard?'

'No, I had no idea!' I exclaimed. 'And what was his reaction the next morning?'

'Nothing,' replied my mother. 'Absolutely nothing! He wasn't scared at all. He hadn't seen any ghosts. He was completely fine. Came back home next morning with innovative ideas for his projects and said he really relished the peace and quiet. And then he started sleeping alone on the terrace every night.'

I felt a shiver run down my spine. I had heard stories about a brahmadaitya, *the spirit of a murdered Brahmin, who haunted the big wood-apple tree in our neighbour's compound. We could often hear loud footsteps from the terrace at night and Grandma often said that it was actually the* brahmadaitya *walking. Many people in the neighbourhood had reported seeing him. A man from Chowdhury Bagan had even fainted because apparently the bored spirit had asked him some juicy questions while he walked past the tree. When I was a child, I couldn't even dream of going to the terrace all alone late in the evening, let alone sleep there at night. But as I grew older, I started believing less and less in that story. However, there was a part of me, a residue from my childhood perhaps, which was apprehensive at the mention of that wood-apple tree.*

'Did he ever see the brahmadaitya*?' I asked.*

'Nope,' my mother replied. 'He saw a huge civet instead and threw a pillow at it. But that didn't stop the civet from visiting him every night. I think he eventually started feeding it.'

'Wow!' I chuckled. 'He's one of a kind, seriously.'

'When I was young,' my mother continued, 'my father

hardly bought me new clothes before the puja. My mother had just a few sarees which she wore. Whenever she had to go out somewhere, I had to drop in at one of my aunt's places and borrow some sarees and ornaments for her. She wore their clothes and jewellery whether she liked them or not.'

'Why didn't he buy her stuff?'

'He would always be rolling his money back into business,' replied my mother. 'Or investing in small plots of land. Land was comparatively cheaper back in those days. He didn't like unnecessary spending.'

'That was a very wise and economical decision on his part,' my father interrupted to say.

'Don't talk about being economical while you're spoiling your kids with unnecessary items every other day,' said my mother.

My father and I exchanged glances.

'I don't think I'm spoiling my kids,' my dad said. 'I'm just trying my best to be a good father. There might be times when I go overboard. But all I want is for them to feel happy and loved. And I've missed you all so much for the last couple of days!'

'So, what have you brought back for me?' my mother teased. 'You brought two boxes of chocolate for your son. A new bag for your daughter. What about your wife?'

My dad coughed in reply. And then he said, with a mischievous glint in his eyes, 'Look in the other fridge.'

My mother looked at him doubtfully, but there was a hint of pleasure in her smile which made it clear that she was secretly impressed. She strode with an air of self-satisfaction towards the fridge, opened one of the doors and let out a happy little scream.

'Almond cubes and cream rolls!' she beamed, holding the bright pink box from Flury's in her hands like an award. 'I've been looking for cream rolls everywhere. I thought they didn't make them anymore. How did you find them?'

'Seek and you shall find,' my father responded proudly.

'He's not just a good dad, but a good life partner too,' I told her.

I could see the child in my mother as she impatiently bit into the almond cube and then relished it with her eyes closed. 'Thank you, honey!' she uttered through her mouthful of cake.

'That will keep her preoccupied for a while,' I whispered to my dad. 'Please continue what you were saying.'

'Well, I don't remember what I was saying,' my dad stroked his chin, a little embarrassed. 'Oh yes… I remember!'

'Great! Go on, I'm listening.'

'I admit I'm not a very good investor,' he began. 'However, that doesn't stop me from appreciating your grandfather and wanting to be like him. In fact, what I admired the most about him was that he didn't squander his money in keeping up appearances or showing off how much wealth he had. He invested it all, thinking about the future, for us, for you and Bonny.'

'Yeah, he has never been extravagant. That's true.'

'Simple living and high thinking, that was his mantra. I've always wanted to be like him.'

'Your grandfather definitely believed in simple living and high thinking,' my mother chimed in, finishing her almond

cube. 'But at the same time, he was also conscious of the fact that important dignitaries often paid us a visit. So, an outward show of affluence was expected of him, which is why he made this house and bought a second-hand car even when he did not have the means to. Since he borrowed a lot of money, he knew how to value money. He never spent it on useless things. Nevertheless he was very generous and maintained a large family.'

I nodded.

'Your grandfather wasn't only an artist,' Dad piped in. 'But he also had a pretty strong business acumen.'

'He definitely did,' my mother agreed.

'If you look at it closely,' my father turned to face my mother, 'you'll realize that your father never kept any idle cash, he was continuously either rolling the money back into the business or investing it instead of wasting it all on clothes and cars and luxury. He was amazingly farsighted too. He went about securing not only his future but also ours. Till today he gives sound financial advice. We ought to give him credit for that.'

'My father would have gladly kicked me out of the house and adopted you as his only son had he met you in the late 1980s,' commented my mother, breaking a cream roll into half. 'Anyway, now I have to go help Bonny pack his bag for school tomorrow. You two continue your discussion.'

'Well, Dad, is there anything else that you remember?'

'That is all I can remember right now,' replied Dad, standing up. 'But I'll let you know the moment I remember something interesting. I'll go take a shower now. It's been a hectic day. Three flights in a row.'

'Sure, and thank you so much, Dad!' I expressed my gratitude. 'This was one of the best discussions I had about Grandpa. It's exactly what I needed.'

'You're very welcome,' he smiled warmly at me. 'Let me know if you need my help with anything else.'

13

My Grandfather's Reflections

As the light in my eyes grows dim and the myriad memories of the past seventy-six years suddenly come knocking at my door, I don't know how to entertain them. Should I let them in? Or do I not answer the door? I was afraid to decide. But there you stood, looking at me expectantly. Your cheeks devoid of colour. And your smile, not as bright as it used to be. 'I haven't been feeling well lately,' you told me. It broke my heart into a million shards, and that's when I knew the decision was not mine to make. I opened the door, I let the memories in. I would do anything to help you heal.

It was because looking at you, I didn't see a nineteen-year-old woman. I saw my little angel, wrapped in an orange towel, wriggling in my arms, just an hour after she was delivered. Your large, dark eyes adorned with thick lashes, were the most beautiful I had ever beheld. They seemed to light up the entire hospital room! Your faint cry was almost inaudible and yet so pleasing to my ears, like the chiming of bells. It touched a chord in my heart. It was such a strange feeling. So frail and delicate you were! So absolutely perfect yet so defenceless. I knew not when a tear had sneaked out through the corner of my eye and splattered conspicuously on the tip of your little nose. That's when I realized with a pang that I'd never felt for my own daughter the way I felt for you on that cold, blue February morning.

That's when I knew you were mine to protect, nurture, cherish and be proud of. So, what if I hadn't been able to be a good father? I could still be a good grandfather!

'Sumitra! What a beautiful little girl she is!' I remember calling up your grandmother soon after. 'So fair! Such large eyes! And she's got so much hair on her head, you won't believe me until you see her with your own eyes!'

'All that is fine,' your grandmother's anxious voice crackled through my old cellular phone. 'But what about our daughter? Have you seen her? Is she alright?'

'What are you saying? I can't hear you!'

'What about Mini?' she screamed. 'Is our Mini alright?'

'I… I don't really know. I have to go check.'

'You didn't ask about your daughter? What kind of a weird person are you?'

'Ah! Don't worry, she must be alright! What can possibly go wrong? Why do you panic all the time?'

'Please, go check on Mini and call me immediately.'

The memories have refused to settle, they linger around me. Their voices have an unusual quality, they drown me in a drowsy stupor. And as I give in to the lull, the past comes back to life once again. Several images, several sights, sounds and emotions whizz past me like speeding bullets casting technicolour shadows.

'Boiled eggs for lunch! One for each!' I can see myself crying out loud. It is probably the earliest memory I have.

I see Vikash, wrapping his arm around my shoulder. I see his face, his smile, his clear, sparkling eyes. 'You can do it, Sridhar!' I hear him say. I can smell the fragrance of his hair oil, feel the freshness of his clothes and the way my heart leaped whenever he dived in for a hug. The images flash one after another in an unrestrained way. I see him as a teen, a young man, a husband, a father, a dear friend, a middle-aged man standing on the threshold of death and finally I see an old picture of him hanging on the wall, with a string of flowers suspended from its frame. It hits me hard. My best friend who had once promised me that he would never let go of my hand, had suddenly ceased to be. It has taken me several years to let that sink in and I have never been the same since. It brought me closer to the truth that one day I too will have to share the same fate. I too will be enclosed within the frame of a picture, a few old photographs, newspapers, documentaries and awards.

When I first succeeded with the underwater lights, I remember coming back home all happy and glowing. My mother looked at me through the corner of her eyes. She didn't utter a word of encouragement. Instead, she complained that my elder brother hadn't yet received his salary from the mill and that the household had run out of groceries. I laid all my hard-earned money at her feet, expecting to see a smile light up her face, expecting her to be proud of me, expecting her gentle hands to caress my head affectionately. I wanted to tell her, 'Look, Mother, I made it!' She simply kept the money aside and sat there in the kitchen, kneading the dough, while I saw my tiny expectation go up in flames.

That was one thing I could never quite figure out. Why was my mother so cold to me? How could she treat one son with so much indifference while showering abundant love and affection on all the others? Was it because I didn't work in the jute mill? Was it because I had married Sumitra against her will? But that was much later. What exactly was the cause of her grievance? The memory of her face, her eyes cold and hard, her unmoving lips and relentless indifference gives my old nerves a shudder. She was the only person I had ever tried to impress. And I had failed, every single time. I try to close my mind to the oddly unsettling memories of my mother, but they sit there still, staring back at me. I can feel their cold eyes boring deep into my head like razor-sharp icicles. Now that she too was gone, will I never find closure? Have I unknowingly treated my daughter the same way?

I have had seventy-six eventful years. Not all these years were the same. They arrived with their own share of ups and downs, they were laden with sorrows and joys, triumphs and failures. But what I had learnt at a very young age was that nothing in life comes for free, definitely not the good things! Everything must be paid for one day with something or the other. Everything arrives with a price tag. And sacrifice is often the only acceptable currency.

My struggles are over, my little one. I have paid my price. My days are numbered, the light in my eyes shall soon fade away, my body shall wilt and turn to dust but your life has just begun. You have several mountains to climb, several oceans to cross, several milestones to reach and hurdles to overcome. You won't always succeed but you must make sure that you never give up. There will be good days and bad, days of sunshine and days of rain, and nights that bring impenetrable darkness. There will be phases when everything goes wrong, and even your most loved ones will refuse to have your back, your most trusted accomplice will give you away, and that is when you will feel like giving up. But don't. Don't give up. Hold on. Hold on just a little longer. Better days lurk right around the corner. Get up and keep walking. You'll soon get there.

When you asked me this morning, 'Grandpa, now that you have accomplished all your goals, how do you feel?' I shied away from telling you the truth. I was afraid I might break down and end up making you sad again. The truth, my dear, is not easy to articulate, or even accept. If there's anything that rules my thoughts right now, it is the haunting fear of death. Death, the ultimate truth, the one reality we can only ignore but never avoid. Each day, with every breath I take, I can see myself inching closer to that reality. And every night, when I close my eyes to sleep, I close my eyes to the fear of never waking up again. Death in sleep would probably be the easiest and most painless way to die but the very thought of never opening my eyes to see you again is unbearable.

I don't want to leave you. You are the reason I'm still alive. You are the one who has pushed me on and on to be better each day. When I was young, my work was all

I lived for. It's what gave me a purpose. But ever since I retired, you are the one who has given me hope and a purpose to keep going.

'You are really a wizard, Dadu!' I can still hear your shrill voice as you cried in happiness after the success of my Nursery Rhymes procession.

Your grandmother often tells me that you are probably my mother, reincarnated as my granddaughter. She tells me that my mother has come back to this world again to pay her dues. I never believed her because I have never believed in the concept of the afterlife.

From a little new-born, I have seen you grow. You've always been very different, unique. All you cared about is your story books, your brother, and the medals you won each year from school. I remember how years ago you stood in the middle of my office one day, and with your hands on your hips, declared, 'One day my prizes will outnumber yours!'

And when I asked you what you wanted to be when you grew up, you thought about it for a very long time and said, 'I want to be a farmer. I want to have my own little farm! Like the children of Willow Farm!'

'What?' I had asked.

'The children of Willow Farm! They're my best friends!'

'Are they from the book you've been reading?'

'Yes!' you had replied, your eyes large and glittery. 'But they are real! They are all real to me!'

I still see you dancing in the little plot of land I later bought and turned into a tiny farm for your sake. I installed a swing, a slide and see-saw there too, because you loved frequenting the parks in the Strand Road. I see you lying down under the mango trees and posing for pictures. I see you watering the plants, tending to the flowers, drenching yourself at the sprinklers. I see you waiting for the lemons to grow and the tomatoes to turn red. I see you swinging higher and higher, sliding down the tunnel slide and balancing your way along the whole length of the see-saw, unafraid. I hear your little voice that was so sweet to my ears, your lilting laughter that always sounded like the chiming of bells. I see you evolve from a baby to an adult. Now that I've let the memories in, they don't want to leave.

I want to live to see you living your dreams. I want to live to see you become a writer and publish many books. I want to live to be a great-grandfather, with my great-grandchildren sitting on my lap, playing with my laurels. I want to see your awards outnumber mine and your name shine like the brightest star in the sky. But it all seems impossible. I don't have the slightest doubt as far as your capabilities are concerned but it's just that I'm not sure of myself anymore.

'Just one more year,' is what I tell myself each day. I don't want to think of the time when I'd have to say, 'Just one more day,' because it terrifies me.

They say that the novelty of being a celebrity wears off eventually. Is that why all my achievements mean nothing to me now? All the days that I spent being a celebrity, the nights I spent working in my factory while your grandma slept alone, come back to ridicule me. I wish I had spent more time with you when you were a kid. I wish I had spent more time with my family when I was a young man.

I wish I had been a more affectionate and appreciative father, a more caring husband who expressed his love to his wife more often. I wish I had been able to strike a balance between my personal life and my professional life. But that's the price I paid. That's the life I sacrificed. Today, I can't help asking myself every now and then, 'Was it all worth it? Did I pay too high a price?' I think I have an answer, an answer I'm not brave enough to acknowledge.

I have never believed in the afterlife. But as I grow older, I can't help hoping for one. What scares me more is the fact that I don't know where I am going. Is it a happy place? Is it somewhere I can start my life anew? Is it somewhere I'll get to meet all my friends who have left me? If there's a place like that, I'd definitely like to be a part of it. However, only after I've been cleansed of all my earthly memories, because I cannot possibly live there happily without you, without my family.

All my life I've only prayed for one thing, and that is to leave the world before any of my loved ones did. And now that my time has come and my days are numbered, I don't want to go. I want to live my life all over again, not as a busy man with no time to spare but as a simple man who can cherish the little things that life has to offer. But that goes against the laws of Nature.

Thank you for being my hope, for loving me in a way no one ever did, for making me feel like a star even when my light was on the wane, for making me feel like a 'wizard'. Thank you for usurping all my interviews and wanting to draw all my new designs, for accompanying me to all the awards functions. Thank you for giving me a taste of what a simple life looks like. It's in you that I have been able to experience all the little joys of life that I had missed out on during my youth. It's in you that I have seen my daughter grow. It's for you that I want to hold on to life endlessly.

We can't have the best of both worlds. And even though I've missed out on most of the simple joys of life, I know that when I'm gone, I'll be remembered. The industry that I once started with three empty tins and a bunch of cellophane papers will continue generating livelihoods and feeding thousands of families. They still come to me, the younger chaps, the ones who dream of making it big in the industry someday. They touch my feet and seek my blessings before all their important undertakings. And every time it brings tears to my eyes as I behold the dreams sparkling in theirs and I wish them well from the bottom of my heart. My successors shall carry forward my legacy. Chandannagar shall always occupy a place in the pages of history and automatic lighting will never go out of fashion. My house will always be a landmark and my name shall never fade into anonymity. I'll live as long as this industry lives and they will always remember me. And what has it been, if it hasn't been a life worth living?

I would like to think that when I die, I'll still be alive. Alive in every hand that has ever nailed copper plates on rollers, twisted the leads of the LED, or wrapped a piece of cellophane over a miniature. Alive in every procession panel and every glowing mechanical figure that ever traverses the streets of Chandannagar. Alive in you and alive in your words if they ever find their way to print. Alive in all my laurels and certificates. Alive in every newspaper that ever bore my name.

Alive in memory. Alive in art.

Epilogue

People of my town usually dress up gorgeously during the Jagadhatri Puja. They discard their regular T-shirts, ripped jeans, casual clothing and splurge on traditional, ethnic outfits and accessories. Everything, starting from the strands of their hair to the nails on their feet sparkle and shimmer like the dazzling lights that festoon the streets and enliven every nook and cranny of my beloved town. Amidst the ceaseless inflow of tourists and visitors, the familiar arrival and departure announcements at the railway station, the streets bustling with people, kids running helter-skelter in their new outfits, vendors with their colourful wares displayed on the pavements, through the burgeoning explosion of balloons and candy floss, cartoon masks and soap bubbles, the sound of plastic whistles and toy guns, the rhythm of the *dhaak*, the smell of flowers and incense, I walked the streets.

It was Nabami, the fourth and the last day of the puja, and I was dressed in a baggy T-shirt and jeans. I didn't mean to look odd, it's just that every time I dressed up in flashy clothes or wore makeup and accessories, I felt so conscious of my appearance that I failed to absorb the essence of the puja. Since it only happened once a year for four days which seemed to pass by in the blink of an eye, I wasn't prepared to let it slip by this time.

'Hey, Sammy!' I heard a familiar voice call.

I turned around to see a bunch of familiar faces, all smiling brightly back at me.

'Hey guys!' I was surprised. 'How have you been?'

'How have *you* been?' they asked me.

'It's been two years since we left school and you never bothered to keep in touch!' one of them complained.

'I changed my phone and lost all my contacts,' I explained.

'No! You can't pull that off this time!' another one said. 'We are not stupid!'

'And you're not even on Facebook or Instagram!' added another. 'What's the matter with you?'

'Nothing's the matter,' I replied.

They were all dressed up, looking beautiful in their gorgeous kurtas and designer sarees. Next to them, I couldn't help but feel a little underdressed. But it was okay. I was comfortable in my own skin and that's all that mattered.

'Why don't you join us? Let's do some pandal hopping together.'

'I actually have some plans tonight,' I replied, remembering that I had to talk to grandfather about a few things. 'But let's fix a date and meet up after the puja, shall we?'

Even though I had social anxiety, one thing that I was

really good at was masking it. I could talk to others just fine when I had to.

'Of course! You give me your number, I'll add you to our WhatsApp group and we'll fix a date,' said my friend.

I didn't know if I wanted to be added to a group. I liked a calm WhatsApp environment where I wouldn't be flooded with notifications.

However, my old friends were being exceptionally nice to me and I had no reason to act like a jerk and withhold my phone number. I told myself that it wouldn't do me any harm to keep in touch with a handful of people, and one meet-up with my old school friends wouldn't be too stressful. So, I gave them my number. At that moment, all I was concerned about was the puja. The clock was ticking and soon the sun would be setting the eastern sky on fire, the idols would be loaded onto the trucks, the street lights would be taken down, the stalls along the streets would be wheeled away and the town, now all ablaze with the lights of revelry, would stretch its tired limbs, turn over and go to sleep. Soon it would all be over. I could feel the urgency. It was unnerving. So, I quickly bade them a fond goodbye and walked on.

As I walked, I realized that I had changed. I had started interviewing my grandfather to keep myself preoccupied but it ended up working wonders for my mental health, pulling me out of the darkness that I had unwittingly plunged into. This had been my hope all along but I wasn't sure if it would be feasible. It was only afterwards that I realized how spending time with my grandfather had altered the whole course of my life.

So, there I was, out on the bustling streets, being unapologetically me. The lights all around me were mesmerizing. Even though none of those panels were made by my grandfather, I could see his imprint emblazoned on each one of them. The Chandannagar Jagadhatri Puja procession, with its grand display of lights, is believed to be the second longest procession in the world after the Rio De Janeiro carnival. I wondered what would have happened if my grandfather had given up. I wondered what would have happened if he had taken the mill job instead, or deterred by all the criticisms and obstacles, he had quit working. Would the Jagadhatri Puja be half as glorious and celebrated as it presently was? It wasn't likely.

My grandfather had turned a blind eye to whoever tried to humiliate him, paid a deaf ear to all the criticisms and ignored the people who tried to do him harm. He kept his focus intact, had confidence in his own abilities and always tried to come up with something bigger and better, something new. And that's what took him so far.

'Quitting is easy,' he had said in one of his interviews. 'Bouncing right back up after the greatest fall takes real guts. Begin again right from scratch even when all the odds are against you. It's only when we're able to put all our inhibitions and inconveniences on the backseat and accept the truth that good things never come easy that we can achieve anything worthwhile in life.'

Tiny carousels and Ferris wheels were installed along some of the streets and the line of kids and toddlers waiting for their turns was never ending. The people in charge of the stalls selling chaat, bhelpuri, jhalmuri and fuchkas always had their hands full. The smell of samosas and jalebis could make one's mouth water but I was more drawn to the ice creams and popsicles even though there was a chill in the air and my throat was sore.

Before I went back home that night, I visited the ostentatious puja pandal next to my house for one last time. As I made my way through the entrance, I could hear the *dhaakis* still playing their *dhaaks* and it made me extremely nostalgic. It reminded me of how I used to be a Kumari when I was a child. Any girl child from the age of five to ten could be chosen as a Kumari and be Maa Jagadhatri's representative on earth for a day. For four consecutive years from age five to age nine, every Nabami morning I used to sit at the feet of the idol all dolled up in a saree and garlands, and was worshipped alongside the Goddess. The *dhaakis* would play their *dhaaks*, the priest would chant his mantras, the people attending the puja would touch my feet, seek my blessings and place their offerings in front of me, and that would make me feel important and honoured. But later on I was disgusted to learn that in most of the mandaps, being a Kumari was something that was restricted only to savarna children and in many cases, specifically Brahmins. As a child, I knew nothing about these things which is why my excitement about the puja was of a different kind altogether. Besides, back then my grandfather was still in business, he illuminated the streets every year, won several prizes, celebrities often paid a visit to our house, clicked pictures with me but more than any of those things, it was the Kumari Puja that I looked forward to every year. It made me feel close to the Goddess, as though She and I were almost one.

I was inside the pandal now. It was teeming with people. And there She was, Maa Jagadhatri, almost 25 feet high, sitting on Her ferocious blue-eyed lion, looking resplendent in Her gorgeous red Banarasi saree and heavy golden jewellery. For one last time, I looked into Her large, hypnotic eyes and then I joined my hands, closed my eyes and bowed my head in prayer. She already knew what I wanted. She always did.

And then I walked back home.

'Hey, look! That's Sridhar Das' house!' I heard someone on the street say as I opened the front gate. They all turned to look at me curiously. I smiled at them, they smiled back and then I went inside.

This wasn't unusual, but every time someone said that while passing by our house, it made me smile. Who could have imagined that the boy who dropped out of school at the age of fourteen would be a household name someday? Albert Einstein had once famously said, 'The true sign of intelligence is not knowledge but imagination.' Knowledge isn't something my grandfather had to begin with. All he possessed was imagination and the willingness to back it up with hard work. Imagination showed him the way, timely action made him grab every opportunity and knowledge chased him of its own accord. There must be a number of people like my grandfather who have contributed to society in their own little ways but have never really been acknowledged. Nevertheless, as Longfellow had once written, they have all left their 'footprints on the sands of time'.

The sun rose the next morning and it was a brand-new

day. A brand-new start. I was happy to be alive. It was Dashami, the day of immersion. I woke up early and was determined to be productive. Leaving the warmth of my bed, I went to wash my face. When I looked in the mirror, I couldn't help noticing with a bit of self-satisfaction how the colour had returned to my cheeks. And a sudden feeling of warm delight hit me like a wave and left me feeling light and happy. I didn't want to disturb it. Was the dark cloud of gloom finally lifted off my head?

Coffee was ready, my laptop was charged, the weather was incredible. I looked out of the window and saw two little puppies playing in the middle of the street without any care in the world. The structures of bamboo planted along the streets were being taken down for the procession. The sun was still hidden behind some clouds but the sky was streaked red and orange. The early birds were twittering and chirping as they welcomed the new day. And there I was, sitting by the window in my cozy recliner gazing at them all with a desire to seize the day, a desire to make the most of my life, like my grandfather did.

Why was I ever depressed? I didn't have an answer to that. Perhaps I'll write about it all someday. But that day wasn't today. Every narrative doesn't need a perfect resolution.

While I sipped on my cup of coffee, I couldn't help being a little proud of myself. I recalled the darkness that my grandpa had also recently plunged into along with me, the phase where he couldn't remember little things, couldn't express what he had in his mind clearly and just slept in his dark room all day. And when I look at him now, I can see a whole new person. I see a person who can stand tall once again, a person who went out on his own, riding his bike to meet one of his old friends, and then came back home safe and sound a little before 10 p.m. looking confident and unperturbed.

Seeing my grandfather healthy and hearty once again gave me a new lease of life. And knowing his story changed me as a person. It gave me a new perspective on life. I did not want to let life pass me by. He had once told me that we never get exactly what we desire. 'We get what we deserve. And what we deserve depends on what we think we deserve. So, always dream bigger, be willing to walk the extra mile and don't stop until you've reached your goal.'

When I had asked why he never took action against his enemies, his reply was, 'Forgive and forget. Nursing a grudge is unhealthy. It consumes your creative juice and prevents you from letting your imagination fly. Besides, we all have a very short time here on this planet and living each day itself is a miracle. Forgive them. You never know what the next moment has in store either for you or for them. Every individual is fighting his or her own battle. Live and let live.'

I switched on my phone and was surprised when I saw the WhatsApp notification that said '122 new messages.' I opened WhatsApp and realized that I had been added to a new group by the friends I met last night, a group with forty-eight members in it. I opened the group and was blown away by the number of people talking about me. They were all waiting for me to make my presence felt in the group and answer their questions regarding my whereabouts, how I'd been, how things were at Jadavpur University and if I was still single. With a smile on my face, I tried to reply to all their curious enquiries and, for the first time, I felt strangely happy about getting in touch with them again.

And then I heard my grandfather's voice in the living room.

'Can I have some tea?' he asked.

I heard my mother pouring him a cup.

'You look very fresh today,' she said cheerfully. 'And you woke up pretty early too!'

'Yeah,' he replied. 'I didn't want to miss the sunrise. It's so calm and peaceful in the morning.'

I didn't know if I could do justice to his story. I was still not sure if I was the right person to be doing this. I had not yet been able to figure out the perfect beginning for the book. Nor the perfect ending. But then again, reality is hardly perfect and life has never followed a neatly structured narrative. It's the mess and the chaos that teaches us how to live. I swallowed the last of my coffee and opened my laptop.

'You don't have to be perfect,' something inside me said. 'Just do it.'

And then I typed the first line of this book.

Acknowledgements

I shall always remain indebted to my grandfather for trusting me with the story of his life. Additionally, I also want to thank my grandmother Sumitra Das, and my parents, Sanghamitra Das and Debyendu Mohan Roy, for being major contributors to this story, for making me who I am today and for always being there to help me navigate through turbulent times with dignity and grace. I also want to thank my little brother, Swarnendu Mohan Roy, for not giving me too much trouble and being extremely willing and cooperative whenever I needed to use his printer.

I am grateful to Professor Rimi B. Chatterjee for being one of my very first readers, my reservoir of inspiration and support, and for helping me edit the initial chapters of the book. I cannot forget to mention Professor Santanu Biswas for playing a transformative role in my life as a teacher, mentor and philosopher; Professor Rafat Ali for always encouraging my offbeat research ideas and appreciating my academic endeavours; Professor Abhijit Gupta, Professor Ramit Sammadar and Professor Pinaki De for offering the most fantastic courses, recognizing my creative and academic efforts and guiding me effectively whenever I needed help. A huge thank you to all my friends from Jadavpur University for seeing me through some of the toughest years of my life.

I would also like to thank Nandita Palchoudhuri, Neline Mondal, Ujjal Mondal, Amiya Das, Shipra Das and Kalyan Chakraborty for furnishing me with extremely vital pieces of information which I would otherwise not have had access to and without which the book would have forever remained incomplete. Thanks to my loving uncles, Avijit Das and Surojit Mukherjee, and my aunts, Lopamudra Mukherjee and Sagori Chatterjee, for making me happy every single day and being there for me through thick and thin.

Most importantly, I would like to thank my literary agent, Dipti Patel, my publisher, Renuka Chatterjee and my editor, Tahira Thapar, from the very core of my heart. Without you, I would never have had the opportunity to present this book to the world, let alone take pride in it. Thank you so much, Speaking Tiger Books, for recognizing and acknowledging my efforts when I had almost given up all hope. I guess the Universe conspired to make this happen.

ALSO FROM SPEAKING TIGER

JOURNEY AFTER MIDNIGHT

A Punjabi Life: From India to Canada

Ujjal Dosanjh

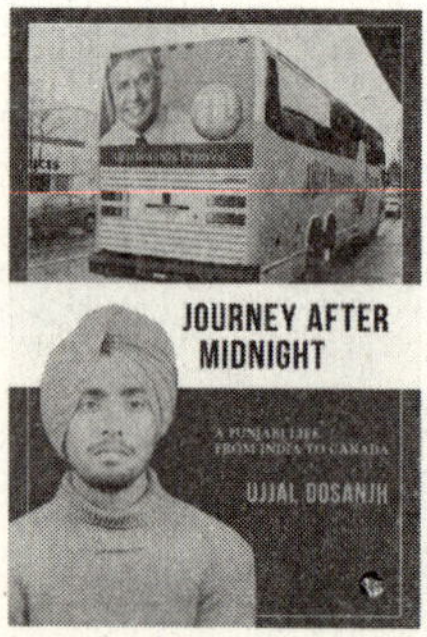

Born in rural Punjab just months before Indian independence, Ujjal Dosanjh emigrated to the UK, alone, when he was eighteen and spent four years making crayons and shunting trains while he attended night school. Four years later, he moved to Canada, where he worked in a sawmill, eventually earning a law degree, and committed himself to justice for immigrant women and men, farm workers and religious and racial minorities. In 2000, he became the first person of Indian origin to lead a government in the western world when he was elected Premier of British Columbia. Later, he was elected to the Canadian parliament.

Journey After Midnight is the compelling story of a life of rich and varied experience and rare conviction. With fascinating insight, Ujjal Dosanjh writes about life in rural Punjab in the 1950s and early '60s; the Indian immigrant experience—from the late 19th century to the present day—in the UK and Canada; post-Independence politics in Punjab and the Punjabi diaspora—including the period of Sikh militancy—and the inner workings of the democratic process in Canada, one of the world's more egalitarian nations. He also writes with unusual candour about his dual identity as a first-generation immigrant. And he describes how he has felt compelled to campaign against discriminatory policies of his adopted country, even as he has opposed regressive and extremist tendencies within the Punjabi community. His outspoken views against the Khalistan movement in the 1980s led to death threats and a vicious physical assault, and he narrowly escaped becoming a victim of the bombing of Air India Flight 182 in 1985. Yet he has remained steadfast in his defence of democracy, human rights and good governance in the two countries that he calls home—Canada and India. His autobiography is an inspiring book for our times.

ALSO FROM SPEAKING TIGER

THE BRASS NOTEBOOK

A Memoir

Devaki Jain

With a Foreword by Amartya Sen

In this no-holds-barred memoir, Devaki Jain begins with her childhood in south India, a life of comfort and ease with a father who served as dewan in the Princely States of Mysore and Gwalior. But there were restrictions too, that come with growing up in an orthodox Tamil Brahmin family, as well as the rarely spoken about dangers of predatory male relatives. Ruskin College, Oxford, gave her her first taste of freedom in 1955, at the age of 22. Oxford brought her a degree in philosophy and economics—as well as hardship, as she washed dishes in a cafe to pay her fees. It was here, too, that she had her early encounters with the sensual life. With rare candour, she writes of her romantic liaisons in Oxford and Harvard, and falling in love with her 'unsuitable boy'—her husband, Lakshmi Jain, whom she married against her beloved father's wishes.

Devaki's professional life saw her becoming deeply involved with the cause of 'poor' women—workers in the informal economy, for whom she strove to get a better deal. In the international arena, she joined cause with the concerns of the colonized nations of the south, as they fought to make their voices heard against the rich and powerful nations of the former colonizers. Her work brought her into contact with world leaders and thinkers, amongst them, Vinoba Bhave, Nelson Mandela, Henry Kissinger, and Iris Murdoch.